Praise for Soteria: Through Madness to Deliverance

Part case history, part case study, and part personal odyssey, this book tells the story of the Soteria project through the voices of psychiatrist, Loren Mosher and his long-term colleague Voyce Hendrix. The two were the parents of Soteria House, creating it, caring for it, and seeing it through over a controversial, tumultuous, and fascinating moment in the history of community-based psychiatric care. For mainstream psychiatric professionals, many of the ideas and opinions in this history will be viewed as marginal if not heretical. Yet for social scientists and humanists, Soteria illustrates the applied interpersonal phenomenology of a meaning-seeking social movement and of an island of innovation in the quest for humanized care for society's disturbed and disturbing members.

—Holly Wilson, RN, PhD
Professor Emerita, School of Nursing
University of California, San Francisco

The results of the Soteria Project sounded a thunderclap throughout the field in the 1970s. They completely and permanently changed my view of how to practice psychiatry. The passage of time has only increased the importance of these findings and endorsed their validity.

—Richard Warner
Medical Director of the Mental Health Center Boulder,
County, Colorado
Professor of Psychiatry and Adjunct Professor of
Anthropology University of Colorado
Author of *Recovery from Schizophrenia: Psychiatry and Political Economy*

As a psychiatric survivor, I hope Soteria stories will be told and retold, again and again, because they illuminate an exhilarating path toward deliverance gone mad.

In this book, Soteria's stories about how people can support and help others experiencing extreme mental and emotional crises emerge in loving (and sometimes humorous) detail. Here, the authors detail how dissident mental health workers, professionals, and researchers heroically championed an historic project in the face of a tidal wave of repression from the arrogant, tradition-bound psychiatric profession. These stories teach us how to survive a confused, drug-addicted, authoritarian, and, at times, deadly mental health establishment. For all those who—when confronted with psychiatry's crimes—ask, "But what's the alternative?" *Soteria* offers an elegant reply. It tells the inside story of an effective, hopeful, commonsense, empowering alternative to mainstream mental health practices.

David Oaks
Director
MindFreedom International
Eugene, Oregon

For at least 30 years, Dr. Mosher has been a burr under the saddle of mainstream psychiatry. However, no one can argue with his central message: "If you treat people with dignity and respect and want to understand what's going on, want to get yourself inside their shoes, you can do it." The Soteria team identified crucial steps that persons with serious and persistent mental problems take to reclaim their lives: 1) connecting 2) partnering 3) communal identification 4) extending to outside relationships, and 5) network balance. Here are clinicians willing to talk about what worked and what didn't. There are important lessons to be learned from Soteria's history.

Courtenay M. Harding, PhD
Senior Director, Center for Psychiatric Rehabilitation
Director, Institute for the Study of Human Resilience
Sargent College of Health and Rehabilitation Sciences
Boston University

Soteria

Soteria

THROUGH Madness to Deliverance

Loren R. Mosher, MD

Voyce Hendrix, LCSW

with Deborah C. Fort, PhD

Not everything that counts can be counted;
not everything that can be counted counts.

—*Albert Einstein*

A man should not strive to eliminate his complexes but to get into
accord with them: They are legitimately what directs his conduct in
the world.

—*Sigmund Freud*

"That crazy bastard might be the only sane one left."
—*Dr. Stubbs, of Yossarian, in Joseph Heller's* Catch-22

TO the staff—physicians, students, groupies, gurus, therapists of every stripe, researchers, psychics, mental health professionals, and volunteers who came into these unique social contexts

TO the residents whom they may have changed and who certainly changed them

TO the pioneers (whom few of us know) who, inspired by Soteria, are trying to change their clinical approaches by implementing its principles in contexts worldwide

Let them multiply.

Contents

Foreword   xi

Preface   xv

Introduction   1

The Staff   45

The Residents   63

Soteria Years   103

Some Problems and Some Solutions   125

Getting It Together   165

Structure   203

Learning from Soteria   247

The Voices of Soteria   281

    Loren R. Mosher, MD   281

    Voyce Hendrix, LCSW   311

References   325

Appendices   331

Foreword

DURING THE 1970S, our country's care of the severely mentally ill went through a defining moment. Today, of course, "antipsychotic" medications are the centerpiece of psychiatric care in the United States, but 25 years ago, there was still an active discussion about whether these drugs really benefitted people over the long run. As a result of that debate, there were a handful of experiments conducted that provided "schizophrenics" with social and community support but minimized the use of the drugs. The result? In every instance, people treated psychosocially did as well as or better than those treated conventionally with drugs, and, naturally, they didn't suffer the many adverse effects caused by the medications, like Parkinsonian symptoms. But that was not an outcome that mainstream psychiatry—and the pharmaceutical industry—wanted to hear, and the experiments were brought to an end.

In this book, Loren Mosher, Voyce Hendrix, and Deborah Fort have revisited the most visible of those experimental programs, the Soteria Project. By doing so, they provide us with a powerful reminder of what we, as a society, lost when we failed to embrace care of this kind.

We regularly hear today about the progress that we are making in treating "schizophrenia"—that we now know that it is a brain disease and that we are developing ever better drugs to treat that disease. Unfortunately, this is a claim that just isn't true. Researchers at Harvard Medical School have found that outcomes for "schizophrenia" patients have *worsened* since the 1970s and are now no better than they were

100 years ago, when the treatment of the day was to plunk people in bathtubs for hours on end. Even more damning, the World Health Organization has found that "schizophrenia" outcomes in poor countries like India, Nigeria, and Colombia, where only a small percentage of patients are regularly maintained on antipsychotic medications, are much, much *better* than in rich countries like the United States. The difference in outcomes is so dramatic that the World Health Organization concluded that living in a rich country like the United States is a "strong predictor" that a person diagnosed with "schizophrenia" will never fully recover.

And therein lies the tragedy: Soteria showed us the possibility of a better way, but we ignored it.

The fundamental philosophical difference between the two types of care—treatment centered on drugs versus treatment focused on environmental support—can be vividly seen in how the providers of such care talk about "madness." If you read articles in medical journals on the merits of drug treatments, you'll find that they always discuss how the medications reduce *symptoms*. What you won't find in those reports is any sense of the *people* who are being so treated. There is no sense that we are talking about an individual with a life history, and that there was a path—most likely one filled with trauma—that led up to their psychotic breaks. Nor is there any discussion of how the medicated patients are faring as human beings. Are they forming friendships, pursuing ambitions, able to feel the world? These questions aren't addressed. But at Soteria, as you'll see in this book, the discussion was all about people. People with names, with families, and with hopes.

As a result of this different philosophy, at Soteria there wasn't the usual drawing of a line separating the "crazies" from the "normals." Go to a psychiatric hospital and that line is carefully drawn. But at Soteria, the philosophy was one that emphasized a shared humanity, rather than how different the "mad" are from "us."

Indeed, as I read this book, I felt envious of those who worked at Soteria. They had the opportunity to "be with" unmedicated people who were battling with "madness." They clearly learned a great deal from this experience. They may have found it frustrating at times and often emotionally draining, but always rewarding and meaningful. The disappearance of a place like Soteria from our society is not just a loss for those who might find a refuge there, but also for those who work in the field of "mental health."

The authors don't sugarcoat Soteria's story. They candidly tell of the many problems associated with running the two Soteria houses, staff burnout among them. They don't claim that a Soteria approach will produce miracles. Some people so treated will recover, and others will continue to struggle with their delusions and behavioral problems. Providing people in severe distress with care of this type—a place to be, staffed by people who will care about them—is not an easy thing to do. It is, in fact, easier for a society to rely on medication as the treatment of choice. It requires less of us. But it is also a societal response that—as the World Health Organization studies revealed— does not do well by those in need.

We can, of course, learn from the past. I only hope that this book will help inspire many to think about how we can reform our care, and how we, as a society, might choose one day to "be with" those who struggle with "madness."

—Robert Whitaker
Author
Mad in America: Bad Medicine, Bad Science, and
the Enduring Mistreatment of the Mentally Ill

Preface

WE—LOREN R. MOSHER, MD, Voyce Hendrix, LCSW, and Deborah C. Fort, PhD—have stitched together in this volume the story of the Soteria Project. It created for certain young and disturbed persons two Bay-area refuges (Soteria House and Emanon), which operated in California between 1971 and 1983. During those dozen years, the project provided to a number of young, single individuals recently diagnosed as "schizophrenic" affordable, workable—and mostly drug-free—alternatives to hospitalization on psychiatric wards.

The two sets of primary documents are Loren's (with various collaborators) formal papers and reports, written over a period from the early 1970s on, along with many heretofore unpublished pages describing day-to-day life at Soteria House over its full dozen years written by Voyce, the project's program and house director and general administrator. Soteria originator Loren's frequent coauthor on the early Soteria papers was Alma Zito Menn, ACSW, a major project administrator, to whom Loren and Voyce offer special gratitude. Though there are significant differences, Soteria House also acknowledges with appreciation the precedent set by its progenitor the Philadelphia Association's Kingsley Hall in London.

Both Loren and Voyce's accounts draw heavily upon taped and written records provided by the part- and full-time staff who worked at Soteria and Emanon. Deborah, a Washington, D.C.-area writer and editor, sewed these various materials into this book, a kind of patchwork quilt.

Over the years, Soteria matured in many ways—the staff learned new ways of relating to people and developed the ability to tune in to altered states of consciousness, to share rather than repress such states. In this book, Loren and Voyce draw upon the community's memory to convey a sense of what happened in a special place and to describe some of the kinds of approaches used to deal with the kinds of problems encountered there. These experiences offer *at best* guidelines, not a cookbook, and *certainly* not a prescription. To remain consistent with the tenets of interpersonal phenomenology, each social context and the individuals interacting in it must be regarded as unique.

The community dealt with a plethora of situations—some expected, some unexpected—in a multitude of ways, some more successful than others. What worked in one situation did not always help in another, however, and the persons with whom the community interacted could not be forced into following preestablished procedures. Each was treated individually.

To follow are accounts of individual successes and failures. Besides being interesting in themselves, they may be helpful to those who wish to learn from Soteria or imitate it. But disciples, take note: Soteria was an ever-changing expression of the people there, and its whole was greater than the sum of its parts.

In the end, Soteria stories will not provide steps to guide sufferers from psychosis to health.

These stories cannot so serve; indeed, they would not if they could.

Loren R. Mosher, MD
San Diego, California
Voyce Hendrix, LCSW
Madison, Wisconsin
Deborah C. Fort, PhD
Washington, D.C.
2004

Introduction

S OTERIA, THE GREEK word for deliverance,[1] was the name of a community-based, experimental residential treatment facility offering refuge to people, most young, most diagnosed as "schizophrenic," and all suffering severe psychological distress. Surviving in the San Francisco Bay area of the 1970s and early 1980s, Soteria House brought together a number of disparate clinical notions. It embraced elements of practice from the era of "moral treatment" (J. Sanbourne Bockoven's description [1963] of America's mental health practices in the 18th century). The importance Soteria placed on the healing potential of human relationships was drawn from psychoanalytical pioneers, especially Henry Stack Sullivan (1962), but also Frieda Fromm-Reichmann (1948); therapists who have described growth from psychosis (Karl A. Menninger, 1959; John W. Perry, 1953, 1962); a group of psychiatric heretics (Ronald D. Laing, 1967; Thomas S. Szasz, 1961); and chroniclers of the development of psychiatric disorder in response to life crisis (George W. Brown and James L. T. Birley, 1968). Its phenomenologic stance vis-à-vis the persons for whom it cared came from a long-standing European

---

[1]   Discussing Pope John Paul II's use of the concept "soteriological" in his *Crossing the Threshold of Hope* (1995), William Safire noted that "The Greek etymon was *soteria*, "deliverance," from *sozein*, "to save," growing out of *sos*, "safe, sound." *The Oxford English Dictionary* has the earliest use recorded in Webster's 1847 dictionary but asserts that "the theological meaning took over a generation later." It would seem a term whose time has come.

philosophic tradition that had been translated into practice by Laing (1960, 1967), David Graham Cooper (1967), Medard Boss (1963), and others. Soteria was also an attempt to develop an alternative model for care in response to the well-developed critiques of psychiatric institutions. The best-known is Erving Goffmann's *Asylums* (1961), based largely on his study of Washington, D.C.'s St. Elizabeth's Hospital in the late 1950s. Finally, the Soteria project tried to operate and study a setting that could test the validity of the critiques of the "antipsychiatrists," such as Laing, Cooper, and Franco Basaglia (1987).

The Soteria project stands out from other community-based mental health residential facilities in several ways:

> ✎ Although it was not a hospital, and its program was not run by doctors (or nurses by delegation), it admitted only clients who would have otherwise been hospitalized.
>
> ✎ Neuroleptic drugs, the standard treatment for "schizophrenia," were used as infrequently as possible and preferably not at all.
>
> ✎ The nonprofessional staff had primary treatment responsibility, power, and authority.
>
> ✎ Most importantly, unlike the thousands of group homes[2] established nationwide since the mid-1970s to serve as post-hospitalization halfway houses for previously institutionalized patients, Soteria (and its descendants—both those born in California 30 years ago and its Eastern United States and European grandchildren) offered an *alternative* to hospitalization rather than a follow-up to it.

Three settings based on the Soteria model (but admitting individuals with any psychiatric diagnosis and using psychotropic drugs conventionally) are operating in Washington, D.C., and its suburbs: Crossing Place opened in 1977; the Care Program in 1982; McAuliffe House in 1990. A random assignment study, similar in some ways to the original Soteria Project, in the 1990s compared treatment at McAuliffe

---

[2]   One of them is eloquently described in Michael Winerip's *Nine Highland Road* (Pantheon, 1994).

House with that usual in a psychiatric ward in a general hospital (see *Result Seven*, pages 263–266). It differed from the original Soteria study, however, in that clients deemed in need of hospitalization were admitted regardless of diagnosis, duration of illness, and age.

Over the centuries, many Europeans emigrated to the New World, often to escape repressive social systems. Now, in a reverse migration, the freedom Soteria offered for a dozen years to the mad, quashed at home by the threatened and threatening medical establishment, is being reestablished in the Old World. A pure Soteria replication has been operating in Bern, Switzerland, since 1984 (Ciompi, 1997). Another descendant was established in Zwiefalten, Germany, in the late 1990s, and a third opened in Munich in 2003. Several others have been proposed but have not yet been implemented in Hanover, Germany, and Budapest, Hungary; one is also being planned in Auckland, New Zealand. Another operated for six years in Stockholm, Sweden, but closed most of its beds when it was integrated into a generic crisis program. Soteria's clinical practice in interpersonal phenomenology has been profoundly influential in "moral" hospital settings in many parts of Germany and Scandinavia.

At the moment, people diagnosed as "schizophrenic" in the West have a much *worse* prognosis than those so labeled elsewhere. Robert Whitaker puts it baldly: "Suffer a psychotic break in a poor country like India or Nigeria, and chances are that in a couple of years you will be doing fairly well. But suffer a similar break in the United States or other developed countries, and it is likely that you will become chronically ill" (2001, p. xiv).

Perhaps the time has come for a Soteria renaissance in the United States.

Getting Started

In April of 1971, nine people, including this volume's authors, psychiatrist Loren R. Mosher, MD, and Voyce Hendrix (now LCSW) came together to continue the work of certain philosophic pioneers (notably, Sullivan, Laing, and Cooper) by founding Soteria House.

Soteria was designed as the first in a series of successors to Kingsley Hall, the London-based commune designed to help individuals in varying degrees of psychic distress started by the Philadelphia Association in 1965. Organizers chose and leased a 2-story, 12-room, 1912-vintage, wooden house on a busy thoroughfare in San Jose, California. True to its heritage, Soteria House sat in the midst of a transitional multiethnic, working-class neighborhood. Bordering the house on one side was a nursing home and, on the other, a two-family dwelling.

However, it had a number of advantages over its East London parent: First, substantial numbers of college students and former state hospital patients lived in the area, one federally designated as qualifying for assistance because of its poverty. Hence, transience and deviance were not unknown. Second, by painting the exterior of the house and replanting its rundown yard, Soteria's members won a certain acceptance in the community. Third, the house and its staff attempted to conform to neighborhood social norms. (The community surrounding Kingsley Hall had been instrumental in closing it.) Fourth, explicit rules prohibited certain behaviors. (See below, pages 227–228.) Fifth, paid staff assured attention to life's prosaic necessities.

Perhaps the most important notion that guided practice at both Kingsley Hall and Soteria was the shared and innovative conception of the psychotic experience—usually viewed as irrational and mystifying— as one which, if treated in an open, nonjudgmental way, could be valid and comprehensible. The altered states of psychotics' consciousness, resulting from crises in living, thus were potentially healthful steps in reiterative processes. The project's purpose was to find out whether Soteria's approach and milieu were as effective in promoting recovery from madness as that provided in a nearby general hospital's psychiatric ward, where the most valued treatment was antipsychotic drugs.

Changing Patterns

The project survived in an atmosphere of uncertainty about continuation of funding. It was site-visited and reviewed by National

Institute of Mental Health committees more than half a dozen times during its 12 years of research support. Although the project acquired subjects slowly and followed their progress for two years, its longest research grant support was for only three years. Closures of both Soteria (1983) and its replication, in San Mateo, Emanon (1980), resulted when research funds ran out.

This history would not be possible, however, without more than 10 years of taxpayer-supported research, granted by the National Institute of Mental Health and designed to answer a simple question: Could persons newly labeled "schizophrenic" and deemed so dysfunctional as to require hospitalization be successfully treated in a small, homelike, nonhospital setting without antipsychotic drugs? How would their clinical outcomes compare at six weeks, six months, and one and two years, to those of a group of similarly selected and studied persons who received the usual inpatient and outpatient follow-up care? (*Outcomes* meant whether factors such as hospitalization, medications, and psychotic symptoms continued and whether levels of psychosocial functioning improved or deteriorated.)

If the progress of the groups treated experimentally and traditionally were comparable, then this new treatment was as good or better than current practice, and a phenomenon had been defined. Its component parts could then be studied to attempt to disentangle the reasons for its effectiveness. If the experimental group did worse, the research ended, and the status quo was preserved.

The question is deceptively simple. Answering it was difficult. One would expect that, after more than 10 years of research (plus the establishment of a second experimental facility lasting for 6 years), a clear answer would have emerged. In fact, Loren believes that it did with the publication of his and social worker Alma Zito Menn's study of two-year outcome data from the original cohort of Soteria subjects (1978b).

Unfortunately, this 1971–1976 study had a *putative* scientific flaw— lack of *strict* random assignment. Despite the comparability of the two groups on a myriad of variables assessed at admission, the scientific establishment eventually denied research funds to study what elements in the setting were critical to its success. In spite of this, data analysis was finally completed in March, 1992. For further discussion of Soteria's research—setbacks, triumphs, and findings—see *Learning from Soteria* (pages 247–279). In this uncertain atmosphere, keeping a core staff intact was difficult. From the perspective of *research*, the involvement of Loren and Alma were the only constants. From the Soteria *community's* point of view, Voyce was its continuity.

The house-based staff also turned over a number of times over the project's life. Alma, Voyce, and Loren estimate that several hundred people had important clinical involvement with Soteria and/or with its descendant, Emanon (*no name* spelled backwards), which opened four years later. So called to distinguish it from its older sibling, Emanon turned out to have some serendipitous lexicological relationships with *emanant* (from Latin *emanans*, to flow out, arise). The intention was to provide an immediate replication of the original milieu in a new community with different staff and leadership but with the same research design. For further information on Emanon and another of Soteria's near relatives, Diabasis (from a Greek word meaning "crossing over"), see below in this chapter and pages 110–116.

Day by Day

When operating at full capacity, Soteria's 12 rooms housed six residents (young, unmarried persons newly diagnosed and labeled as "schizophrenic"), two full-time staff members, usually a man and a woman, and various volunteers and part-time helpers. In addition, each facility had a house director and access to a quarter-time project psychiatrist. Due primarily to licensing laws, Soteria and Emanon could each accommodate only six residents at one time, although as many as 10 persons could sleep there comfortably. One or two new residents were admitted each month, usually remaining for a period of three to six months.

The core staff at Soteria, usually about seven paid full-time-equivalent employees plus volunteers, made for an average of six to eight ratio of staff to residents compared to the control group's six to nine paid personnel of all types to patients. Actually, at times of high activity—usually 4 PM to midnight—Soteria tried to have a 50–50 mix of persons in crisis with ones functioning more or less normally, including residents who had recovered sufficiently to be helpers. This nonprofessional staff aimed to provide a simple, homelike, safe, warm, supportive, unhurried, tolerant, and nonintrusive social environment. While typically imbued with counterculture values, the staff did not tend to be militant. Soteria staff believed that sincere human involvement and understanding were critical to healing interactions. Most staff worked 36- to 48-hour shifts to provide an extended opportunity to relate to "spaced-out" (their term) residents continuously over a relatively long period of time. The house director was friend, counselor, supervisor, and receptor of staff's displaced angry feelings. The part-time project psychiatrists supervised the staff, served as stable, reassuring presences, and fulfilled their formal medical and legal responsibilities.

Staff and residents shared responsibility for household maintenance, meal preparation, and cleanup. Persons not "together," however, were not expected to do their full share of the work. Over the long term, staff did much of the upkeep, stepping in to assume responsibility if a resident could not manage an agreed-upon task.

Although they believed in the work and the *residents* (or sometimes *clients*)—not *patients*[3] (a label Soteria staff resisted as both too medical and too passive)—such staff members resented the intrusion of logical positivist research into the phenomenological-existential interpersonal world at the facility. Writing notes, tracking particular behaviors, setting goals, planning treatments, managing cases, conducting formal psychotherapy sessions, and the like, were usually anathema. Hence, much of the project's contribution to the field

---

[3]   And certainly not the mentally ill "consumers," the absurd term that Winerip reports was briefly applied to the residents of the halfway house about which he wrote (1994).

cannot be written; it lives in the experience of the myriad of persons involved. It was for them a time, a place, a context to be experienced; to be lived; to be loved; to be frightened by; to be "bummed out about."

Soteria and Emanon were not observational experiments with controls. Staff were not Audubons sketching schizophrenic birds in protected parts of the forest. They were Janes or Joes trying to relate to, *be with*,[4] and understand persons whose means of communication and behaviors were often unlike anything the staff had encountered before. Staff came in most cases to have an experience that would leave an indelible imprint, an experience on which they would have an impact, an experience that would be reciprocally formative. Staff were explorers in an uncharted frontier; they were in a place where few people without preconceived notions had ventured before, and they were there without the usual trappings of power to control madness. Staff did not carry the highly symbolic keys to freedom: There were no locks on the doors; there were no syringes and few medications; and there were no wet packs, restraints, or seclusion rooms.

Being There

During the 12-year span, only three figures were consistently on the scene:

1. **Loren,** the project's designer, chief theoretician, analyst, spokesperson, and writer. Between 1976 and the project's end in 1983, his formal role was that of collaborating investigator.

Prior to 1976, when he was, in effect, research director (a post he later assumed formally), Loren had a hands-on role. He helped select and train the original staff and worked directly in San Jose and San Mateo with clients and staff. He also designed the research procedure, directed its start-up, and sent his Washington, D.C.-based research assistant to California to help.

Also important was the fact that Loren's National Institute of Mental

---

[4]   For more on *being with*, see *Getting It Together*, pages 165–201.

Health office received and analyzed all data collected during the project. After 1976, his role became more peripheral, when a review committee recommended that the project recruit a research director to be located at the Mental Research Institute, the Palo Alto-based grantee institution, and directed that all data analysis be transferred there. When the project closed in 1983 and the research staff left because of insufficient funding, Loren became research codirector with psychologist Robert (Bob) Vallone, PhD. In addition, Loren has remained in close contact with many members of the Soteria community and worked extensively both on this volume and on the final grant report (1992). (His autobiography appears on pages 281–309.)

2. **Alma** was the first full-time employee of the project. Hired by Len Goveia (briefly a part-time principal investigator), she took on many of the project's early responsibilities when he became ill prior to the opening of Soteria. After selecting the initial staff, she was officially designated principal investigator, a role in which she remained—sometimes alone, sometimes in collaboration—throughout the life of the project. With the opening of Emanon, she turned over clinical responsibility for Soteria to Voyce.

3. **Voyce** was actively involved with the project from its inception in 1971. Starting as a staff member, he became the senior staff person, then house director, then director of both Soteria and Emanon. When the project closed, he wrote its day-to-day history and then left to earn graduate degrees in social work. (See his autobiography, pages 311–323.) Over the years, he continued to provide information, review, and comments on this book.

In the tradition pioneered by Sullivan, however, Soteria's full- and part-time staff were not mental health professionals. The administrators and researchers had degrees in various mental health fields—Alma is a social worker; Stan Redd, Ken Woodrow, and Richard Poe (at Emanon), who were on call and visited frequently, are psychiatrists;[5] so is Loren, who had studied with Sullivanian analysts at Harvard and with Laing in London in the 1960s. Voyce, however,

---

[5]   Other consulting psychiatrists included Bob Spitzer and Howard Siegel.

had had little formal mental health training when he was at Soteria, although before coming there he had worked as an attendant on wards in state hospitals for both the mentally retarded and the mentally ill in California.

The nonprofessional staff on the job were asked to "provide a warm, supportive, protective, flexible, nonauthoritarian, and nonhierarchical environment" (Hirschfeld, Matthews, Mosher, and Menn, 1977, p. 158). Over its 12-year history, Soteria staff and volunteers included graduate and undergraduate students in psychology and other fields, Comprehensive Employment Training Act (CETA) workers, and a wide variety of miscellaneous interested others. Most had little or no mental health training when they started work. They tended to be young, middle-to-lower class, and moderately educated.

This part- and full-time, paid and volunteer staff, along with the administrators and mental health consultants, as well as the house's residents and the community's friends, provided the text below. Out of the oral and written records they set forth, as summarized by Loren and Voyce, emerge Soteria's purpose as it touched on the clients, staff, and volunteers working in the house, and the family, friends, and professional community that formed its broader ecology.

In this book, Loren and Voyce explain Soteria's demystifying process as a basis for treatment. They describe attempts of staff and residents to work *through* psychosis to health, the community's expectations for treatment, and the patterns of response produced. Often, the particular technique to achieve the therapeutic end was a modified vigil, during which staff members stayed continuously with a client in crisis in one place until s/he worked through the difficulty. The vigil evolved, at Soteria, into the less formal concept of *being with*, a communion that could and did occur anywhere in the house or community. (On these approaches, see *Getting It Together*, pages 165–201.) Finally, Loren and Voyce examine Soteria's attempt within the community to develop and transfer basic relationships during the interactive process.

Alma, Voyce, and Loren, along with the handful of psychiatrists who consulted regularly at Soteria, are among the few members of the

Soteria community whose identities have not been disguised. On occasion, persons playing administrative, temporary, and/or theoretical roles also appear under their own names. Those of all other staff and, of course, all the residents have been protected.

Philosophy

In 1970, Loren set down Soteria's fundamental philosophy, as well its original theory about how a milieu designed to deal with developmental crises should function. He planned that Soteria's staff would learn to view the "schizophrenic" reaction as someone's altered state of consciousness in response to a crisis. If a "psychosis" developed, it evolved in and affected the psychosocial matrix of the entire family or other intimate group forming the disturbed person's ecology. Thus, often, the disturbed and disturbing person's entire surrounding community—which could not easily tolerate or coexist with the strange behaviors stemming from an altered state of consciousness— experienced crisis, not just the individual labeled "mad."

Few clinicians would disagree with a description of the evolution of psychosis as a process of fragmentation and disintegration. Loren also believed (and believes) that the affected individual's state usually involves personality fragmentation with the loss of a sense of self. As modalities of experience blend with one another, inner being becomes difficult to distinguish from outer, ambivalence reigns, and the disturbed person's terror is reinforced by the fearful reactions of others in his/her environment, who feel their own sanity challenged by the events taking place. Mystical experiences are common in this state beyond reason.

Such a view of "schizophrenia" implies a number of therapeutic attitudes. At Soteria and Emanon, the disruptive psychotic experience was neither aborted nor forced into compromise but was seen as having potential for reintegration and reconstitution. Staff were to try to see as many aspects as possible of the "schizophrenic's" experience as real and, in spite of the fragmentation process, to treat his/her feelings as potential for psychological growth, reconstitution, and reintegration on a more whole or higher psychosocial developmental level. Staff were to take the experiential and behavioral attributes of the "psychosis"—including irrationality, terror, and mystical experiences—as the extremes of basic human qualities they are. Staff, therefore, were not to view such expressions as ones to invalidate, as nonhuman, or as symptoms of disease. Staff were to relate to such experiences personally rather than through detachment. Soteria saw the individual experiencing a "schizophrenic" reaction as someone to *be with*—tolerated, interacted with, indeed appreciated.

Soteria set limits, when individuals were a danger to themselves and/or others, but not because of inability to tolerate madness. Because they regarded residents' experiences as real, capable of being understood, and valid, the staff's major function was to help provide an atmosphere accepting of strange states of mind and facilitating their integration into the residents' lives.

Staff were also taught to regard mystical qualities as metaphorically valid and comprehensible, both in relation to cultural background and to the dynamics of the family. Operationally, the staff were to *be with* the residents (in much the same way as an LSD "trip guide" used to stay with the person experimenting with the drug's effect). For such interactions, the staff were specially selected, trained, and supervised, so they could tune in to the resident's consciousness in order to provide reassurance and protection. Each staff member was asked to aim to be someone with whom experience could be shared (as long as neither staff nor resident suffered intolerable levels of fear or anxiety).

The lines of authority and roles were not clearly delineated. Staff would neither wear uniforms nor pretend to be authorities with solutions. Loren planned few *prescribed* expectations to which residents would be pressured to conform—all such limitations would aim to avoid harm to residents, staff, others, the community, or the program. Instead, the staff would encourage participation in a variety of activities, such as yoga, massage, art, music, and the like, aimed at the development of a sense of self, physical and psychological, while allowing solitude and safety in the turmoil an individual might feel, need, and choose to express. Loren saw the dyad as the primary interpersonal unit, with the program developing out of the participants' needs and changing over time in consonance with the emergence of new priorities.

Loren planned Soteria's milieu to provide a context in which "schizophrenic" residents could differentiate and validate their selves or identities. Thus, he taught staff to emphasize individuality, tolerance, equality, respect, and interest, with minimal pressure for conformity. He viewed the social context as making available to the residents a setting in which the implicit demand is for them to sort out what they wish to be from that which *others* want them to be. (A crucial aspect of this attitude is the position that the staff is not *right,* that they do not have *the answer.*) The latter attitude, Loren thought, would emerge through the application of old, or the development of new, problem-solving techniques based on a resident's own experiences, past and present. This empowering view immediately establishes his/her experience as both valid and potentially useful.

Loren arrived at his view of the importance of aberrations in the sense of self or self-image in "schizophrenia" in part through his readings of a number of earlier works, including studies by Sullivan, Erik Erikson (1959), W. Ronald D. Fairbairn (1952/1994), Seymour Fisher and Sidney. E. Cleveland (1958), Thomas Freeman, John L. Cameron, and Andrew McGhie (1958), Harry James Samuel Guntrip (1969), Laing (1960), and Paul Schilder (1950). Their terminologies vary, but all these writers see the major issue in "schizophrenia" to be the establishment of a valid sense of *self* as differentiated from the attributions of others (especially the family). This model seemed especially relevant to the subjects of Soteria's research, the relatively young still attached to their family networks.

While Loren's experiences at Kingsley Hall were keys to the development of the Soteria project, the difficulties he noted with the treatment of psychosis in hospital settings also provided a major impetus in shaping the particular type of facility Soteria became. It was planned as a home where "schizophrenics" who would otherwise have been hospitalized lived through their psychosis with a nonprofessional staff. Hospitals—even well-staffed, progressive ones—have institutional characteristics that create barriers to the relationships that could help recovery from psychosis.

A Few Constants

At Soteria, there was no one to whom to turn to obtain "the answer." Staff and residents alike found themselves in an environment that refused to affirm the existence of a solution to madness.

Although a remote descendant of Laing's ruleless (at least explicitly) Kingsley Hall in London, Soteria, thanks to Loren's experiences in London, opened with three prohibitions. (For further discussion, see *Structure*, pages 203–246.) Soteria's original rules follow.

1. Insofar as it was preventable, violence to self or others was forbidden. From the outset, Soteria's planners believed it important to make this expectation explicit. Providing the safe, quiet, protective, containing, predictable environment essential to natural recovery from psychosis demanded freedom from violence.

2. Tourists were not allowed without prearrangement and agreement of the current residents of the house. (Family members and friends of residents were of course, welcome, although the community preferred to know in advance that they would be visiting.) Just as no one should invite a stranger into someone else's house without asking, the community exercised a veto. In addition, clinical experience had taught Loren that persons disorganized enough to be labeled psychotic frequently reacted poorly (for example, they withdrew, ran away, or became angry and assaultive) when confronted by strangers.

3. No illegal drugs were allowed in the house. When Soteria and Emanon were in operation, much of the nation was involved in drug use and abuse. Both to continue to be in good standing with the federal funders, however, and, equally importantly, to coexist peacefully with the local community, the facilities could not afford to be seen as drug scenes.

Furthermore, Soteria was attempting to conduct an experimental protocol as free from drugs as possible. There were no clear guidelines as to what effect illegal drugs would have had on the course of recovery from acute psychosis, and the community did not wish to muddy further the already opaque waters of madness. In practice, the project's participants rarely used illegal drugs.

Note that sexual activity, very commonly proscribed in community residential programs, went unmentioned when Soteria opened. Eventually, the community would have to add a fourth rule in that regard. Part of the project's uniqueness grew from the freedom to find and furnish a facility, to hire staff, and basically to turn them loose in it with only the three original rules. Otherwise, all were free to operate as they saw fit, except that two staff members were to be on duty at all times. About the same time that their burnout dictated devising a regular ongoing staffing pattern, events also conspired to bring about a fourth rule.

One of the project's early admissions was an excited, overactive, incoherent young woman. One of the expressions of her psychosis was to disrobe, climb into a male staff member's lap in front of others, and invite him to have intercourse with her. Although potentially attractive, when admitted to Soteria, she was not bathing or brushing her teeth; had lost 25 pounds, dropping to a skeletal 85 pounds; and obviously lacked ordinary judgment based on an assessment of what was appropriate.

Staff had been trained to *be with* the residents, to try to put themselves in the situation of the disturbed person rather than interrupt or disrupt his/her experience. This young woman's behavior, therefore, created a situation with conflicting injunctions: The project's clinical gurus usually encouraged staff to go along with what the clients wanted so long as it was not dangerous. In this case, however, doing what she asked would exploit her vulnerability. Hence, staff had no trouble in applying a normalizing rule, recognizing a woman looking and acting like her found in ordinary social context should be helped, not seduced.

Because she continued this behavior for several weeks, staff decided to consider a general rule prohibiting sexual relations between staff and residents. Such a policy would relieve them of dealing with these contradictory dictates. A house meeting was convened and in the end the community affirmed an incest taboo on sex between staff and residents—not between staff members or between clients. In 12 years of operation, this taboo was violated only once, and by someone who was neither a staff member nor a resident but a guest.

(Soteria solved this single violation by redefining the guest's role. The next day, after open discussion by the house membership, he was officially defined as a live-in volunteer, an acknowledged staff-like role. The problem did not reoccur.)

Other rules came and went at Soteria, most commonly a ban on alcohol when it was being abused by someone living in the house. However, these four—*not more*—endured, a remarkable accomplishment in an open residential setting dealing with usually unmedicated acutely psychotic clients.

Holly Skodol Wilson (RN, PhD), a medical sociologist, observed Soteria closely during the 1970s, often in juxtaposition to her study of patient-staff relations on psychiatric wards (see pages 27–30). Of social interaction at Soteria, she wrote,

> The dynamics of social control touch the lives of all persons who are attempting to participate in group endeavors. Sensitivity to this fact of social life is not the exclusive domain of the poet's, hero's, or madman's "discerning Eye." At Soteria House conventional formal arrangements for social control are muted, denied, and discarded. Under the espoused freedom characterizing Soteria, a tacit infra-controlling process has emerged in place of elaborate, formal control structures to deal with problems of social control. Infra-control comprises three implementing processes, each of which addresses problems presented by a corresponding population of resident patients, staff, and external control agencies. These implementing processes are presencing, fairing, and limiting intrusion. Presencing

refers to ways in which the physical presence of other people is used to influence and modify residents' behavior (Kneisl and Wilson, 1976). Fairing refers to the management and distribution of work according to tacit, implicit understandings among staff members about what is fair (Kneisl and Wilson, 1976). Limiting intrusion refers to the process by which Soteria restricts the potential control that might be exercised on its operation by external agents (Wilson, 1977). The definition in the Oxford English Dictionary of the term infra—is denoting "below or beneath in respect to condition or status as in infra-red." The term infra-control in this study refers to a control process that is largely emergent, intuitive, tacit, and improvised. The formulation of infra-control organizes many events that superficially appeared to be disconnected or paradoxical. Furthermore, it enables major patterns of interaction to be discerned, despite the tendency of persons involved in the setting to discount patterned events in favor of the uniqueness of each situation. (1983, pp. 43–44)

Mission

In most psychiatric institutions, it is assumed that the priority is to help patients, who should therefore be the most important people in the system. On the surface, this position appears unarguable. But *should* and *are* are not synonymous. Most psychiatric hospitals pay lip service to a patient-centered philosophy, but, even to an untrained observer, it becomes quickly clear that the staff in fact enjoys number one status on the ward.

Administrations usually attempt to control their clinical staff by appealing to their sense of humanity, and, indeed, no one could argue with the idea of the patient's welfare as paramount. Whenever the staff begins to feel that patients' rights are gaining precedence, however, it takes control. And, when administrators aren't around, the staff unleashes its anger on the patients—sometimes to the point of physical abuse.

At Soteria, on the contrary, the understanding was that the house was there for all the groups—although not necessarily to fulfill the same purpose for each—and that no group was favored above another. If *any* group disappeared, Soteria wouldn't be Soteria. Because each group was a necessary part of the total program, to make the residents the focal point could have created an inequity leaving them vulnerable to the staff's anger at the administration.

Frequent, regular discussions prevented this kind of injustice from poisoning Soteria's atmosphere. At Soteria, the primary focus was on growth, development, and learning. Decision-making powers and responsibility were shared. The staff were there neither to treat nor to cure the residents, but to *be with* them.

New Ground: Avoiding Drug Therapy

Soteria's emphasis on the possibility of growth from psychosis, although firmly based on theories earlier articulated by Laing and Menninger, led to its creation of a uniquely organized milieu. Soteria had few established precedents to follow as it transmuted theory to practice. Although the medical model has demonstrated heuristic value, its application to psychiatric disorders has had unfortunate (and unintended) consequences for individual patients. Soteria proposed no alternative model; as yet, none seems to satisfactorily explain the condition(s) labeled "schizophrenia." Instead, Soteria worked from an alternative *attitude* or *stance* or *view:* It endorsed an interpersonal phenomenologic approach to "schizophrenia," as staff attempted both to understand and share the psychotic person's experience—without judging, labeling, derogating or invalidating— as well as their own reactions to it. As time passed, the community developed new ways of dealing with disorganized behavior—ways that did not, however, involve the traditional devices of medication, restraints, or seclusion.

In 1979, Loren and Alma explained Soteria's approach as follows:

We live in an over-medicated, too frequently drug-dependent culture despite ambivalence which is resolved by creating two categories of drugs: good ones like alcohol and bad ones like LSD. Psychiatry's attitude is no different from that of the wider social context: We are all still looking for the magical answer from a pill. The antipsychotic drugs have provided psychiatrists with real substance for their magical-cure fantasy applied to schizophrenia. But, as is the case with most such exaggerated expectations, the fantasy is better than the reality. After two decades, it is now clear that the antipsychotic drugs do not *cure* schizophrenia. It is also clear that they have serious, sometimes irreversible, toxicities, . . . that recovery may be impaired by them in at least some schizophrenics, . . . and that they have little effect on long-term psychosocial adjustment . . . These criticisms do not deny their extraordinary helpfulness in reducing and controlling symptoms, shortening hospital stays, and revitalizing interest in schizophrenia. One aim of the Soteria project is to seek a viable informed alternative to the overuse of these drugs and excessive reliance on them, often to the exclusion of psychosocial measures. We use drugs infrequently and, when prescribed, they are primarily under the individual resident's (patient's) control. That is, s/he is asked to monitor his/her responses to the drug very carefully to give us feedback, so we can adjust dosage, and, after a trial period of two weeks, s/he is given a major role in determining whether or not s/he will continue to use drugs. (p. 73)

Because of its experimental design, Soteria clients did not ordinarily receive the then available antipsychotic drugs (neuroleptics, major tranquilizers) such as Thorazine, Haldol, Prolixin, or Stelazine (there were 18 on the market in the 1970s[6]) during their first six weeks in residence. The experimental reason for this delay was to allow a fair test of Soteria's psychosocial approach. The staff believed it might well take six weeks before important relationships could form and before the special qualities of the culture there could be meaningfully transmitted. At six weeks, each client's progress was evaluated, and, if no improvement had occurred and if the resident, the staff, and the consulting psychiatrist all agreed, a trial drug treatment usually was initiated. Since some antipsychotic drugs were well-established as efficacious for treating psychotic symptoms, withholding a "proven" treatment indefinitely could have been unethical.

Over the course of the project's life, drug trials during the first six weeks became more common at Soteria, although they remained infrequent compared not only to patients in the control group (100 percent) but also to residents in most conventional treatment facilities. In the initial five years, less than 10 percent of the residents received neuroleptics continuously. In the last seven, just under 20 percent did. This change probably results from a certain waning of the original enthusiasm for, and commitment to, a purely interpersonal approach. It may also be partly the result of the generally increased use of various *il*legal drugs during the late 1970s.

During the initial six-week "no drug" trial, the use of antipsychotics was permitted if

- it was believed that the drugs could quell otherwise uncontrollable violence or suicidal impulses
- the resident was in unrelenting psychic pain that could not be relieved by interpersonal means
- the resident asked for medicine to help him/her reorganize

The limited use of antipsychotic drugs at Soteria House contrasts with the fact that nearly every subject studied treated in the general hospital wards that served as comparison settings received neuroleptics during their entire stays.

Loren and Voyce now see the irony that, as they write almost three decades after the start of the Soteria project, antipsychotic drugs were

---

6   The atypical antipsychotic drugs did not arrive on the market until the 1990s. Initially hailed as being more effective and having fewer adverse side effects than their predecessors, they are proving to be similarly effective with different but also harmful side effects.

not withheld to avoid tardive dyskinesia (late-appearing muscle movement dysfunction) and other adverse side effects. Tardive dyskinesia, characterized most often by uncontrollable movements of the tongue and face, had been little noted by the psychiatric profession until the mid-1970s—*although the first case reports appeared in 1956.* Of these reports, Loren was as ignorant (as in denial?) as, apparently, were other members of his profession, which now gives tardive dyskinesia at least cursory notice as a serious problem. It is chilling to note that, out of four patients started on neuroleptics, one will develop this iatrogenic (doctor-produced) disease, a cosmetically disfiguring and untreatable condition perceptible by anyone who looks, within five years. Tardive dyskinesia immediately sets its sufferers apart and makes stigmatization nearly inevitable.

By the end of the century, in spite of continued widespread application of antipsychotic drugs, a number of people were criticizing their use.[7] A second WHO investigation, undertaken because disbelieving researchers said the result was so unexpected that the study must be flawed, came up with the same finding (Jablensky, 1992; Leff, 1992). Peter R. Breggin (1990, 2000) was among the most emphatic. He wrote, for example,

> In summary, the neuroleptic drugs are chemical lobotomizing agents with no specific therapeutic effect on any symptoms or problems. Their main impact is to blunt and subdue the individual . . . . They also paralyze the

---

[7]   While this is not the place to go into the implications of a massive 1979 World Health Organization (WHO) study of "schizophrenic" outcomes showing a correlation between low reliance on neuroleptic medication and recovery, Soteria's findings agree. *The fewer antipsychotic drugs, the better the chance for recovery.* While more than three quarters of third-world individuals diagnosed "schizophrenic" had either recovered or were doing fairly well five years after their diagnosis, only 25 percent of such patients in rich countries enjoyed a similar level of success. A second WHO investigation, undertaken because disbelieving researchers said the result was so unexpected that the study must be flawed, came up with the same finding (Jablensky, 1992; Leff, 1992).

body, rendering the individual less able to react or to move. Thus they produce a chemical lobotomy and a chemical straitjacket. Indeed, there is relatively little evidence that they are helpful to the patients themselves, while there is considerable evidence that psychosocial interventions are much better. The drugs are also the cause of a plague of brain damage that afflicts up to half or more of long-term patients. (1990, p. 67)

[and]

Rather than treating a disease, the neuroleptics create a disease. (1990 p. 71)

Loren agrees. The abnormalities researchers have found with brain scans, he thinks, are the results of taking antischizophrenic medication, not those of the "disease" itself. The Germans, who invented neuropathology, looked at the brains of thousands of "schizophrenics" before there were any neuroleptics, he points out, and they were unable to find any specific cellular pathology.

Studies show that people treated with neuroleptics have changes in brain structure associated with drug treatment, dosage, and duration that increase over time as drugs are given.

Forty-three percent of the 82 clients treated and followed up in the experimental[8] settings of Soteria and Emanon received no neuroleptics whatsoever during the two years of the study. Others received drug therapy for limited periods of time. While few became paragons of mental health, most were at least spared iatrogenic disorders. *All* of the subjects in the comparison group are at risk for tardive dyskinesia and other side effects induced by neuroleptic drugs.

---

[8]   Many clients who did not meet the research criteria for the study stayed at the two houses (see pages 64–65).

Change Soteria-Style

Once residents' needs for warmth, food, and shelter were met, and once they understood that those needs would continue to be met, the community encouraged changing roles in terms of function and power at Soteria.

The staff at Soteria embraced the notion that recovery from psychosis was not only possible but probable and to be expected.

Loren's comment: You start there, and you're way ahead of the game right away.

The Roots of Madness

Rather than seeing psychosis as an unfathomable mystery, Soteria staff treated it as an understandable coping mechanism comparable in some ways to shell shock.

In that trauma, in spite of the fact that an individual soldier survived a horrendous battle, he often went out of his mind later. Shell-shocked individuals rant and rave—so do acute psychotics. The difference is that the soldier's trauma—the overwhelming experience to which he is reacting—is obvious.

In contrast, what drives "schizophrenics" over the edge tends not to be readily identifiable; Usually, it is a response to cumulative experiences rather than to a single event.

A number of scientific studies over the years have traced various psychosocial factors leading to "schizophrenia."

For example, more than half of adult admissions to psychiatric hospital wards have histories of sexual and/or physical abuse, contributing factors not receiving attention until the 1980s, after Soteria's demise.

Two aspects of family life are consistently associated with what's called "schizophrenia:" parents' communication deviance (inability to focus and to be clear) and parents' hostility towards their children.

No single factor can be said to be the sole cause of "schizophrenia," and not every person who's been sexually or physically abused becomes psychotic. Some don't; some do. But when someone goes crazy, it's often in response to numerous problems, usually triggered by a particularly distressing event like a romantic rejection, the death of a parent, or excessive involvement with recreational drugs.

If sexual or physical trauma is compounded by a hostile, critical, fuzzy family—and then someone breaks your heart—your chances of going to pieces are pretty good.

Going crazy is a way of coping. What the psychotic person is saying is, "Hey, folks, I'm out of here. I'm constructing this world as it pleases me. I don't need to pay attention to the world out there that is hurting me. Instead, I'm going to live in this one, which I made."

The mad person's chances for returning to "normal" life in the outside world depend on how much they been hurt and how far they have retreated. Some people have been so damaged by relationships that they give up all hope. But that's a small minority. And the majority will try again.

Complementary and Symmetrical Relationships

Relationships were central to Soteria's therapeutic environment. Said one staff member: "When I was first hired for the job at Soteria, I felt as if I had been adopted into a family." Her experience resulted from the community's style of interpersonal relationships. Its aim was not only to provide tangible examples of and personal participation in honest, affectionate, caring, and trusting interactions, but also to instill the skills necessary to initiate such contact with others. Soteria created the opportunity for such relationships for both the staff and the residents. If this base did not develop, a resident's progress could be greatly inhibited, and much of what was unique to the Soteria experience, which rested on interconnections and a sense of community, would be lost.

Soteria stressed the necessity of developing symmetrical as well as complementary relationships. In the former, two people exchange similar types of behavior—for example, mutual criticism, support, or advice. While symmetrical relationships can become competitive, symmetry—balance—is the focus. In complementary relationships, on the other hand, the behaviors exchanged reinforce each other: One gives and one receives; one teaches and the other learns, and so forth. The tendency in this case is to develop roles of power and dependency, roles that are by definition imbalanced.

Soteria fostered neither symmetrical nor complementary interactions exclusively. (Constructive, balanced relationships are made up of constantly shifting elements of both kinds.) Hence, interactions at Soteria, which aimed to offer a corrective interpersonal environment, provided new relational experiences for residents.

It would be simplistic to describe the activities at Soteria only in terms of these two dimensions. Interrelationships among members of the community were far too complex to describe only in terms of complementarity and symmetry. Still, these concepts usefully describe certain community practices. For instance, symmetrical interactions among staff and clients were encouraged at the time of separation. Because of the crises that many residents were experiencing when they moved into the house, symmetrical interactions usually weren't immediately feasible, and complementary relationships emerged at first.

The Past—Not Always Prologue

Compared to more causally based models of treatment, Soteria's focus on interpersonal phenomenology neither assumed nor focused extensively on but explored what preconditions caused behavior patterns to emerge. This approach distinguished Soteria's methods from most—if not all—other major approaches to treatment. At Soteria, no preconceived notions about the causes of madness separated what individual members of the community saw as "what is" from what the program defined as "what is." Everyone was entitled to his or her view of "reality."

Because this condition was essential, staff members were selected because of their strength of character, compatibility with the others, tolerance, and flexibility. Identification and emulation were major components of change at Soteria; therefore, staff members were chosen for their abilities to serve as role models as well as to be comfortable with the maelstrom that often characterizes acute psychosis. Although everyone had an individual view of the nature of "reality," the staff and program director were the purveyors of Soteria's culture. Thus, the *program* conformed in many ways to conventional realities, while it at the same time recognized the *individual's* right to harbor an idiosyncratic one. Soteria's process, thus, allowed its members to establish a community that had the support and protection of a group identity to guide it through the broader social context.

How Patients Change: The Control Groups

The Valley Medical Center, part of the Santa Clara County Hospital, included two locked 30-bed psychiatric wards, which served as controls to the experiments at Soteria and Emanon. Prospective admits to Valley Medical Center meeting the research criteria were alternatively referred to Soteria or to the hospital's wards. Emanon was similarly served by an equivalent county hospital, Chope, in San Mateo.

Valley's wards were well-staffed, active treatment facilities oriented towards crisis intervention. Staff administered high doses of neuroleptics, made rapid evaluations, and aimed as immediate goals to place patients in other parts of their treatment networks. All of the control patients received antipsychotic medicine during their inpatient stays. During the 12 years of the study, only one patient was discharged drug free.

The hospital staffs were generally well-trained, experienced, and enthusiastic; they believed they were doing a good job. Each patient was assigned to one of five treatment teams operating on each ward and to a therapist (a psychiatric technician, a community worker, or another specialist), who with the team took a major role in planning treatment. Each day, each patient met with his or her treatment team, saw a physician (for a half hour), and went to occupational therapy (one and a half hours). Other groups met less frequently—While crisis groups often met for an hour and a half, five times weekly, other groups often met only once a week. For instance, patients and spouses (two hours); a psychodrama group for those able to participate (two

THROUGH Madness to Deliverance

hours); a women's group (two hours); and a survival group for readmitted patients (one and a half hours).

Valley's inpatient service accepted patients from all over Santa Clara County (it was the only facility with a 24-hour-a-day psychiatric emergency service and locked wards); therefore, most patients were referred back for outpatient care to one of four regional facilities nearer their homes. That care could include partial hospitalization (day or night); individual, family, or group therapy; and medications. Also available through the county was an extensive board and care system of semisupervised boarding houses as well as eight halfway houses for adolescents and adults.

It cost about four times as much daily to treat patients labeled "schizophrenic" at Valley or Chope as to maintain residents at Soteria or Emanon. Experimental subjects, however, stayed much longer—about five months—than controls—about one month. (See *Result Seven*, pages 263–266 for details.)

"Dispatching" on the Wards

For six months in the 1970s, as part of her doctoral study, Wilson went to observe the two local 30-bed wards, where the project's control subjects were admitted and treated. As a former nurse, she was qualified to describe hospital ward processes. Her report is based on 120 hours of participant observation on the wards, which included time spent on all shifts, attendance at all meetings, review of all the wards' written documents (e.g., guidelines for medical coverage, nursing notes), and informal interviews with all types of staff. In 1974, Wilson's dissertation described the wards' primary overall functioning as a "dispatching process" with a variety of subprocesses as follows:

1. *Patching.* Staff's initial contact with patients often revolves around the imposition of a variety of behavioral controls such as the use of seclusion rooms, mechanical restraints, verbal instructions, and particularly heavy doses of psychotropic medications such as Haldol, Prolixin, or Thorazine. In essence, violent, out-of-control, or inappropriately bizarre patients are *patched together* by

subduing their socially unacceptable symptoms as quickly as possible.

2. *Medical screening.* Because the psychiatric dispatching process (a term used to encompass the multiple, complex operations employed for "processing patients through" a clearinghouse model of care) takes place in a "medical" setting under the direction of physicians for the most part, a standardized routine of physical testing and diagnostic procedures is immediately initiated for all new admissions. These procedures include a physical exam, blood work, urinalysis, EEG, and a selected variety of others. Such screening also serves as an information-gathering strategy in that on occasion a patient's psychiatric problem is discovered to be a consequence of a medical or physiological disorder. Properties of this process of screening are that it is extremely time consuming for staff, that it requires accurate and proper completion of a multitude of requisitions and forms, and that it is rigidly imposed, even though a patient who is readmitted may have undergone the same screening process within the same week.

3. *Piecing together a story.* Proportionately speaking, the most staff time and energy is devoted to this dimension of the dispatching process. In order to make subsequent decisions about distributing a patient to the appropriate aftercare placement, as well as the more immediate decision of which course of medications to begin, a diagnosis must be made. Thus, information-gathering and intelligence operations consume staff's focus during the first 72 hours of a patient's confinement. The interaction of staff attempting to sleuth out and uncover information about a patient in order to engage in fate-making decisions, with patients who are attempting to cover up what they believe is damaging data about themselves, constitutes another key focus for staff/ patient contact. The major modalities for this contact are the "Group Intake Interview" wherein a newly

admitted patient is confronted by a group of staff in an interview room and questioned, and the "Second-Hand Report" where bits and pieces of data are passed along from shift to shift verbally and on the patient's chart and then used to make generalizations about the patient. Properties of this process are its preconceived tendency, a reliance on speculations which easily become "truth," and the trickery involved in "finding things out."

4. *Labeling and sorting.* Once there is sufficient data to justify some decisions, patients are stamped with a psychiatric label. For the most part, patients in the study setting fell into the following diagnostic categories: schizophrenic, manic-depressive, alcohol or drug abuse, or violent character disorder of some type. Labeling acts as a key in deciding which medications to order and which aftercare placements to begin exploring. It also provides staff with an additional source of control in their dealings with patients, for with diagnoses comes an increased sense of being able to predict patient behavior and the ability to deal with patient communications and behaviors as typifications—"That's her hysterical personality coming out; those are just delusions," etc.

5. *Distributing.* The official goal of community mental health legislation in California also includes a goal of moving mentally ill persons back into "the community" as rapidly as possible. Yet, psychiatric professionals in the study setting are constantly balancing this mandate against their perceived mandate to act as protectors of society and their patients. Consequently, staff act as fate-makers by distributing their "charges" to one of a variety of placement options for follow-up and aftercare. A property of the distributing stage of dispatching is its revolving door nature. Many of the setting's patients are "old familiars," who periodically rotate through the study setting and back out again. A number of patients are *tracked* by community liaison workers, who contribute additional data, which are taken into account when

distributing decisions are made. Reports include the fact that one aftercare facility or another "won't take her back again," so the options become limited by virtue of exhausting some of them over time.

The above conceptualization of "usual psychiatric care" in the study setting conveys, I hope, the complex nature of the psychiatric decision making and deposition process that goes on. Consequences of these operations include (a) A very hectic and busy pace of work for staff while the hours "drift by" for patients. (b) A low accessibility of staff for patients—sitting and talking with patients has very low priority in view of all the tasks that must be accomplished. (c) A substitution of technology for potential face-to-face contacts (e.g., there's a mechanical cigarette lighter on the wall to discourage patients from bothering busy staff for lights; medications are announced over a loud speaker instead of passed out by a nurse who seeks out patients around the ward, etc). (d) Staff spend the majority of their time in interaction with other staff—in report, team meetings, intake interviews, and other meetings. (This observation differed on the two wards with more staff/patient contact on Ward I, in ritualized formats such as "anger group," "feelings group," etc., but these contacts were low on spontaneity, low on openness, and high on superficiality and control.) (e) Staff are the constants on the units with patients only passing through, thus a lot of energy is devoted to intrastaff conflict, problems, and the distribution of labor. (f) Most staff have a lot of integrity about their work—their value systems are relatively congruent with conventional psychiatric and medical model explanations of madness. (1974, pp. 77–81)

A View from Inside

Complementing Wilson's careful observations and author Kate Millett's horrific experiences on her "loony-bin trip" (page 258) is the following eloquent retrospective of a former patient about the treatment he received five years earlier as a 20-year-old on the psych ward of a general hospital.

As I've said, I feel pretty lucky for the way things turned out for me. I've never been bitter about the nonsense I went through at the hospital; in fact, it became great fun after a while. But there is a point that chills me sometimes and amazes me to contemplate.

It disturbs me to think back on the effort that was made to fit me with a permanent label and to persuade me that I had a brain disease, that my situation was fixed, and that there was little point in considering my view of what had happened. There was no interest in my version of events, except insofar as the details could be made to corroborate and solidify the diagnosis. Yes, when I emerged from my third break, I could look back— and simply understood how I had arrived at that place, and why. With that clarity, I felt certain the whole thing was over. I could also see real value in it. God knows, it was frightening to my loved ones, but on a personal level, it was profound. When I hinted at this in conversations with my doctor—well, that is when a peculiar contest arose between us.

At that point my doctor began awaiting—even praying?— for my next psychotic break, and I began fighting much harder than I needed to, to keep it from happening. When it did not go his way, my doctor got downright nasty; he seemed deeply disappointed. It was during this period, I think, that my personal records came to contain all manner of bullshit notations like "residual symptoms," some of which now seem comical to me, because I know very well in some cases just how appropriate my "inappropriate" affect was becoming.

The point, in my eyes, is that the result could have been much different. This is what disturbs me to think about sometimes, and I think my own case is a good example of this problem. Suppose that my doctors had been able to persuade me that I did indeed have a brain disease, and suppose I had taken to repeating the catechisms I was expected to memorize. Suppose I had stayed on medication for the recommended 6 to 12 months. It is conceivable that, when I discontinued, I might have had that reaction that some people get when they go off the medication—the one that looks like a relapse. Where would I be, if that had happened? I was never encouraged to read anything but E. Fuller Torrey's

Surviving Schizophrenia, so how would I have known what to make
of it all? I might well now be convinced that "schizophrenia" is a
disease—"just like diabetes"—and be spending my time trying to
publish my personal testimony in Reader's Digest. (personal
communication, 2002)

Five years later, this supposedly chronically ill young man has a full-time job
and a passionate artistic avocation. Since discharge, he has taken no psychotropic
medications, nor has he been rehospitalized.

How Patients Change—Social Rehabilitation Models

Social rehabilitation facilities mainly serve individuals *after* they been treated in hospitals.[9] The social rehabilitation movement won greater acceptance in the 1980s, after hospitals had emptied large numbers of their disabled clients into communities that lacked facilities to care for them. A high percentage of these refugees had never learned, or had lost through disuse in the institutions, the basic social and instrumental skills needed to survive in the community. In social rehabilitation models, the disabled change when they are taught basic living skills that enable reentry into the mainstream of society. The implication is that the recovering person, at one point in the past, was "habilitated" and needs only to learn or to regain those skills to return successfully to the community. Hence, residential social rehabilitation settings provided some responses to the widespread criticism of the process of deinstitutionalization.

In this system, staff and patients have some potential for normal relationships. Social rehabilitation models, reflecting psychosocial paradigms, are less medically oriented than hospital ones. These community-based settings employing paraprofessional staff members operate with the expectation that learning basic living skills can assist the client's integration into the community. The role of the staff, therefore, is to train rather than to do therapy, to cure. Change in

---

[9]   Winerip's 1994 book describes one example of this type of facility.

community-based models comes from teaching—the staff instructs the patients in life skills.

How Residents Change—Soteria Model

The Soteria model incorporates aspects of both the hospital model and social rehabilitation models, but it differs from both in that the primary cause of change is based neither on therapeutic intervention nor in learning basic living skills. Change occurs through the normal interactive processes, when the system's members come into contact with each other. As a result, issues surrounding the nature of relationships between and among staff and residents become central to change Soteria-style.

Soteria staff believed that almost no one was too crazy to talk to.

> *Loren comments: If you believe that there is a person in that disoriented head, and you can really speak to him or to her, in only a few instances will you be thwarted. During my stint in psychiatric hospitals, when attendants presented me with their most psychotic inmate, I would sit down with this very, very crazy person. Then, he or she and I would have a conversation, which—after the first five minutes or so—everyone listening could understand. The observers invariably explained that this coherence resulted because the patient "was having a good day today," not because we two were communicating.*
>
> *I don't see it that way. If you treat people with dignity and respect and want to understand what's going on, want to get yourself inside their shoes, you can do it.*
>
> *And it doesn't take very special training to develop this skill. What it takes is attitude and interest and intensity and willingness to sort of suspend your own reality and not worry about it.*

The relationship between physician and patient is by definition unequal. To elaborate: The implication is that the doctor, by virtue of his/her role, rules. When the patient becomes capable of exerting acceptable self-control, s/he will likely be discharged, terminating his/her active participation in the therapeutic network.

In contrast, many of Soteria's graduates kept in close touch with the community. Continuing involvement is important because of the high level of the personal commitment among members of the Soteria community. The relationships were *personal* and, therefore, had implications beyond separation, for the clients as well as for the staff and volunteers. At Soteria, therapeutic involvement went beyond the boundary of the official relationships framed by admission and discharge.

Why? Because relationships were critical: If they didn't happen at Soteria, neither did change. It was nearly impossible not to develop *some* kind of relationship in the Soteria process. The issue became a question of *what* kind should be encouraged. In hospital or rehabilitation settings, relationships between staff and clients often developed around the degree of a patient's dependency upon a particular staff member. Such a relationship was usually abruptly terminated upon discharge.

Size also plays a major role in how relationships form in institutional and noninstitutional settings. (See *Structure*, page 203 for elaboration.) It also dictates some aspects of structure: Large groups of people require more elaborate sets of controls to maintain a functional system than do small groups. If the desire is to develop the capacity to follow orders, as in the military, then a large institutional process is appropriate. If the intention is to develop the capability to maintain a productive existence in the broader community, it is unnecessary— or even harmful—to instill that degree of conformity.

The nature of the Soteria involvement was not to "do therapy" with clients but to interact with them in as normal ways as possible given the conditions. Put another way, Soteria believed in *being with* instead of *doing to.*

Space for Interpersonal Networks

Soteria made sure that its philosophical belief in the paramount importance of relationships was matched by a physical and psychological setting wherein they could develop. Interpersonal networks take time, energy (physical and mental), and *space*. This space differs from that available for *involvement*—the kind that occurs between people having only limited or one-time contacts, such as those between clerks and customers or among people sharing a common space, such as neighbors. It also differs from *intrapersonal* involvement, the time spent alone.

Areas of personal contact are of limited availability but play a major role in one's interaction with his/her environment. Because interpersonal relationships among community members were key factors at Soteria, the house strove to establish a milieu conducive to such lasting interactions. This concept deviates significantly from traditional modes of treatment and calls for several operational factors:

    ✎ a willingness on the part of the staff to view a client as a potential peer

    ✎ a process that allows and/or encourages both clients and staff the opportunity to establish and maintain a shared, equal relationship

    ✎ available network space

The last point is of critical importance.

Interactions are more affected by network availability than most people think. Staff working in hospitals are discouraged from personal interactions with patients through overt rules, through implicit programmatic procedures, and through covert training techniques. Hospital staff are typically instructed not to touch clients any more than necessary, for example, and to keep relationships with patients on a professional level. Staff at most hospitals have a well-established network system that includes other staff members and excludes patients. As a result, staff has little room for interpersonal involvement with patients. These patients, isolated from their normal networks by the trauma of being hospitalized, have an enormous need to fill the void. No wonder hospital staffs do not want to open up potentially endless floods of involvement, especially given the large number of patients who generally fill psychiatric wards.

Other typical hospital procedures distinguish sharply between the duties of the staff and the patients; Soteria's did not. Most hospital workers attempt to treat patients rather than to coexist with them, an active-passive set of roles that helps to reinforce differences. Hospital staff gives medication, for example, with or without their patients' consent.

As noted earlier (pages 19–22), Soteria's policy towards drugs was decidedly experimental. While medication was under certain circumstances offered to residents as an option, it was never administered against their wills.

In Sum

The differences between the hospital and the Soteria model are clear. Not so clear is how Soteria differs from social rehabilitation models. The potential for a process like Soteria's to occur in a social rehabilitation facility is high. Such institutions are usually staffed by less medically-oriented people than psychiatric wards; they are usually located in minimally institutional settings like houses; and they are usually small. It is the inherent difference in the concept of change that points out a basic dissimilarity.

If the predominance of the healer's work is finished when the client has learned his/her basic living skills, then it becomes unimportant for the two to continue to interact. For Soteria, however, interpersonal interaction *was* the work. The potential for ongoing relationships, therefore, existed as a natural part of the process without the expectation that they would end after discharge.

In fact, the Soteria program existed mainly to bring people together to establish ongoing relationships. A secondary reason was protection. Like social rehabilitation programs, Soteria temporarily sheltered the disabled by making available food, lodging, and other essentials at a time when individuals could not provide for themselves. So social rehabilitation programs might, like Soteria, protect and establish relationships. Because of their other mission, however, they would not be able to do what Soteria believed critical—establish and encourage appropriate long-term relationships. The rehabilitation policies of discharging clients to other programs—independent living centers, halfway houses, daycare centers, and other after-care programs—affirms their expectation that the healed would move on without the support formerly necessary.

In short: The relationship of patient to hospital is unequal and temporary; that of client to rehabilitation center, tutorial and transitional; that of resident to Soteria, equitable and—potentially— permanent.

The history of one resident's stay at the house, which concludes this chapter, was not atypical of the general course of events many residents experienced at Soteria even though she was not a research subject. At the same time, what occurred is uniquely hers.

Deirdre: A Soteria Cameo

When admitted to Soteria for her 12-week stay, Deirdre was 17. Her three other sisters (one a nonidentical twin) and brother were attending college at the time Deirdre was hospitalized. Her parents appeared to have a good relationship, although her father may have had a problem with alcohol.

Deirdre's early history showed difficulties that stemmed from her feelings of inferiority to her twin sister, especially at school. She appeared phobic and frightened during her first five years of public school, though she was not in academic trouble: Her grades were above average.

In retrospect, Deirdre's family felt that the problem leading to her hospitalization began several years earlier when she was about 14. Subsequently, her parents noticed signs of severe disturbance in Deirdre's last month of high school. After enrolling in but before entering college, she experienced her first major crisis. The particular events in Deirdre's life that coincided with the onset of her crisis were adolescent dating, high school graduation, and college registration.

She stayed briefly in San Diego with her cousin, stating that he "willed her into insanity." Shortly before being admitted to the hospital, she had seen a psychiatrist, who prescribed Mellaril, a tranquilizer used primarily with psychotics.

On her return to San Jose, Deirdre became so upset that she had to be hospitalized at Valley Medical Center for six weeks. Her records from Valley Medical Center show that she had been given several different drug regimens.

Her mother said,

> All they did was give her medications, which seemed to make her worse. They put her on one kind of medication; then, they took her off that and put her on another kind. We just had to find her some place else to be, so we took her to Kaiser-Permenente Hospital in Richmond.

Deirdre liked the Kaiser approach better than Valley Medical Center's. She remained there another six weeks, remembering

> At least the doctors were more friendly; in fact, I made some friends there. They seemed to care more about me as a person. I think the medication was helping me, but it made me sleepy most of the time.
>
> I also liked it better there because they had more groups. People just spent more time with you there.

Deirdre's fatigue was a common side effect of most of the drugs used to treat psychotics. She was given similar medications for short terms at both facilities, but there seemed to be more person-to-person contact at Kaiser, and Deirdre voluntarily visited the ward once after she left the program.

Deirdre's parents had heard about Soteria from friends and decided to try to get Deirdre into the program because they worried about the effects and dosage of her medication. They had heard that antipsychotic drugs can be physically dangerous.

They also wanted Deirdre closer to them, so they could more easily visit; however, Deirdre felt that her family, more specifically her parents, were intruding too much.

Arriving

When Deirdre arrived at Soteria, Voyce observed that she was

> very nervous and disorganized at times. She feels that
> someone is trying to rape her and somehow feels that it
> would be good for her. She complains of feeling sleepy most
> of the time.

Deirdre's psychiatrist at Kaiser opposed any change in her drug treatment:

PSYCHIATRIST. I can only agree to let Deirdre go to your
program if you agree to keep her on the medication
we have her on now. We have heard that your program
is against medication, and Deirdre's treatment calls
for it at this time. It would be irresponsible to take her
off, because she would immediately regress, possibly
without being able to recover.

VOYCE. Have you ever withheld medication?

PSYCHIATRIST. Yes, and she started immediately to regress.

VOYCE. Then what happened?

PSYCHIATRIST. We reestablished the medication before she
had regressed too far to recover.

VOYCE. We have found that some people taken off medications
regress first but then do better without the medications.

PSYCHIATRIST. I'll believe that when I see it. I believe that
Deirdre will be schizophrenic—and probably
medicated—for the rest of her life.

VOYCE. Our psychiatrist is well versed pharmacologically, and
he will probably see things as you do. I would like to be
able to consult with you whenever possible on Deirdre's
progress, and I will have our psychiatrist contact you
tomorrow when he's here.

PSYCHIATRIST. We think we have found her optimal level
now. She seems to have some kind of control.

First Days

Deirdre arrived at Soteria taking 1,000 milligrams of Thorazine, 30 milligrams of Haldol, and 2 milligrams of Cogentin. Under the influence of these massive doses of neuroleptic drugs, with nearly identical therapeutic profiles, Deirdre had difficulty staying awake and, when awake, could barely move.

After talking to Deirdre's psychiatrist at Kaiser, Stan, Soteria's house psychiatrist, found it advisable to continue Deirdre's medication for at least a month before gradually withdrawing it. But Voyce, in consultation with Alma, Soteria's project director, disagreed. Voyce advised withdrawing medication at once. And Deirdre wanted to get off the medication as soon as possible. A compromise was reached: Staff immediately began to reduce her medication with the plan to eliminate it entirely after two weeks.

The first few days, Deirdre complained of constipation and stomach pains but appeared otherwise comfortable in Soteria's environment. Except for some small confusion, Deirdre had an uneventful first week.

Changes

As the medications wore off, she became disorganized, sexually preoccupied, as she put it—"getting into being nude . . . ." Her sleeping patterns became erratic; she stayed up late at night and took periodic short naps.

Voyce's notes from that period:

> Deirdre is deep into her "madness," as the drugs are reduced. Tuesday night Thomas [another resident] told me she came into his room, and they had sex, without intercourse. In the morning her behavior was regressed: She was speaking "baby talk" and urinated on the kitchen floor and over herself.
>
> She quickly got back into age-appropriate behavior; however, her confused state of being needs constant attention. Luckily, she is very open, bringing out many emotions, so it is easy to *be with* her. She does lots of crying,

especially while listening to the radio, to record albums, to my guitar or to the songs I sing to her.

TV, on the other hand, gets her extremely angry. She had a difficult time sleeping Wednesday night, and Frederick [a volunteer] and I stayed up with her. I remained with her till 4 AM.

Katy [a staff member] and Deirdre slept together in Deirdre's bed.

Katy's notes add,

In the morning, she wanted to breast feed from me. I gave her a baby bottle instead, which pacified her. For about an hour she was into a deep regression; then, she emerged, but in continued confusion.

Deirdre has changed greatly this shift. On Sunday and Monday, she was very spaced out and scared. Staff members stayed with her. Monday night, she slept 11 hours and woke up Tuesday, appearing a lot calmer. She went to the park and played and had a quiet, lucid conversation with me regarding sex. She is anxious to talk of her experiences with other residents and staff.

This period was clearly difficult for Deirdre, however. For instance, she ran away to Kaiser for a few hours before deciding to return to Soteria. Similar unusual behavior continued for at least two weeks before she began to move towards reorganization.

Recovering

Staff member Sidney noted that, after the third week,

Deirdre is continuing to do better, still talking a lot with anyone who's willing. She is able to be alone more, reading, writing, embroidering, and watching TV. Her fears continue, but not to the point that she loses control.

At about this time, Deirdre expressed her sense of pain and
isolation in poetry:

> Silence means peace
> drowning in a Kleenex
> letting all the fears slide
> down to the
> center
> of earth
> peace of mind
> will come one day
> perhaps tomorrow the pain
> will die
> and good feelings will come
> a hard night
> from all the sorrow
> pain and hatred
> all these emotions
> collected on the small
> brain
> of a child
> trying to become an
> adult
> but still drowning
> in anguish
> will the headache
> go away soon?

From four weeks on, she made continuous progress, interrupted
by some short bouts of anxiety, one of which centered around going
home for a visit.

Katy's notes continue:

> Deirdre is increasingly clear and secure. She participates
> more and isn't as afraid of noises or intensity. We went to
> Planned Parenthood, where she was fitted for a diaphragm

after participating in a "rap" there about contraception. She has a vaginal infection for which she was given medication. All went really well—in spite of a four and a half hour wait! Her sister is coming home from Wednesday to Sunday, and Deirdre would like to visit her at home on Thursday.

This feels all right and good to me now. She's increasingly stable.

Six weeks into her stay at Soteria, Deirdre started to look for work. Staffer Nelly remembered that she went with Deirdre to a job interview and she "got it!"—i.e., a position as a gift wrapper at Penney's. Afterward, the two went shopping and out to dinner.

"Deirdre has been in an active positive space since then," Nelly exulted, but added, "I'm a little concerned she may be taking on too much (frequently adding, for example, to her list of courses at school)."

Reintegrating

Four days later, this report:

Deirdre went to work at Penney's today from noon to 9 PM. She was anxious and missed the bus this morning, but Stuart drove her over and she made it through the day.

At 10 weeks:

Deirdre has resolved the school issue for now: She is going. She is still working at Penney's and around the house. She appears to be in an OK mood.

At 11 weeks:

Deirdre is now mobile, literally. She borrowed the family car and drove people to the beach. She also takes people shopping, and she still plans to go to school.

Deirdre's graduation note at 12 weeks:

> Deirdre is enrolled at San Jose State and lives in the dorm, as
> of today. She agreed to come to the house every other day, if
> she is having problems.

Epilogue

After leaving Soteria, Deirdre continued working and completed a
BA in psychology. She stayed in contact with members of the
community. Eventually, she become a forest ranger, living in a state
park with a boyfriend for several years.

Deirdre talked about wanting to write a book about her experience
but had difficulty getting started. She and Voyce have kept up a regular
correspondence since Soteria closed.

Twelve weeks on medications in psychiatric wards helped Deirdre
not at all; after the same amount of time at Soteria, with support from
her sympathetic family, she emerged healthy and able to live effectively
and responsibly on her own.

The Staff

I T WAS NOT even revolutionary during Soteria's days to employ nonprofessional mental health workers to deal with persons labeled "schizophrenic." It certainly is not now.

Soteria's decision to use carefully trained nonprofessionals as primary staff was well-considered (see Mosher, Reifman, and Menn, 1973, and Hirschfeld et al., 1977, for retrospective personality and psychological test characteristics of the staff). Loren believed that the inexperienced and psychologically unsophisticated can adopt useful interpersonal-phenomenological stances vis-à-vis psychosis more easily than highly trained MDs or PhDs, because the former work from no theory of "schizophrenia"—psychodynamic, organic, or both. Because they are unburdened by preconceived theories, nonprofessional staff members are free to be themselves, to follow their untutored responses, and to be spontaneous with psychotic individuals.

Highly trained mental health personnel often replace this freedom with cognitive, abstract, learned responses that, if the professional's theory-based behavior is not congruent with the patient's needs, can invalidate the latter's experience. Professionals sometimes also use their theoretical knowledge defensively when confronted, in an unstructured setting, with anxiety-provoking behaviors by psychotic persons. For example, patients' often *justified* fears that professionals are trying to control them could be described by their psychiatrists as "projected needs to be controlled." This pattern of response is neither so readily available to nonprofessional therapists nor is it reinforced by the status and power of a professional degree or hierarchical context.

Sullivan had been using such nonprofessional personnel to work successfully with schizophrenics in the 1920s at the Sheppard and Enoch Pratt Hospital in Towson, Maryland—his rate for patient recovery or improvement was 12 of 16, or a remarkable 75 percent, as compared to 25–30 percent for those treated by professionals. Soteria's overall recovery rate—largely achieved without the use of antipsychotic drug treatment—was similar to Sullivan's. In addition to a theoretical preference for nonprofessional staff, Soteria used them for a practical reason as well—money. At the time, administrators were aware that the staff were not well paid; now, in retrospect, it seems to Loren that, at about $10 per hour in today's dollars, they were exploited.

The original staff members were recruited by word of mouth in the consciousness-raising underground of the Bay area in the early 1970s and from a number of other sources. Some came from a project at nearby Agnews State Hospital, where a Laingian-type ward housed a medication experiment. This project, which was directed by Maurice Rappaport, MD, and Julian Silverman, PhD, and included John W. Perry, MD, a Jungian analyst, in a consultant's role, also furnished Soteria with some of its original staff. Silverman was closely connected to the Esalen Institute in Big Sur, the birthplace of the human potential movement, which also produced a number of Soteria staff members. For further details on the Agnews experience, see pages 165–170 and Rappaport, Hopkins, Hall, Belleza, and Silverman (1978).

There were many more applicants for Soteria's opening staff positions than places available. Project organizers knew of no demographic predictors for the ability to work well with unmedicated psychotics, so they selected staff members based, in the case of applicants who had not worked at Agnews, on performance evaluations and additional skills—for example, music, carpentry, massage, yoga, wrestling—that might conceivably benefit the project. Some performance evaluations consisted of the applicant's spending time with a psychotic and an experienced mental health worker. Applicants whose interaction with both was promising entered the pool of potential staffers. Gender balance was also important.

Loren, his research associate Ann Reifman, and Alma early on defined original staff selection procedures. They noted that, because of the potentially threatening questions the Soteria project raised about traditional mental health practices, organizers tried to select a fundamentally apolitical staff whose beliefs would not actively conflict with the status quo. The staff were neither conservative nor liberal, they explained, continuing,

> We believe that an apolitical staff is important for two reasons. First, the work in the house is so draining that it would be an unusual person who could both work with psychotics and actively pursue anti-Establishment activities. Second, because we are located in a community, it is not possible . . . to be insulated from the existing order . . . . If staff were to set themselves up in an adversary role, the community would soon make it impossible for us to operate . . . . Problems with our neighbors would be difficult enough without adding unnecessary conflict. (1973, p. 393)

On-the-Job Training

Soteria's first six months of existence served as a training ground for its nonprofessional staff. The learning process was informal—no lectures, readings, classes. Instead apprentices worked beside experienced therapists, following each session with a free-ranging discussion among staff members, with or without the project director or one of the consulting psychiatrists. During these encounters, participants probed their feelings, doubts, fears, insights, and hopes about approaches that were helpful—or compromising. "At Soteria," wrote Loren and his colleagues, "a therapeutic session can last anywhere from 10 minutes to 3 weeks, since, in our experience, psychosis does not fit well into 50-minute hours" (1973, p. 393).

The training approach, thus, fell into a traditional apprenticeship model. The major focus of the therapeutic relationship emphasized the importance of coexisting with psychotics rather than curing them (see below pages 169–201 for an extended discussion). Although Soteria's nonprofessionals did not typically intellectualize, like their more traditional colleagues, they sometimes needed to curb impulses to manipulate, distance, categorize, or demand. And they needed, on occasion, help with tolerating, supporting, and empathizing with residents without giving in to fear or stress.

The following episode illustrates training Soteria-style.

A new resident, Owen, with a history of violent outbreaks had since admission been quietly trailing after a staff member, Tim, helping with household chores and errands. On the third day, Owen became extremely quiet, began to weep silently, and retreated to his bed. Tim waited half an hour; then, wanting to help but not knowing how to, he called the consulting psychiatrist who asked what Tim wanted to do for Owen.

"Go into his room," Tim responded.

"Go ahead," said the psychiatrist. "I'll be along soon if you need help."

By the time the psychiatrist arrived, Tim and Owen were in deep conversation and, while the psychiatrist let Tim know he was available, he did not interrupt and left without seeing either. Tim stayed with Owen all afternoon and late into the evening.

The next day, Tim, the psychiatrist, and the rest of the staff discussed the incident in detail. The experience had been a breakthrough for Owen, who had for the first time felt able to express some terrifying thoughts. It had also served Tim. By not responding immediately to Tim's request for help, the psychiatrist demonstrated his belief that Tim could both understand Owen and deal with any hostility that might come out. Tim knew, on the other hand, that, if need be, he could rely on the psychiatrist.

In a later paper, Loren and Alma joined two colleagues to study the personality characteristics of staff in two traditional mental health programs in comparison to those of Soteria's original staff (Hirschfeld et al., 1977). A battery of self-report personality questionnaires were administered to first-year staff from Soteria, to personnel from a university psychiatric ward, and to workers in a community-based program. The results showed

> an over-all similarity of personality profiles in the three groups.
> All . . . demonstrated . . . the ego-strength qualities of self-
> assurance, emotional maturity, independence, and autonomy

and the affective qualities of warmth, sensitivity, and empathy. However, . . . Soteria staff possessed significantly more intuition, introversion, flexibility, and tolerance of altered states of consciousness. The authors speculate that it is this last set of characteristics that allow the Soteria staff to function in the program's intensive, unstructured treatment environment. (p. 273)

Basically, over the life of the project, the staff continued young (usually under 30), middle-to-lower class, and free of therapeutic or political rigidity. Thus, the characteristics of the "ur-group" remained typical of the other staff who worked at Soteria during its 12 years of existence. Later on, when staff came in significant numbers from the California School of Professional Psychology and from individuals working under the auspices of the Comprehensive Employment and Training Act (CETA), the level of formal education went up. This increase was not always a positive development: The amount of education did not predict, positively or negatively, success as a staff member at Soteria. When university students became staff, in fact, they frequently arrived with academically acquired belief systems inappropriate to Soteria's milieu. When such staff tried to apply their theories, the result was occasionally conflicts needing resolution. See *Soteria Years*, pages 103–123.

Still, often the difference between Soteria's staff and its residents was like the one Carl Jung defined between James Joyce and his psychotic daughter, Lucia. Jung explained to the writer that the two were both like people heading for the bottom of a river; one, however, was diving and the other, drowning. Since Sullivan's experiment, "there have been many studies of the efficacy of nonprofessionals as mental health therapists. Overall, results of such studies have clearly demonstrated the nonprofessionals' effectiveness in the treatment of a variety of mental disorders. Interestingly, in certain situations they may even outperform professionals" (Hirschfeld et al., 1977, pp. 257–258).

During the course of the project, some 25 full-time staff members worked at Soteria and Emanon with about 200 clients. (In its 12-year span, Soteria housed about 125 residents; Emanon, about 75.) Of these 200 or so people, about 75 were clients who, for one reason or another, were not part of the formal study—for example, they remained for less than the 28 days required by the research protocol. In addition, after 1978, no research subjects were admitted and studied. In the following pages, both professional residents and staff, along with the approximately 15 part-timers and scores of volunteers—as many as 14 different individuals per week—have been simplified into *representative* males and females. The names of the nonprofessional staff (except for Voyce) and all the residents have been changed.

Who Worked at Soteria?

Soteria and Emanon's full- and part-time paid staff and its many volunteers have been distilled into the people listed below.

Women Staff (Including Volunteers)*

Della—a part-time staff member

Evie—a volunteer dance teacher

Katy—a part-time staff member

Kay—a part-time staff member

Kim—a staff member who shared a full-time position with her husband Tom

Kimberly—a full-time staff member and a former resident

Natalie—a middle-aged volunteer

Nelly—a part-time staff member

Ophelia—a California School of Professional Psychology graduate and former volunteer

Susannah—a member of the initial staff

Tabitha—a staff member and a musician

Tara O'Neill—a member of the initial staff

Zaida—a volunteer

* Names have been changed.

Men Staff (Including Volunteers)

Adam—*a full-time staff member*

Bart—*a volunteer*

Daniel—*a member of the initial staff*

Ed—*a part-time staff member*

Elmer—*a volunteer*

Frederick—*a part-time staff member*

Geoff—*a part-time staff member*

Hal—*a part-time staff member*

John—*a part-time staff member*

Keith—*a veteran Soteria staffer, working on his dissertation from
    the University of California at Santa Cruz*

Leonard—*a volunteer, a graduate student at the California School
    of Professional Psychology*

Lewis—*a middle-aged former expatriate*

Luke—*a volunteer*

Ned—*a volunteer*

Saul—*first a resident, then a volunteer*

Stuart—*a Soteria veteran, formerly a psychologist's assistant*

Tim—*a part-time staff member*

Tom—*a staff member who shared a full-time position with his wife
    Kim*

Names have been changed.

Administrative Staff

Alma Zito Menn, ACSW, *Project Director of Soteria and link to
    Mental Research Institute, Palo Alto*

Loren R. Mosher, MD

Voyce Hendrix

Stan Redd, MD—*house psychiatrist from the project's beginning
    (the first cohort) to 1976*

Ken Woodrow, MD—*house psychiatrist who took over Stan's role
    until the project's end (the second cohort)*

Richard Poe, MD—*principal psychiatrist at Emanon*

Stanley Mayerson—*the first person responsible for setting up the research and for screenings at the local inpatient unit*

David L. Rosenhan, PhD—*a Stanford professor, member of the Soteria Board, and fundraiser extraordinare in Soteria's closing days*

Len Goveia—*director of a behaviorally focused private nonprofit group home and, briefly, a part-time principal investigator when the Soteria project was being planned, who left the project after the National Institute of Mental Health reviewers essentially cut out his study from the proposal*

All in a Day's (and Night's!) Work

Ideally, staff members were able to sense nonverbally when residents needed someone to *be with* them. (See *Getting It Together,* pages 165–201, for a full discussion of this therapeutic approach.) Often staff stayed up all night talking with a client, whether that individual was in a crisis state or just wanted companionship. But staff members also reached a point where they had to assert their personal needs. Thus, the emotional requirements of both the resident and the staff person combined to determine the degree of interaction. Early in the history of the project, Alma tried to investigate this process with one of the project's original staff members, Tara.

> ALMA. When you describe what happens with Naomi, you make some kind of judgment that it's better for Naomi to go to sleep than for you to sit up with her. When you decide to sit up with Iris, you make some kind of judgment that you're not going to bring in a male staff member. I'm sure it's some kind of diagnostic evaluation of what's going on with them as well as a diagnostic evaluation of what's going on with you—that is, if you can tolerate what's happening. I'd really like to know how all that works.

TARA. I don't know. It all depends on a lot of things. Sometimes you have an all-nighter with Naomi, and you want it to be an all-nighter because she just seems ready and needy. There are other times when I'm too pissed off at Naomi to stay up with her all night—like if she's been very hostile, and there doesn't seem to be any way to break through that. If I'm really too tired to handle it, then I won't. I don't know how you make your judgments. I imagine everybody does it in different ways. A lot of times Naomi will be really straight and whisper to me, "Come outside," and explain that she's scared, that certain things are upsetting her, and that she wants to talk. Most of the time, 99 percent of the time, when Naomi approaches me in that way, I'll stay up with her as late as she needs, unless physically I'm so worn out that I have to beg off.

Everyone had an individual tolerance level for dealing with a particular situation or resident. The staff tried to acknowledge and reinforce individual differences, realizing that psychotic behaviors (as well as individual personality traits) can eventually try anyone's patience. Susannah offered an example of such a time:

That was one of the times Tamara was resisting being changed or bathed, and she was beginning to offend everybody, so I said it was time to give her a bath. She resisted me all the way to the bathroom. She started to take her pants off and got her hands full of shit and smacked me in the face with it really hard. But more than the smack, it was the shit in the face that was too much for me to bear, and I really thought that I was going to lose control.

It made me very angry, and it just gave me added incentive to get her clean. I said she couldn't do that and threw her in the tub and washed her. I got her nice and clean. She would always like it after we'd get her out of the tub, dry her off, put clean pants on her, and put baby powder on her. She always liked that feeling. It never lasted long because she'd be messing herself a half hour later.

Another time, Tamara wanted me to sleep with her, and it was at that time that if she slept an hour a week that was really something. She would get really tired, but she was too scared to sleep. So she would want somebody in with her. But I wasn't allowed to sleep. She would be very scared if I would even close my eyes, and she would shake me and say, "Don't go to sleep, don't go to sleep."

I'd be trying to pry my eyeballs open because I was so tired. Once I just succumbed and fell asleep. She got pissed off at me for falling asleep and slugged me in the stomach. That kept me awake for the rest of the night.

I was very angry with her. I yelled that she couldn't do that any more, and she immediately told me that I shouldn't have fallen asleep: That was a "No, no." I had to stay awake to protect her from all the "things" that were coming at her— bugs and spiders coming out of the ceilings and out of the walls and stuff like that.

Understanding Limitations and Setting Limits

Some staff members believed that the staff as a whole set itself unrealistically high goals. Tara spoke of her early expectation that she would always work at maximum effectiveness in this very demanding job.

I'm starting to realize that sometimes I'm going to be really good, and other times I'm going to be on a bummer.

There is a lot of expectation in general of staff being this and staff being that, and lately we've started to talk in what I consider a pretty good vein about the fact that there is an inconsistency in the whole setup here. One of the things that we're constantly saying is that residents must be

free to be where they're at, to freak out if they need to, to be
totally real.

But while we're saying "Oh, well, that's fine for you
people to do that," we staff members have to remain perfect,
always together, and super-strong.

That's just unreal, and we don't do it either. I think what
we're all doing now is to recognize our limitations, to try to
stop before we get too stressed, but to forgive ourselves when
we fail. It's a lot more risky. But in the long run, it's so much
better.

It is not surprising that a staff member who has worked long hours
with an acutely disorganized individual experiences tension and
exhaustion. Staff members acknowledged their tendency, in such
situations, to take out their feelings on other staff members as well as,
at times, on residents. One staff member, Geoff, believed that more
open communication could alleviate this situation.

I think that *not talking* has taken up an awful lot of energy
and led to staff discord. Maybe some of that is inevitable
because we're working so closely and under a lot of tension,
but if we could get into the habit of encountering each
other immediately instead of letting things build, feuds start,
and scapegoats emerge . . . I think it would make all the
difference in the world.

It seems that people start getting frustrated with the
situation. Everyone's overtired and overworked and starts
feeling underpaid and resentful—and then they decide to
find a cause. I think part of it happens when we don't really
talk to each other at meetings, when we leave a lot unsaid.
When I hold my gripes back and want everybody on the staff
to work the way I do, think the way I do, have the same
energy level that I do, then I get in a lot of trouble. I start
placing unrealistic expectations on myself and everyone else.

One cause of friction was Soteria's lack of theoretical orthodoxy.

The fact that staff members had unique ways of dealing with particular situations or individuals, however, gave Soteria's approach variety and richness. It also produced some internal conflicts. Explained Geoff, continuing the point he made above,

> We have a staff here of all different kinds of people, and we all have different methods . . . . I think I work best with people who are pretty open. I like a lot of nurturing qualities. When I get with somebody who works really differently than I do, I have a lot of trouble dealing with that. But when I actually sit down and talk with that person about where my feelings are, about how his or her approach makes me uncomfortable with what's being done, I usually find out that we're both really aiming at the same thing anyway. And then we get a lot closer.

Another way of dealing with individual limits on tolerance was to establish staff schedules that realistically reflected the length of time each person could effectively work. As staffer Hal explained to Alma,

> HAL. Geoff and I alternate: Four days on; four days off. Then it moves one day forward each time, so each of us ends up working every day in the week and being off every day in the week. Nobody gets stuck with weekends all the time. This was kind of for Geoff's and my convenience. It gives us a chance to work with everybody. After four weeks, you end up having four weekends off.
>
> After four days, you are ready for some time off and need a new, fresh person. What Geoff and I have been doing a lot is whoever has been off comes in on the fourth day, and both of us work. I'll be working on Geoff's fourth day and stay and work that night because he is pretty well worn out by that time. He also comes in on my fourth day and it allows me to relax a little bit, and if I am really exhausted, he will do that night. I go to bed early and get some sleep if I need it.

ALMA. Can you recollect how long it took you to get to this schedule? Did you experiment a lot, or did you—

HAL. When we figured out the schedule for Geoff and me, we worked around Voyce. We added up the days and the time slots and inked out when Voyce would be here, figuring what was left would be when Geoff and I would fill in. We both kind of laid out what we wanted, which was not to be on every weekend. Because of the pay thing, I was going to work for five days, and Geoff, three.

But Geoff said he didn't like that—he wanted it to be equal. So, we first set it up with five days on and five days off. We figured that was going to be kind of a long time span. So, we went on to four days on and four days off. The whole thing took maybe an hour to set up.

Geoff and I get along well. We like and enjoy each other, and we both felt, to begin with, that we both were willing to do extra to let each other get time off—we were willing to protect each other. It was a kind of acceptance of equality, I guess.

Help from Many Places

Volunteers gave the staff some time in which to relax. Also, as residents became better integrated they were able—often very effectively—to understand and help out other residents. One such client, Deirdre, remembered,

I could relate to Thomas a lot because we were almost the same age—we were both in the same place! With Naomi, I didn't relate too much because she was on a whole different trip. Once I saw where she was at, we got along better and better. I could understand where she was at, because I once had overweight problems too and because like her I have an

acne problem, and I can understand the feelings she has
around people . . . the jealousy and stuff. I could understand
when she got really mad at Kelly one day, because Kelly was
showing the pretty things she made. Naomi came out and
just really got down on Kelly, not that she was mad at Kelly.
She was mad at herself. She was jealous.

Help with residents from residents was one of Soteria's staff's
somewhat unusual sources of assistance. That those seeking help
often became those giving help had a good deal to do with the
contributions of Loren, who believed truly helpful relationships
eventually become reciprocal. Hence, there was an expectation
that someone who had been helped would at some point also
help.

Soteria's staff also had support from various administrators,
among them project director Alma Menn. She originally acted as a
liaison between the house and its program and the community at
large, thus freeing staff members to devote all their energy to working
within the house. Alma also served as a confidant and advisor to
staff and residents, not as a timekeeper or disciplinarian. People
at the house were able to talk out their frustrations, uncertainties,
and fears with Alma—someone who knew the situation intimately
yet was able to provide a different perspective on it. Said one staff
member, Katy,

> Alma's really good to have around. I wish she could be here
> more. She's a very strong woman, and I really admire that.
> She's dependable. I don't have the feeling that she'd ever
> crumble under something.

Hal, another staff member, described the role of house psychiatrist
Stan Redd.[10] Stan knew, Hal thought, when to help—and, just as
important—when not to help:

---

[10]   Stan was replaced as house psychiatrist in the mid-1970s by Ken Woodrow, MD,
who stayed on for the project's duration. (See *Soteria Days,* page 205–226.)

A couple of times I felt in a crisis situation, and I kind of turned to him and what he said made the clearest, most beautiful kind of sense and helped me immeasurably. I have tremendous respect for what he does. I really like the way he acts when he comes in here and deals with people. He's just very much himself. He'll come in and sit down at the table and be part of the group here and just relax. I think it would be totally useless and almost a disaster to have somebody who'd come in and play doctor. There's something trustworthy about Stan. He cares, he really cares about people.

Of course, Voyce was the most important source of administrative continuity and strength. There when the project opened, there when it closed, Voyce was both staff and liaison, colleague and leader. Often working a 70- to 80-hour week, Voyce served Soteria in many roles: When Alma became less directly involved with the house, he was given the title of "senior staff," which he shared with Tara until her departure. He was then appointed house director, then clinical director; then, when that position was abolished, he returned to his post as house director, which he held until Soteria died. A mainstay for the project in many ways, Voyce's imposing 6 feet 4 inches and 250 pounds were sometimes as calming an influence as his sensitive, caring approach. Staff and residents alike turned to Voyce for comfort and help in good times and bad.

No single staff member and no single administrator expected (or was expected) to be all things to all members of the community. Each had one or more particular talents; their different gifts combined to provide a rich, effective environment for residents. This philosophy relieved pressure; if one staff member's particular strength did not fit a situation, others coped with it. The person who couldn't help in a particular instance was not labeled a failure or expected to "improve." Insofar as possible, as in the case of its approach to the residents, Soteria affirmed individual staff members' differences, which it recognized, allowed, and encouraged as useful—even essential—to the overall functioning of the house.

Why Work at Soteria?

Staff at Soteria, comprising two overall groups (locals and out-of-towners), worked out of a sense of purpose as well as to make the pittance paid. In today's dollars, they made about $18,000 a year. Both groups included former volunteers and "graduates" among their numbers.

Former residents "graduated" from the Soteria program in the sense that they were sufficiently enriched by their learning to function autonomously, not in the sense that they severed their ties with it. Usually, on the contrary, clients who moved out stayed in the neighborhood and kept in close contact with the community that had helped them. Calling former residents "graduates" is in keeping with Soteria's emphasis on growth and learning as integral to the process of recovery from psychosis. It is also normalizing in that many residents were in late high school or early college years. *Contrast "graduation" with the hospital term for the same event, "discharge."*

Some staff, especially students, were attracted by the "block time" scheduling; it was possible to complete a week's shift in two days, leaving five days to study and attend classes. Some staff members simply wanted Soteria experience on their résumés. Others were curious to learn how the process worked.

The out-of-towners, people who were looking for a new social network, included graduate students, people who came because they had heard or read about Soteria, and others who were attracted by its communal aspects after moving to the area. None of the out-of-towners had a local primary group, so Soteria provided both a potential support network and a source of income. The out-of-towners were among Soteria's most effective but also most destructive staff. Their potential for interpersonal involvement was so high that it was essential to hire selectively.

It is not a secret that a number of mental health workers choose this field because they need to *be with* people they find "crazier" than they are. Individuals like these, who had usually left their previous networks not by choice or not in good standing, often caused so much turmoil at Soteria that normal processes couldn't evolve. The out-of-towners, ultimately, became the individuals most destructively engaged with Soteria.

The local staff generally established a primary network that included individuals from within Soteria. After the workers from the area left Soteria, their networks gradually became less centered on the community, just as did those of the residents who graduated. Both locals and former residents usually remained part of the extended Soteria community, however, by dropping in periodically, by socializing with community members, and by attending official functions. Among those continuing this kind of involvement were people who had been part of Soteria since its inception—over the entire 12 years of the project.

Also important to Soteria's well-being were the volunteers who happened to be working when a staff position became available. Often, they were people who simply were interested in working with the psychologically distressed.

Some, in fact, volunteered specifically until a position became available, and, whenever feasible, replacement staff came from among the volunteers whom existing staff believed to be tenable candidates. Finally, Soteria employed a number of former residents. Their motivations and patterns of behavior were similar to those of other staff members for the most part. But there is one exception: One subgroup of former residents became staff members as a validation of their achievement of health. These graduates felt equal in status to staff only when they were paid to work rather than paying to stay. Other clients sought the same end by getting a job outside of Soteria.

See pages 242–244 for detailed information on staff recruitment and selection.

The Residents

B ECAUSE OF THE research selection criteria (see below), clients at Soteria were usually unmarried and well under 30 years old. Early in the project's history, some residents were as young as 15; later, in response to legal considerations, admissions started at 18. The residents, whose average age was about 21, tended to be middle-to-lower class socioeconomically. Soteria's original research design called for the study of two matched cohorts of recently diagnosed schizophrenics deemed to need hospitalization. Members of both groups were chosen at the Valley Medical Center, a county screening facility that processed 600 walk-in psychiatric patients monthly. Members of the originally constituted comparison group were admitted to one of the two psychiatric wards at "Valley," where they received traditional treatment for "schizophrenia," principally medication. Experimental patients—a maximum of six at any one time—went to Soteria, where they were encouraged to live through and eventually beyond their psychoses, ordinarily without drugs. (Later, Chope Hospital would perform the same function for Emanon).

Because of funding limitations, however, as time went on, Soteria began to admit private clients as well as those supported by the research funds and a federal community mental health center staffing grant.

Soteria Bound

Anyone referred to Valley and meeting the following criteria was a potential candidate for Soteria's study. The six selection criteria for a patient's admission follow. S/he had to be

1. *diagnosed as DSM II schizophrenia by three independent clinicians*

2. *deemed in need of hospitalization*

3. *exhibiting four of seven diagnostic symptoms of schizophrenia* used as admission criteria by the National Institute of Mental Health's original (1964) study (which proceeded on the basis of but two symptoms) of the effectiveness of neuroleptic drugs in treating acute schizophrenia*

4. *the veteran of no more than one previous hospitalization for schizophrenia lasting 30 days or fewer*

5. *aged 18–30*

6. *single (including divorced and widowed)*

In reviewing the literature on "schizophrenic" individuals' prognosis, Research has shown that people without spouses suffering an early onset of "schizophrenia" more often need chronic care than those who are married and/or are afflicted later (Strauss, Kokes, Klorman, and Sacksteder, 1977).

**The seven are thought or speech disorder, catatonic motor behavior, paranoid ideation, blunted or inappropriate emotion, disturbed social behavior and interpersonal relations, hallucinations, and delusions.

The selection criteria were designed to provide a relatively homogeneous sample of individuals diagnosed as schizophrenic and at risk for prolonged hospitalization or chronic disability.

Because of the changing demands of the research grant, residents at Soteria were divided into two cohorts, 1971–1976 and 1976–1983. There were 37 experimental and 42 controls in the first group, and 45 experimental and 55 controls in the second. The second cohort includes residents from Emanon. These numbers include only those research subjects who stayed at least 28 days in Soteria/Emanon or 7 days in a control ward after their initial admission. Many other individuals were admitted to both groups but left before fulfilling these research criteria. Over Soteria's dozen years and Emanon's six, some 200 people (including residents who were not research subjects) lived in the experimental houses.

Subjects meeting study selection criteria were identified but were not told to which group they would ultimately be assigned until after they agreed to participate. After learning about the nature of the Soteria project's experiments, potential residents were asked to give their informed consent (as well as that of families or significant others, if available).

In most cases, the longer clients stayed at Soteria, the more often they received medication. In keeping with the research protocol, residents were given drugs at Soteria when they were stuck, when they couldn't make progress. This could happen as early as six weeks into their stay. Staff, however, were usually unwilling to define a client as unresponsive after such a short time.

In the 1971–1976 study cohort, because of limited experimental bed availability, subjects were assigned on a consecutively admitted, space-available basis to Soteria House. Subjects in the 1976–1983 cohort were assigned on a strictly random basis to Soteria, to Emanon, and to the corresponding hospital wards. Both types of assignment produced demographically and symptomatically similar experimental and control groups.

Working It Out—with Oneself and with Others

At Soteria, in addition to dealing with the manifestations of their psychoses, residents focused on the business of day-to-day living in a community. Most clinicians agree, wrote Loren, Alma, and Ann,

> that psychosis evolves as a process of fragmentation-disintegration. But at Soteria, . . . the disruptive psychotic experience is also believed to have unique potential for reintegration and growth . . . By guiding [clients] through altered states of consciousness rather than repressing them,

Soteria's milieu [aimed] to help its clients emerge from their life crises as stronger, better educated persons with the ability to pursue [means of living] that they themselves consider to be successes . . .

Soteria staff took all manifestations of the psychotic experiences as real . . . and viewed them as having potential for growth and reintegration, if expressed under therapeutic guidance, rather than being negated . . . (1973, p. 392)

Given the preponderance of evidence that people labeled "schizophrenic" are often unable to develop or maintain close interpersonal relationships and supportive network systems not centered around their immediate family groups, Soteria believed that interventions leading to long-term success ought to focus on developing basic interpersonal skills. The key factors in Soteria's treatment of the mentally distressed are embodied in its constant attention to the relationships necessary to fruitful interactions.

A sampling of the 200 residents—names and identities disguised—at Soteria and Emanon has been distilled into the 17 female and 29 male clients listed below.

Who Lived at Soteria?

Female Residents

Bonnie, Cassie, Charlotte, Christine, Deirdre, Ida, Iris, Kate, Katherine, Kelly, Marcy, Naomi, Nora, Tamara, Tammy, Toni, Tracy

Male Residents

Bill, Brett, Chip, Chuck Starr, Conrad, Curtis, Earl, Ethan, Evan, Harry, Henry, Howard, Hugh, Ike, Jim, Kevin, Kris, Leo, Mel, Mike, Nicholas, Orville, Owen, Sam, Sidney, Spence, Stephen, Thomas, Todd

*Names have been changed.

The Dynamic Interpersonal Interaction Processes

At Soteria, staff found that the growth of basic relationships between and among individuals in the community often happened as they progressed through certain processes. Relationships were important beyond basic survival and included essential elements that evolved over a long period. Without these ingredients, no positive social interaction—and, consequently, no meaningful change—was possible. A full progression included five separate stages, which normally occurred in the order described below. On certain occasions, however, developing relationships skipped certain stages; at other times, the steps took place in different sequences.

Stages of the Dynamic Interpersonal Interaction Processes

1. *Break—when the client takes the initiative to make a significant contact (beyond that necessary to survival)*

2. *Friendship—when the client establishes an interpersonal relationship with another person at Soteria in which the client sees him/herself as in a partnership with someone else*

3. *Communal identification—when the client feels a member of the Soteria family, not simply a member of the house**

4. *Extending—when the client begins to establish relationships outside of the Soteria community (at this point, the client may no longer live at the house but is still part of its network)*

5. *Network balance—when the former client's support system includes persons from outside Soteria as well as within*

*Another critical stage is the process of separation from this Soteria family, discussed on pages 98–102.

Break

Because of the admission criteria used to select Soteria clients, most arrived still seeing themselves as part of their families of origin.

Although they ordinarily preferred Soteria to hospitalization, their first choice, usually, was to go home. When they found that returning home was not an option, they almost always chose to stay at Soteria. Given this situation, an important part of Soteria's mission was to provide the client with an incentive to develop and maintain a surrogate-familylike relationship with the Soteria community.

Most entering clients initially rejected involvement with the group except insofar as it met their basic needs—for food, shelter, and the like—needs they were often unable to fulfill for themselves because they were in acute crisis. At this point, residents spent a major part of their time, as one client put it, "inside their own heads." For the client first experiencing a major crisis, the "break" (the first interpersonal crisis) typically came soon after s/he emerged from the acute phase. Remembered a staff member, Adam,

> I had been up most of the night with Henry. All night he just wandered around the house, talking to himself, apparently not paying any attention to anyone. When I asked him anything, he would seemingly not hear, but after what seemed like a minute or two, he answered or asked, "Did you ask me something?" (He's been that way ever since he arrived.)
>
> The next morning, though, he seemed different. I saw him asking one of the other residents where he could clean up. After he showered, he came to me and said, "I have to do something about my voices. Sometimes they scare me." This took me by surprise. He didn't seem like the same person I had been with the night before.

Both Henry's anxiety about his voices and his wish to be clean were changes in his usual behavior patterns. Often a break had to occur several times before it gained enough momentum to carry it to the next stage, but in Henry's case, one break was enough.

Another kind of break occurred for Spence, a privately paying client not part of the formal study. In treatment for about a fourth of his life, Spence had been diagnosed as a "chronic schizophrenic," Voyce recounted, coming, according to his parents, to Soteria as a last resort. Spence had spent the last three years of his 10-year patient's career in a Veterans' Administration hospital. His records indicated very little or no change in his behavior in the last two of those years. His last decade had been spent in virtual isolation.

Spence spent most of his days at the hospital smoking cigarette after cigarette, taking multiple doses of medication, sleeping, and eating. For the first four months at Soteria, Spence continued all these patterns except one—he stopped taking medication. Occasionally, he became agitated, and twice he threatened (verbally) members of the staff who tried to engage him in conversation.

Late one night I got a call from Ophelia (then a volunteer, later a full-time staff member). She sounded excited. After she calmed down, she reported that Spence had "asked me to give him a shower," a request so extraordinary for him that it reverberated through the Soteria community for days.

In this case, Spence went through the break and the next stage, "Soteria friendships," nearly simultaneously—an astonishingly quick progression in someone with his history of illness. The break occurred when he deliberately attempted to change his behavior. At the same point, he began a relationship unnecessary for basic survival.

This was the first time he consistently referred to a specific person by name. In order to know when Ophelia came to Soteria, he had to know what day it was. Thus, he had to become less disorganized: Change became an essential element in his life.

Voyce recalled with pride a number of clients' breaks. One graduate, who had been out of the program approximately two years, described his break to Kay, a staff member, as the two lunched together. Kay wrote,

Ethan and I were having lunch last week at the Harvest Inn when somehow we began to talk about what happened when he tried to jump out the second floor window at Soteria.

(Ethan had been in treatment for many years before being admitted to Soteria.)

He spent most of his first month in his room (and over three weeks in his bed). We at first thought that he had slept for most of the first two weeks, but, as we found out later, that wasn't the case. Feigned sleep, he told me, was the only way he could deal with "another new world."

One day, when he was able to emerge from his room, he caused one of the most frightening experiences the house ever experienced. Here's Ethan's version:

> I can still vividly see myself going out that window.
> Somehow it seemed the only thing that I could do.
> Not I could do, but I had to do. I needed to get out
> of this crazy place in my head, and the only way I
> could do that was to go out that window.

> I asked him how he had thought hurting himself was going to help him get out of anything. His response: "I know you won't believe me, but I didn't see how jumping out that window would hurt. It was the only way I could get out of that crazy place in my head."

He said that that incident was his attempt to change his life. Ethan's break may eventually have saved him, but it also almost killed him. Only Tara's quick reflexes avoided a tragedy. Voyce later described the sequence of events:

> About noon Ethan, who had been coming out of his room only to go to the toilet, came back from a long walk with another resident. Two volunteers from the California School of Professional Psychology, one of whom had spent a great deal of time with Ethan, had just arrived. At this point, three staff members including me and three or four residents were scattered in different parts of the house.

Suddenly, Ethan screamed and ran up the stairs. For
some reason Tara ran after him. Several others followed, not
too far behind. Ethan ran straight to his room and climbed
out the window. Tara caught one leg just before he would
have plunged to the neighbors' concrete driveway.

It's unclear why they both didn't go out the window—
Tara weighed less than 105 pounds, and Ethan, at least 175.
Once the other members of the community arrived, it took
five people to get him out of the window and back downstairs.

Thus, the break—while it generally has positive implications—
can also set up situations where clients harm themselves or others.
When at the break and when separating from their communal
identification, clients are most at risk for suicide or other violence.

The break was a demarcation in residents' processes showing that
they were open to interpersonal involvement with other members of
the community. Until they became aware of their impact on the outside
world and decided actively to change their self images, there was
little potential for relief.

Several breaks occurred before clients were ready to move to the
next stage. Sometimes clients wanted to change because they thought
it was expected of them or would earn approval, but the genuine
breaks stemmed from different motivations. *Real* breaks' major impetus
came from clients' desires to change.

Friendship

If the break came as a client made a gesture at interaction, the "Soteria
friendships" stage of the dynamic interpersonal interaction processes
occurred when the individual singled out a member of the community
for special attention. Clients rarely began this second stage before
embracing the idea that they were, at least in some small measure,
part of the Soteria community.

Most clients accepted Soteria as their residence within the first
three weeks after admission and entered on the second stage of the

process by the end of their first month. Partly due to the personal skills and warmth of the members of the community, new clients committed to Soteria quickly; however, their commitment was often insubstantial and shaky. On many occasions, the visit of a member of the resident's family reversed the processes. But once the pattern of a Soteria friendship was firmly established, backsliding became less of a problem. For example, if former clients were hospitalized, they usually called Soteria for help in getting discharged.

A number of residents neither made a break nor formed an individual friendship during their first time at Soteria. The majority of this group showed only mildly psychotic symptoms when they arrived; most saw themselves as unlike the other residents— specifically, as less ill. Rarely did they stay over two weeks, tending to return home having made only superficial connections. Usually, they failed to experience the break because of their concern about their external physical selves—their hair, their clothes, their general grooming—about which they were often compulsive. When such clients returned—and they usually did—they followed more typical paths. Harry, a 17-year-old admitted to Soteria after an acute psychotic episode, was such a resident. (His case history is presented in detail on pages 81–87.)

Harry's fourth stay at Soteria finally helped, when he at last went through the dynamic interpersonal interaction processes in much the same way as did most successful clients. Without the break and its following stage of individual friendships, the developmental process can fail: The material for changes in relationships is unavailable. Without *interpersonal* involvement, one is left only with *intrapersonal material* as a guide for change. But for individuals in crisis, their own resources are usually insufficient for successful adaptation to the broader community.

Communal Identification

This stage doesn't have a clear demarcation point and sometimes is merely an extension of the preceding "Soteria friendships" stage. It happens when residents join, temporarily, the Soteria community as a substitute for the family of origin they were forced to leave. But it deserves a separate identity because it is part of a developmental progression and leads to new adjustments. *During "communal identification," the residents accepted Soteria—however briefly—as their primary support system, maintained a close relationship with two or more Soteria members, and let others in the house have an emotional impact on them.*

All three changes are critical.

At the friendship stage, clients separate themselves from their families of origin and identify with the larger Soteria network in a way that encourages normal peer-based interaction. When clients see themselves as part of the group, they are motivated to change. The group, then, becomes their major source of support, so available social space—physical and spiritual—is critical. One resident, Kate, felt the lack of such psychological space:

> For the first month I found it hard to make friends with the staff and the older residents because they seemed so close that I felt like an outsider.

In the hospital, she reported a similar sense of isolation:

> The staff seemed to be good friends but wouldn't let me be friends with them. I always felt like a patient with them. I guess I was, but they didn't have to treat me that way.

Kate was asking for more than just attention. She was asking for a symmetrical relationship. (See pages 24–25.) This need for involvement among individuals is the major thrust behind the second and third stages of the dynamic interpersonal interaction processes. At the same time, it carries a potential risk of rejection. This resulting conflict can present a major dilemma for the client embarking in this new territory.

Emanon also ran into this difficulty. Voyce recalled,

> A staff member from Emanon reported that one of their biggest problems with the first few clients was the difficulty

of welcoming them into the group that had had several months
to close ranks before the first client arrived. The original
group's closeness and rapport became an obstruction for the
new residents, who felt like outsiders.

In Emanon's case, what appeared to be a desirable situation—
enough time to work out staff difficulties before involving clients—
had negative consequences. The lesson: Working through conflict,
within reason, with the clients' participation establishes bonds
necessary to develop the skills for survival in the broader society. So
allowing clients the opportunity to participate in the interpersonal
conflicts of the community can furnish the necessary material for
change. A note of caution, however: Clients must never be forced to
participate. Both their wish to join in and their fear of doing so must
be respected. They must set the pace.

Extending

The "extending" stage usually begins when the client has left the
program, when s/he establishes a mode of being independent of
both family and Soteria. To allow the former resident to maintain
relationships external to the Soteria community, however, it is critical
that the three previous stages be firmly established. The earlier steps
give a basic support system on which to build independent
relationships with new friends.

Thus, the client should see him/herself as a part of the Soteria
network, but no longer as a resident—much as does the young adult,
who needs not only independence from his/her family but also
continued contact. In both cases, a redefinition of roles is necessary,
not a termination. This change also allows more available interpersonal
space, as contact with family/community members lessens.

Soteria's commitment to demystification is affirmed here. Activities
there occurred in most homes; communication patterns, for instance,
were similar to those in "normal" families. Members argued about who
should wash the dishes, who should go shopping, which movie to see,
and so forth. Very little jargon came up about psychiatric symptoms,

diagnosis (such as "schizophrenia"), and the like. Thus, clients had to change communication patterns little to talk to new associates. A resident, Curtis, noted the nontechnical, nonmedical atmosphere of the house. Still, the pangs he felt at separation were intense:

> I remember when I left Soteria. Man, I felt like I was out there alone, even though I came over to the House every day.
>
> Then, I met Luke at the 7-Eleven. He was a drummer, and we got together and jammed at his house two or three times a week. Through Luke, I met Karen, and we got to be good friends. After a while I stopped coming to Soteria so much and spent most of the time with Karen and Luke, until I got a job at the San Jose main library.

Curtis's statement reflected both his difficulty separating and his need to have other social contacts. When common interests led to other friends, he didn't need the same degree of contact with the Soteria community. Although Curtis established a degree of independence from Soteria, he stayed in touch for at least three years after he graduated (a not uncommon pattern).

The former residents who returned either to the hospital or Soteria within six months after discharge usually did so because they failed to make the transition from extending—the state Curtis describes above—to the next stage, the "network balance," instead becoming isolated and eventually having another major crisis. Other returnees failed temporarily in their bids for independence when traumatic events—such as a death in the family—led them to return to Soteria to ward off states of major disorganization. Such people usually spent only the night or, on rare occasions, a week or two.

Voyce remembered one particular former resident, however, who came back at least ten times—mostly because of problems with love relationships:

> Marcy never can get her love life together. When I hear that she has another male friend, I expect to see her in no more than two months and, more than likely, in less than one.

Marcy came to Soteria the last time because she had just broken up with someone named Sam. She arrived after work one day, saying that she was tired and didn't want to go home because she and her friend "weren't getting along." As usual, she said she was having difficulty keeping herself together and needed someone to talk to about her relationship with Sam.

We talked for three hours, during most of which time she cried. At dinner, she discovered one of the former residents she knew from the last time she came back, and the two of them went to the movies. When they returned, Marcy spent the night on the couch and went to work the next day.

She called from work to thank me for letting her stay.

Marcy saw herself as having a crisis in the making, a problem she nipped by returning to Soteria for a "fix." The two times she didn't return voluntarily to Soteria after major crises—after her father's death and after her own divorce— she was brought back to Soteria, severely regressed, by her mother.

Extending was a difficult stage, but it was also a transition. If clients completed it successfully, they were on the way to establishing supportive networks that enabled them to survive new crises without formal intervention from the mental health community.

Network Balance

"Network balance" describes consistency within a person's social network. While the network may not be (and should not be) static, the changes within it should still maintain its relative equilibrium. The ideal network combines family members and people from Soteria with friends and other contacts into a larger entity. Its major parts— usually family and Soteria community—are interrelated and balanced but have little or no direct association with either. Through such a network, the individual maintains independence from both family and Soteria, enhancing the chances for successfully rejoining society.

Some find having a few close friends is sufficient for their needs; others need many casual ones. Once again, this pattern is no different for the former client than for anyone else working to sustain a healthy lifestyle.

Soteria Typology: Representative Groups of Clients

Although residents reacted to treatment at Soteria in a wide variety of ways, eight broad kinds of responses occurred with some frequency among the disturbed and disturbing individuals who found their ways to the House.

The Salvageable Young

The 18 to 26-year-old moderately disturbed individuals who were Soteria's most common residents rarely made up a majority population; however, they were usually the largest presence. What difficulties these youth presented to the House usually occurred at the beginning of their stays, when their crises and disruptions strained other members of the community as well as themselves. Such crises often kept staff and other members of the House awake all night. Often, only weeks of vigils seemed to help. (For a further discussion of "vigils" as practiced at Soteria, see pages 168–169.)

These recovering youth usually stayed at Soteria somewhere between three and five months, depending largely on how long it took them to raise enough funds to move out. Even if they applied for it, most were not awarded government disability assistance— Supplemental Security Income—before they left the program. (The federal bureaucracy moves slowly.) As a consequence, many found jobs while they were at Soteria or soon after they left. Most had little or no previous history of psychiatric problems.

Clients like these used little medication at Soteria and distrusted drugs as a solution to their problems. They seemed a group for whom the Soteria environment was especially productive. They moved through the dynamic interpersonal interaction processes (see above) in a predictable and consistent way, usually coming to Soteria in the middle of a crisis, which generally lasted two to four weeks. Once it was over, they went through a reorganizing stage, lasting one to three months, during which time they developed relationships with other community members.

Residents without financial resources prior to leaving had some problems, mostly worsened by a return home to their parents. Going home itself was invariably a negative experience, but most clients who did so actually ended up doing well, at least if they moved out shortly. In most cases, members of the Soteria community continued to encourage graduates to leave home. Most parents were also in favor of this step towards independence, although a few, afraid that their offspring could not survive independently, were unwilling to encourage them to move out.

Like other residents, most of the recovering young left to live in places close to Soteria. Usually they moved in with friends (often ones made at the House) in order to share the same living space. Even though members of this group had the ability to live independently, they stayed actively integrated in the Soteria community. In fact, they were the most involved former residents, both as volunteers and as paid staff members. A number of them completed college degrees. Many developed good social interaction skills and stayed out of treatment; they were among Soteria's most successful clients. As a group, these young adults improved more significantly than any of Soteria's other prototypical members except the "quick trips" (see page 94). Henry's history is not atypical of the pattern followed by many of the salvageable young.

HENRY arrived at Soteria at lunchtime, talking to himself most of the time and paying little attention to others around him, except for Zaida, a volunteer who drove him to Soteria from Valley. While at the hospital, he had begun taking several different medications, which he quit gradually upon arriving at Soteria, coming off all medication in three days. He said the drugs had made him drowsy.

Henry attempted to get work a few days after he had arrived at Soteria but was unable to fill out the forms because he said that he was having too much trouble with his medication. Although he had been off drugs for several days, he was probably still having side effects and was confused most of the time.

As the medication wore off, he began to think more clearly, and in two weeks, he was able to participate in all the activities within the House. Although he was able to do physical labor (he got a job with a company called Manpower), he still had difficulty concentrating. After a month, he was able to go visit some relatives (who lived out of state) for a few days. He returned in good spirits and continued working for Manpower until he found a better job.

Two months after he had arrived, he found himself an apartment and moved out of Soteria, agreeing, however, that he would come over to eat and to use the House until he felt secure on his own. Henry gradually moved away from Soteria and went back to the school where he had been before his "schizophrenic" crisis. He stayed in contact with some of the friends he had made while at Soteria.

Eventually, he graduated from college.

The Recyclers

These residents were not numerous—making up maybe 10 percent of Soteria's population—but because they returned and because of their often disdainful and demanding natures, there seemed to be more of them about than in fact there were. Their recidivism also meant that they spent, on average, twice as much time at Soteria as the salvageable young.

The recyclers often arrived at Soteria showing little evidence of a crisis: Scoffed one, for example, "I'm not like these other people. Somebody must have put LSD into my drink." They tended to be obsessively concerned with their physical appearance. For the most part, they seemed to dislike other members of the Soteria community, who generally reciprocated: One staff member complained about a resident who exhibited this pattern of response, "I don't think we should have to work with people we don't like. I hate being around him." Fortunately, the staff person's wish was not fulfillable.

Such individuals came to Soteria and agreed to stay for the two-weeks' minimum—clients were asked to remain 14 days before deciding if Soteria was right for them—because they weren't welcome at home and they didn't want to go into the hospital. Then, they were usually able to talk their parents into letting them return. Because of such residents' arrogance, staff and other members of the community did not usually encourage them to stay at Soteria. Wrote Voyce of one:

> I had a hard time trying to get the staff to discourage Bill from going home. Part of the problem was that I had a hard time myself trying to talk him into staying because I couldn't stand him.

Although residents like Bill usually showed few symptoms, the staff tended to believe that they were concealing a good many. The result: Whatever originally pushed them into the hospital resurfaced after they left, at which point they were sent back either to the hospital or to Soteria. If the former, they usually contacted Soteria immediately, so they could be released to stay at the House.

When such clients returned to Soteria, they typically showed more symptoms than during their previous visits. About half took this opportunity to go through the dynamic interpersonal interaction processes in the usual way, an action that often led to their eventual recovery. Others, however, repeated the original pattern one or more times and pretended nothing was wrong. Each time they discovered that all was not well, they relinquished some of their pride and resistance to involvement and opened themselves up to interpersonal contact.

The recidivists were more apt to ask for and use antipsychotic drugs during and after their stay at Soteria than any group other than the "prophets of madness" (pages 94–96). Although the recyclers rarely used medication during their first time in the residential program, they tended to be difficult and often seemed to make little progress.

Typically, members of this group were minimally regressed during their first stay at Soteria, but with each return, they tended to become more and more childish. When they did, they often wanted to take medication, which they claimed helped them to stay in control.

With time, these residents became more familiar with the community and lost some of the inhibitions that previously had so restricted their behavior. Still, clients like these were among the most difficult for Soteria to help. They did not usually act violently but often provoked violence verbally. When recidivists did commit violent acts, they were often temporarily but promptly expelled from the program when similar acts by other residents would probably have been tolerated.

When the returnees successfully completed the Soteria process, they tended, like other residents, to move initially somewhere near the House and eventually out into the larger community. But they often took longer to develop adequate relationships in separate social networks. Almost every member of this small group remained involved with Soteria after leaving, often wanting to come back to Soteria when difficulties of any sort presented themselves. For example, one such former resident sought refuge at Soteria after he broke up with a girlfriend.

While some of the recyclers recovered—like Harry, whose case history appears below—others, still denying their illness, would probably still be returning to Soteria had its doors not closed in 1983. As it was, Harry came back to Soteria four times after his first admission; after over four years in and out of the House as a resident and a guest, he finally was able to adapt and function outside in the community.

HARRY, 19 years old, had one sister a year his senior. His parents had been divorced when he was two, and he had never seen his biological father. His mother remarried and moved with Harry and his sister to California in 1959, where the family lived with his stepfather for 11 years. His mother had periods of depression, for which she was treated with psychotherapy and medication.

According to his parents, Harry was "always a good boy," who never gave them "any trouble at all," until just before he was admitted to Soteria. He had graduated from high school, taken a job, saved his money, and bought a car. He had never lived away from home, however, and was reluctant to leave his mother even for a night. He had a history of unusual developmental problems with language.

Suddenly, about the time he discovered his parents were going to move to Arizona, he became increasingly paranoid and withdrawn and began hallucinating. His parents brought him to Valley Medical Center, at which time he was diagnosed as a paranoid schizophrenic and referred to Soteria. He arrived with no apparent overt symptoms, but his medical records from the hospital showed that he had acted acutely psychotic for the previous five days. Although Harry offered no obvious evidence of psychosis when engaged in casual conversation, he did reveal peculiar thought processes and seemed preoccupied when asked about his feelings or possible problems. He said he was not hearing voices.

During his first two days at Soteria, Harry was extremely quiet and suspicious but then became much more verbal, participating in (and even initiating) group activities such as cards, board games, and picnics. During his entire two-week stay, however, he never spent the night at Soteria, always going home evenings to his parents' house. During his last week, he got his old job back and announced that he no longer needed Soteria.

He left for home exactly two weeks after he arrived, in spite of staff attempts to discourage him and his family in this decision.

Stan Redd's Diagnosis

Mental status: *At admission, Harry was quiet and rigid, with torn feelings of ambivalence that almost immobilized him. Mute because of them, he stood like a wooden soldier. His disordered thought processes rendered him unable to abstract or reason. His affect is blunted. Although he seemed very sad at times, when he was near tears, he was able to prevent himself from crying.*

On the third day, Harry's appearance and outlook seemed to change. He became interested in competitive games because they helped him to identify himself as a strong young man. Intelligent and precise verbally, Harry is a neat, clean person—in contrast to the unkempt appearance of many of his contemporaries. Until his breakdown, he had always been well-mannered, polite, and obedient to his parents.

Harry's recent high school graduation and his work—in addition to his (unacknowledged) need to move away from his family—heightened his dependency needs. He could not cope with his aggressive drive to break away from parental bonds and fend for himself.

He has little or no acceptance of his psychological difficulty.
Neither does his family, which had difficulty admitting that Harry
is a schizophrenic.

Diagnosis: Schizophrenia—an acute episode.

The First Return

Harry began to regress approximately three weeks after going home. When he returned to Soteria, he began showing more symptoms of psychosis than before. He was admitted because of his conflict with his family over his potentially violent behavior towards his stepfather. Harry had been receiving medication at Valley Medical Center for about a month. He claimed to be allergic to most medications, but the hospital tried a variety of regimens because both he and his parents were afraid of his violence without medication. He often believed that his father was an arsonist planning to kill his mother and him.

During this stay, Harry participated more in activities, but still went home to sleep at night. He had little involvement with other residents unless they were taking part in an activity that involved staff. Shortly before he left, he stayed away for three or four days while telling his parents he was at Soteria.

He was told that he could return to the House if his parents moved away, and he did not have another place to stay, but after leaving Soteria, he initiated only one contact. He telephoned, asking for Dr. Redd's number and seemed pleased to be invited to drop by. The next day he appeared and announced that he had found an apartment with a friend and was working as a clerk and attending school. Harry engaged—somewhat precariously—in the Soteria community for another three weeks before he talked his family into letting him come home a second time.

The Second Return

Now 20, Harry returned to Soteria with a psychomotor disorganization. Before coming back to the community, he had been treated with neuroleptics and outpatient psychotherapy at Valley. During that period, he had had another acute schizophrenic episode.

Stan Redd's Diagnosis

Mental status: *At this point, Harry is confused, has somatic preoccupations, fears death (especially from suffocation), has difficulty eating, shows marked psychomotor slowing, and presents a blunt affect. His manner is unusual—occasionally, he hugs people as if he were a windup toy, programmed to demonstrate affection.*

His normal intelligence is untempered by either judgment or insight. While he is not hallucinating, he cannot abstract. His concentration is impaired, and he is forgetful, appearing to be in a daze.

The diagnosis has not changed since Harry's original admission.

Diagnosis: Schizophrenia—an acute episode.

Harry's monthlong admission was precipitated by his parents' move to Arizona. Shortly after they left, Harry became disorganized, was hospitalized, and again returned to Soteria. Geoff, a staff member, recalled,

Harry is very very thin, quiet, paranoid, scared of everything, meticulous. He keeps asking to be taken out of the House, to go out to lunch or dinner, or to return to his apartment. He won't talk about problems, asks the same question many times, and apparently forgets the answers. He called some friends who came to get him last night, and he left without saying goodbye to anyone but [another resident] Jim. He seems to be bothered by the lack of order and schedule in the House.

During this stay, Harry slept at Soteria most of the time. Although never popular with the community, Harry failed this time not only with other residents but also with the staff, partly because of his suspicious nature. His regressed condition encouraged staff and others to continue to try to develop a positive relationship, but he remained un- or negatively involved—the latter, Geoff said, in an odd way, was a form of connecting.

This time, Harry remained in Soteria for about two months, showing little improvement and losing weight. For the most part, he was quiet, stubborn, and withdrawn. He did not like to be helped, preferring to try to help himself. His affect was flat. Harry showed very little improvement; although this had been his longest stay, he participated in house business even less than before.

When he again left Soteria, Harry moved not home but to a house nearby with Henry, a former resident who became a friend. Shortly, Harry found a job at a liquor store where Henry one day found him standing behind the counter in a rigid posture, unable or unwilling to communicate with anyone. Henry called a staff member at Soteria who, in turn, telephoned the manager of the liquor store. The boss allowed Soteria staff to bring Harry back for help.

The Third Return

Harry, now 23, resided unofficially at Soteria for a few weeks after the liquor store episode. Then, he formally reentered the program as a resident. His present condition had been manifested in severe departures from reality for the last four to five months, and this stay, which would be his last as an official resident, was his longest, taking another five months.

While he had managed to recover enough for brief periods to function as a liquor salesman, he had recently became disoriented, confused, and withdrawn—standing and staring bizarrely. Before returning to Soteria, he had used Navane with some success—particularly in Arizona with his family following his second major break.

Following his use of Navane at Soteria, however, he became at once animated and distant, still harboring doubts and suspicions about neuroleptics; in response to this discomfort, he discontinued the drug. At this time, he was in good physical health, although he was still losing weight because he refused to eat.

Originally, Harry was disoriented, confused, and disassociated, speaking at times in ways that showed his sense of reality was grossly disturbed. He did not appear to be overtly hallucinating; however, his mannerisms were strange. He had no insight about his illness and seemed unaware of and unconcerned about his condition.

Harry's third stay lasted significantly longer than any of his previous admissions. And, as towards the end of his first residency, he involved himself with other members of the Soteria community, organizing picnics and getting people to go out dancing, for instance. This behavior was very different from his "middle" periods: Harry slowly established himself as an integral part of the House. He began to make what turned into lasting relationships with both staff and residents. He accepted his inability to work at that time and applied for state and federal financial assistance.

Evie, a volunteer who taught dance for a time at Soteria, described Harry's interaction with her:

> Harry participated every time from the beginning. He had a strong, well-developed, but rather tight body with a lot of ability to move and range, but he was stiff. He seemed to enjoy the warm-up exercises and was responsive to my instructions and my hands helping him into stretches. We danced together several times, touched a lot as we danced—which was comfortable for both of us—and exchanged hard hugs at the end of the sessions. His movements were varied and not mechanical.

When Harry left Soteria this time, he moved into the neighborhood with two other graduates, staying involved with the community and making friends with new residents. Several months later, he moved to Arizona to live with his parents.

After a considerable period of time had elapsed, he called. Difficulty with his parents in Arizona prompted him to ask if he could move back to Soteria, temporarily, so that he could relocate in the area. He moved back into Soteria and slept on the couch until he found a place to live.

Although Harry continued to use Soteria as a backup when he was having difficulties, his residencies there—finally—were complete.

The Refugees from Storms

A slightly older group of residents developed a characteristic way of using Soteria as a support group after successfully completing the dynamic interpersonal interaction processes; such graduates used Soteria as a safe harbor when difficulties arose, in the same way that others in trouble might consult families or friends.

Such refugees often feigned "schizophrenic" symptoms after their initial stays to achieve readmission. As soon as they were accepted into the Soteria community, their symptoms vanished rapidly without medication.

Generally the most sociable residents, these individuals were rarely without work—even when they were living at Soteria. Often their work equaled or surpassed the jobs of the staff in wages and status. Several refugees opened their own businesses, and two of them were instrumental in setting up another nearby residential treatment center, O'Neill House,[11] after Soteria and Emanon closed.

Not only did such graduates get good jobs, but also they seemed able to forge meaningful relationships. Most married or cohabited, although not usually on a lasting basis. The foundering of such partnerships were the refugees' major motivation for returning to Soteria.

Rarely were they rehospitalized for treatment, and their return stays at Soteria, unlike those of the recyclers, were usually brief. Perhaps because they were older than most of the other residents, this group had little difficulty staying away from their parents after leaving Soteria.

A veteran staff member, Keith, reported the history of one such client, a young woman of 23.

---

[11] O'Neill House was able—with the help of the state and local aid that had eluded Soteria and Emanon—to offer alternative care for the chronically mentally ill until the late 1980s. Although an alternative facility for the disorganized, it was not modeled on Soteria or Emanon.

NAOMI arrived at Soteria from Valley shortly after her father had a heart attack. She had lived at home all of her life.

During her first two weeks at Soteria, she was incoherent, had periods of rapid mood changes, and demanded many hours of attention from staff and volunteers. She thought that people were talking about her behind her back all of the time. She also had difficulty sleeping for the first few days.

After three weeks, Naomi began to reorganize and became very sociable. She began initiating activities, took responsibility for cleaning the house, and said that she was looking for a job.

While working in a law office before her collapse, Naomi had acquired a good reputation, and another law firm gave her a job within a month after she had arrived at Soteria. After working for a month, she began to spend more time at work and at home visiting her mother; then she moved out into an apartment and continued to work.

Naomi returned to Soteria nine times in six or seven years because of various difficulties. Her stays were usually short—typically fewer than five days—and she was never officially readmitted. On a couple of these occasions, she had shown symptoms of psychological distress, but the staff could never decide whether or not her crises were genuine. Naomi continued this pattern until the house closed, always going back either to her present job or finding another while she stayed at Soteria. On only a few occasions did she stop work.

The Flight from Psychotoxins

Other individuals found frequently at Soteria were those who had been overmedicated prior to referral. Because of their drug reactions, they exhibited unique patterns of response to treatment at Soteria. All the toxic individuals came into the program with treatment histories describing large amounts of medication with bad outcomes. Some were virtually immobile. Their physicians often thought, however, that their patients were at an "optimal level of medication." One such "optimal level"—for Deirdre,[12] a patient standing (or sprawling) 5 feet 2 inches

---

[12] For Deirdre's history, see *Deirdre: A Soteria Cameo*, pages 37–43.

and weighing 105 pounds—was (daily) 1,000 milligrams of Thorazine, 30 milligrams of Haldol, and 2 milligrams of Cogentin. This level of antipsychotic medication made her zombie-like, immobile, and expressionless. Her condition, a severe version of extrapyramidal side effects, made her shake like someone with Parkinson's disease, which affects the cells that control involuntary movement.

Frequently, such patients had received more and more medication for behavior patterns that became more and more fixed. At the point when a physician took them off the medication, such patients seemed to begin to improve; then, however, the physician frequently prescribed a similar drug, and the pattern was reasserted.

When, at Soteria, such patients' medication was withdrawn, they typically spent two to four weeks regressing. In this, they were not unlike certain other less toxic residents.

Voyce recounted the following history of a resident suffering from—and then recovering from—an adverse reaction to antipsychotic medication.

HOWARD, another privately paying client not part of the formal study, was admitted to Soteria after being treated at three different hospitals. The police found him walking on the side of a highway, speaking to himself incoherently. They brought him in and booked him; then they took him to the local hospital where he received medication "to help him regain control of himself."

The admitting hospital staff described Howard's behavior as "loud and out of control," so he was transferred to another hospital in the Bay area. There, his level of medication was raised, but he was still secluded most of the time because of his noisy, disruptive behavior. After two weeks in that hospital, he was transferred to yet another hospital where still more medication was prescribed. There, he took care to isolate himself *quietly* to escape the notice that would alert hospital staff to send him to seclusion. According to Howard, "They just wanted to get rid of me because I wouldn't keep quiet."

All three hospitals were escalating the medication in spite of the fact that his boisterous behavior was increasing. When Howard's mother contacted Soteria, Voyce attempted the intake interview, but couldn't arouse Howard from his fog of medication. Howard's psychiatrist explained the dosage as necessary because the patient was "out of control" on less medication. Howard was now, said the doctor, "at his optimal level."

When Howard arrived at Soteria, however, his stupor had dissipated, and he had become hyperactive and loud. When he arrived, he was taking 75 milligrams of Haldol and 4, of Congentin to counteract his "extrapyramidal side effects," that is, his zombieism. Soteria staff proceeded to wean him from the medication, and, except for his hyperactivity and his loudness, he suffered little thought disorder. Unfortunately, his boisterousness and strident voice were difficult to overlook.

In three days, Howard was off all medication. The following three weeks were difficult during the day, but while he slept heavily throughout the night, the community had a chance to recuperate. This pattern lasted for approximately another three weeks before he began to subside into what he described as "my normal hyperactive self."

Howard gradually reconstituted himself. After six weeks at Soteria, he found a job in a fertilizer-processing plant and moved to a rooming house three blocks away. After living away from Soteria for three months, he returned as a regular volunteer, a position he held until the house closed. Through Howard's influence, his employer hired many of Soteria's current and past residents.

The Institutional Victims

Originally, Soteria's research design focused on newly diagnosed "schizophrenics," or at least ones without histories of previous hospitalization. Because too few such individuals were available and because the project was always on the verge of financial collapse, Soteria also served a number of people who had been categorized as "chronic schizophrenics." Most came to Soteria from private referrals, and most had had a significant amount of previous hospitalization and various other sorts of therapy. Most could pay for their treatment.

They were not research subjects and were, therefore, not studied systematically.

Chronic problematic behavior in these individuals often seemed the result of their past treatment. For example, some people come into the mental health system because of socially unacceptable behaviors that are part of their personalities—not necessarily "illnesses." When such persons arrived at Soteria, they were not treated as ill: Because it basically rejected the metaphor of "mental illness," Soteria did not perpetuate what it saw as a conceptual mistake in diagnosis.

These individuals had to unlearn old behavior patterns and therefore often spent as much as a year at Soteria in contrast to the average resident's stay of three to five months. Because of the program's desperate financial situation, three quarters of the "iatrogenes," who made up approximately 25 percent of the total population of Soteria, were treated during the final two and a half years of the program.

The duration of their stays varied dramatically in proportion to the length and type of their previous treatment. Other factors influencing how long they remained at Soteria were the amounts and types of previous medication, the age at which they became patients, and their family's income and supportiveness. While all these factors had some bearing on the length of stay of most residents, the issues were critical with respect to the iatrogenes, whose average stay at Soteria was six to eight months.

They were given more medication than any other group at Soteria: Approximately 75 percent of these residents took drugs. In most cases, they asked for medication, which they saw as a way to control unwanted behavior.

These clients also went through the dynamic interpersonal interaction processes, but it took longer, often proceeded in unusual sequences, and sometimes included repeats of key stages. The "break," for example, typically didn't occur in the first month but sometimes happened as late as six months into the iatrogene's stay. In fact, these clients' initial isolation from the community often presented significant difficulties.

Residents in this group, ranging from age 25 to 35, were 6 to 7 years older than the average client at Soteria. Their degrees of regression varied widely in both intensity and duration, taking from days to months.

"Success" for the iatrogenes was defined differently than for other residents. If such clients were able to stay out of hospitals and to maintain relationships, Soteria considered them successful. Voyce recalled Sidney, who failed.

SIDNEY'S first difficulty occurred 6 years before he entered Soteria, when he was 19 and in his second year at a university. He had had therapy in high school, was involved with a girlfriend, and was talented and successful.

Suddenly, he spent 5 months at home "freaking out," as he put it, followed by 18 months at two different private treatment facilities. After some improvement, he went home and had day treatment for a year and a half. Then he moved into an apartment and accepted a low-level job as a clerk and messenger in his father's advertising agency.

Sidney went to a community college and completed one semester but dropped out a year and a half before coming to Soteria. At this time, he quit his job. After day treatment, he began taking huge doses of vitamins, becoming a victim of the much ballyhooed "megavitamin orthomolecular treatment," a never-proved approach fashionable in the 1970s and early 1980s for those who could pay.

His former psychiatrist, he said, believed that because psychosis was ingrained early in life, sufferers needed to return to infancy to redevelop into healthy adults. She had, therefore, "regressed him" during "treatment," making Sidney the victim of still another queer and untested psychoanalytic silver bullet; however, she did not legally adopt him as she did a number of her other clients. Her bizarre technique, also briefly in vogue for the wealthy, failed with Sidney, who was sent to another residential treatment facility, where he was forcibly "regressed" to being a two-year-old.

Promises of miraculous if extensive cures for the disturbed seem most tempting to the rich, who can first sustain the psychiatrist and then move on if s/he fails. Unfortunately, the "curer" not infrequently causes harm, sometimes irreparable harm, in the "curee" over whom s/he has power.

Ken Woodrow's Diagnosis

Mental status: At admission, Sidney was disoriented, confused, anxious, delusional, and hallucinatory, doing repetitive motor acts such as rocking from foot to foot or beating his thighs in rhythm. Occasionally, he became lucid and revealed his depth of understanding and superior intellect.

Diagnosis: Schizophrenia—a chronic undifferentiated type.

Sidney's progress at Soteria was originally slow, and, throughout his stay, he slid back periodically. Several months into the program, he had to be hospitalized because he hurt himself trying to jump out of a second-floor window. As a result, he was given a great deal of medication.

His progress was dramatic over the course of the next six months, however: He was able to take some classes at San Jose State University, and, after being at Soteria for a year, he went home for a short stay. Although he returned to Soteria showing behavior similar to—but not as bad as—that for which he was originally admitted, he again made rapid progress.

Eventually, he was able to move into a boarding house near Soteria and then, at his parents' suggestion but against the advice of the entire Soteria community, he moved to his family's house back East. Sidney stayed in contact with members of the Soteria community after leaving the program.

Awakening at 33, however, realizing that he had slept for almost half his life, and finding himself back in the environment that had precipitated his psychosis, Sidney made the irrevocable sacrifice by throwing himself under a subway in New York City.

In spite of Sidney's suicide, his father recognized that Soteria had significantly helped his son and expressed his gratitude both in words and in generous financial support.

The Quick Trips

Residents in this small group—most young and many Latino (an ethnic group that, as a whole, distrusts and avoids the ministrations of organized mental health professionals)—had experienced major crises a few days before entering Soteria. They were usually able to recover in less than a week, sometimes overnight. Because of the brevity of their stays, they also do not figure in formal Soteria research.

The Soteria community often stayed up all night—sometimes several nights in a row—with such clients when they entered the program. While the degree of regression was high, it did not last long enough to put a strain on the community. The beginnings were intense, but the stays short—from 12 hours to 2 weeks. Individuals in this group used no medication and subjects went through the dynamic interpersonal interaction processes in an incomplete or blurred way, often experiencing only the major crisis and the break. They stayed but briefly in the Soteria network, though occasionally they dropped by to see if their experience at Soteria had been real.

After Soteria, such residents tended to go back where they came from—home with their families or to their independent living arrangements. Usually, except for accidental contacts with members of the community, their farewells were permanent.

The Prophets of Madness

All of these clients came to Soteria as private referrals. They shared a conviction that they were psychotic and therefore needed to go through some kind of therapeutic process (which each of them could—and did—explain in detail). Usually such clients had heard or read about Soteria; they often expected Soteria to be the answer to all that plagued them in life.

Such residents, typically in their late 20s or early 30s, had usually previously been in at least two treatment programs. In a way, some seemed to be making a career out of being treated. Among the most common reasons they gave for coming to Soteria was their desire to be regressed and reborn—they "needed" to go through these processes. Often they tried to apply Laing's metaphors literally.

Almost all members of this group had a source of income, which was specifically provided by their family (often as a trust) with some strings attached. This income was usually insufficient to maintain them in the way that they would have liked but enough to keep them ineligible for other kinds of assistance and reluctant to assert financial independence. In some ways, their limited incomes paralyzed them.

Although relatively small, this group had a major impact on the program because its members, who demanded a lot of attention from the entire Soteria community, stayed for at least five months, often for a year or more. When the community responded to these residents' calls for help, caregivers were often accused of insincerity.

The prophets rarely used any medication stronger than Valium but commonly had problems with illegal drugs and alcohol. They used medication more as sedation than to alleviate psychotic symptoms.

The prophets usually didn't go through the first stages of the dynamic interpersonal interaction processes. They showed no regressed behavior, although they talked at length about being regressed. They needed no break because they were never in touch either with their own condition or with that of the people around them. The last parts of the process—extending and the network balance—had the most relevance for the prophets. They were able to leave Soteria (about half of them without entering other programs) and, like other successful graduates, stayed connected to the community's network. Such former clients often stayed in touch by mail with selected members of the Soteria community. They seemed not to be bound by distances. Cassie, whose case history is typical of those of such residents, moved to the East Coast after she left Soteria.

CASSIE, who had been trained as a nurse, arrived at Soteria after being treated at four different programs. She left all of them without resolving her problems, which would go away, she said, when she experienced a regression that "I have to go through."

According to her brother, she was diagnosed as a "schizophrenic-depressed type" at all four programs. Cassie insisted that Soteria staff not contact the places where she had had previous treatment, however, because they would provide inaccurate information.

Her source of income was a trust, left by her father, with whom she had had difficulty getting along. Her brother, the conservator, administered it so as to allow a set amount per month, which, according to Cassie, was "not enough to live on, but too much to let go of."

Cassie put more emotional stress on the other members of the house than almost any other resident. She demanded constant attention but she almost always rejected it because it was "not genuine" or offered "out of pity." She called Voyce at any time—often late at night or early in the morning—to complain that she was not being properly taken care of.

Cassie tried to get prescriptions from different doctors for Valium or other minor tranquilizers. She drank coffee continuously during the day and tried to hide an alcoholic beverage somewhere so that she could get a drink when she needed it.

There was no discernable change in any of these patterns until Soteria told her that she was stretching the limits and that she needed to deal with her brother directly about her financial situation. This challenge initiated a series of events that lessened her self-destructiveness. She moved into a boarding house near her brother, who lived on the East Coast, but she stayed in contact with Soteria for a year after leaving and with selected members of the community for much longer.

She has managed to stay out of inpatient treatment since she left Soteria. She sees a therapist "off and on." It is unclear, however, whether Soteria had any real impact on this therapy addict.

Young Adults in Psychosis

Soteria achieved a reputation for being able to work with clients too young to be treated in adult programs and too old to be treated in adolescent programs. If it looked as if a patient would turn 18 before completing treatment, no one liked to start it.

Soteria succeeded with two such clients from a neighboring county and became a resource both for them and for aging adolescents rejected by other programs. In all, Soteria treated about 15 such individuals, mostly "schizophrenics" from single-parent families. Many of these referrals had sociopathic tendencies and other behavioral problems.

Soteria was usually their last resort before they were sent to a state hospital (and one of them actually came to Soteria *from* one). The aging adolescents usually arrived at the house without psychotic symptoms, but at least half went through some regression during treatment. Their worst tendency was aggression—towards property, towards themselves, and towards others. In fact, this group, representing only about 15 percent of the total resident population, initiated over half of the physical violence that took place at Soteria. Most of it, fortunately, was directed at the facility rather than towards the community. Breaking windows and doors, for instance, was fairly common.

The aging adolescents usually became active participants in the Soteria network after leaving the program. Most became volunteers, and two became paid staff members. None went home; most stayed close to Soteria when they first moved out of the program.

Members of this group either succeeded or failed rather dramatically. Some formed independent, high-quality relationships and got jobs; others mostly remained in the mental health system, managing to spend only short periods of time out of treatment. Few such residents fell between these two categories.

Fortunately, the first group was the largest. Earl, for instance, whose case history follows, matured into successful adulthood.

EARL came to Soteria from a local program for adolescents after he was diagnosed as schizophrenic. He had previously been hospitalized once because of his aggressive behavior towards his mother. When he returned to the hospital, he was referred to Soteria because he was nearly 18.

He arrived at Soteria at a time when the program was helping two similarly diagnosed clients. Their parallel behavior reinforced Earl's. He destroyed Soteria property, and, once, he hurt a member of the community. He locked himself into rooms on several occasions and said that he might hurt himself; this made staff members and volunteers break down doors to stop him. Earl also hurt a volunteer who tripped over the electric mixer he planted in a doorway.

After seven months in the program, Earl's violent behavior subsided. He moved out to a place near the house. He continued to hold his job as a gardener and began college, volunteering at Soteria and staying in regular contact with several members of the house.

Earl has had no more treatment since leaving Soteria.

He completed his BA at San Jose State College and planned to continue his education.

Departing While Connecting: Continuing Contact

When Soteria's first resident, Bonnie, decided to leave after being in the house for two weeks, it was clear to the staff that she was not able to manage on her own. When she was still allowed to go, staff members were disappointed and angry with both Alma and Stan for not using their authority as project director and consulting psychiatrist to force her to remain. Accused Della,

> You sent her home to that dope freak, punk, boyfriend. What if she freaks out again? You sent my work down the drain. She needed this place, and this place liked her and could work for her.

Alma replied that staff had done a good job with Bonnie and had helped her, adding that had the staff been perfect, maybe things would have turned out differently, but that she did not expect perfection even if *they* perhaps aimed for it.

Added another staffer, Ed, "This spoke to my wounded pride for not having cured her, because I think we could have if we had had time and were good enough. She was curable."

Staff members worried about Bonnie's defection, thinking that they had *done* something wrong or *not done* something right, or she would not have left. With increasing experience, however, the staff became willing to allow residents to decide for themselves when to go. For example, when Tracy wanted to leave, although her symptoms were still evident, Susannah said, "What the hell! She is 23 years old;

she is an adult, and you can't take that away from her." Susannah continued,

> That really hit home—they are still people, human beings, and have rights, just plain human rights. One is that they are free to move around, to leave some place—as long as they are not going to be hurt walking in front of a car or something like that.

There were occasionally still differences among staff about clients' exits, however, especially when the residents seemed unable to function on their own. Such departures were in some ways like those of children leaving their parents. Like some parents, staff members had to fight tendencies to control inappropriately. Wrote Tara,

> We [staff] tend to be overprotective at the time when residents are leaving. We want to safeguard them from the outside world, but I have to watch myself that I'm not keeping them from cutting ties that they need to sever if they are going to grow. I have to be aware of that myself—I have the feeling that I could be smothering them.

The mixed feelings about residents' departures that Susannah expressed are typical. Wrote Daniel,

> I feel good and bad when people go away. Good and sad, should be the word. It's like anybody leaving home. You're glad that they're good enough to leave, that they're well enough to leave, but there's a closeness. It's different when they're not there.
>
> I can remember when Tracy left: She left a big chunk out for a while. I think it was because she wasn't organized yet and had required a lot of attention. The other people, most of them, by the time they've left, have organized some and have not required such huge doses of attention right at the end.

Yet, Susannah, herself the single mother of two preadolescents, summarized,

> My feeling is that it's like a family here, and when children
> leave the family, they don't just completely stay by themselves.

In fact, many residents returned to the house after graduation. Some came back as volunteers; others just dropped by to say, "Hi." For many of them, the house had become a surrogate family, for which they felt much affection. One departing resident, Luke, described his feelings to Della:

> It's a really worthwhile thing, and if it wasn't for this place, I
> don't know where I'd be right now. I'd have to be on the run
> if it wasn't for Soteria—14 days they were going to hold me at
> the hospital. Soteria saved me from a fate worse than death.
> Food's good too, food's excellent, good cooks, and there's a
> whole lot of love generated around this place. Caring for
> each other. More so than any other place I've been.

Others, however, came back for help in dealing with personal problems. (See pages 87–88, above.) The staff welcomed such returnees and sometimes located help from outside. For example, recalled Tara,

> Katherine stayed in touch with the house and came back a
> couple of times when she got scared. She felt comfortable
> enough and safe enough to call and say, "Hey, can I come
> back? Maybe just for a couple of hours in the evening?" It
> went from that to her calling me, and she'd say she needed
> to talk. I'd go down to Palo Alto, and we'd sit and talk for
> hours about how she was scared.
>   This was when she was pregnant, in the first stage of her
> pregnancy, the first couple of months, I think. And we'd talk
> about how she remembered things that happened at the
> house. Some things she understood and some things still
> scared her. She thought about it and wondered what we
> thought of her when she was spaced out—and stuff like that.

When she was at Soteria, she *wasn't* pregnant, and everybody knew it. But although Katherine wasn't really pregnant, we all went through her "pregnancy" with her. She ended up feeling better about it. Part of it was she didn't know how much was in her mind, how much was still fantasy, and it helped to check it out with me:

"Yes. It did happen."

"Yes, you did do that."

"You did know what was going on."

That said to her that at least certain things had really happened, and she knew she was not freaking out again. She went through ups and downs during her pregnancy, a lot of them having to do with her living situation and her husband.

I just think she's done amazingly well.

Alma asked what made Tara decide to put Katherine in touch with an old friend named Marguerite. Tara explained that she wasn't sure, but

I just wanted to make sure Katherine was well taken care of. There were lots of times that I couldn't go and see her, because I don't have a car. She needed a woman to talk to about her pregnancy and her fears about her husband. She couldn't talk to any of her girlfriends because they were all involved in the situation and counseling her to get rid of her baby. They were upsetting her, plus most of her girlfriends had crushes on her husband because he had a pretty face.

Tara continued, coming up with more reasons,

Marguerite's in Palo Alto. She could help Katherine out in a lot of practical ways. She's an excellent seamstress, and Katherine had no money and needed to make maternity clothes. I talked to Marguerite. She knew Katherine and liked her and had free time and was more than willing to do it.

So Katherine started dropping in to Marguerite's house when she started getting alone or scared. At first, Marguerite was kind of nervous about Katherine and would call me immediately afterwards and say, "Did I do all right?" I would say, "Yes, yes. You did all right."

Marguerite didn't even need to talk to me after a while. She'd just deal with Katherine. Also I knew that Katherine was having really bad financial problems. Her husband would take her check, cash it, and buy really stupid things—and they would have no food.

I knew there were lots of times when Katherine went hungry. Katherine would come over looking a little pale, and Marguerite would stuff her full of good food. It just worked out well. I felt very safe; I felt Katherine was safe.

Eventually that was how I'd get in touch with Katherine, because she couldn't afford the toll call to San Jose to call me, so she'd call Marguerite for free and say that she needed to see me or talk to me. Marguerite would call me, and then I would call Katherine.

Katherine's pregnancy went to term, she had a healthy son, and her marital relationship improved. Katherine had no more formal treatment.

The history of Soteria's graduates was often a tragicomedy (or a comic tragedy). Too many successful residents met death early— Sidney by choice under a train, Katherine, when her son was four, by accidental drowning while surfing with her husband. By treating everyone as possessing the potential to become what he or she wanted to be, Soteria encouraged participants to take risks, to change, to evolve through life.

For all graduates, leaving Soteria was a beginning as well as an ending. As long as the house's doors were open, its resources were available to any client, past or present, who needed help. Leaving meant developing a relationship with the larger community, true, but it did not have to mean severing one with Soteria.

Even so, Soteria was risky business for all concerned. It was a haven, certainly, but not one for the faint of heart.

Soteria Years

C ONCEIVED WHILE LOREN, on a research fellowship in 1966–1967 sponsored by the National Institute of Mental Health, was spending a year in London with Laing at Kingsley Hall, Soteria— like its model—was planned to offer asylum to people in psychological crisis.

After Loren's work in London, he returned to the United States, first to Yale University and then to the National Institute of Mental Health to serve as director of the schizophrenia center. About a year later, as part of his grant-coordinating responsibilities, he saw Rappaport and Silverman's proposal (see page 46), which detailed a drug/nondrug random assignment study to be conducted at Agnews State Hospital near San Jose, California. An experimental milieu developed by Laing, gestalt therapist Fritz Perls, PhD, and Perry, was planned. Loren laughed when he saw the proposal—three gurus of humanistic psychology running a state hospital ward?

The drug/nondrug portion of the study was approved. The special milieu was not, however, so Loren offered to consult with Rappaport and Silverman to develop another milieu proposal. Although this proposal was unusual and eventually helpful to the Soteria project, a comparative study of milieus was not feasible in the state hospital, because its superintendent would not allow experimental variation. Thus, the proposal comparing a Soteria-type milieu with a hospital ward had to be withdrawn. It is worth noting, however, that, as originally defined, the Soteria project would have occurred in a state hospital.

Because they already had an approved project, neither Rappaport nor Silverman wanted to develop a new study out of the hospital. So Loren identified a community agency—Rehabilitation Mental Health Services (directed by Len Goveia)—that had provided group home treatment for a number of years, and he and Len wrote a grant to study three types of treatment settings for mental disorders (1971). They proposed to investigate the experience of patients on a "normal" psychiatric ward (Valley); clients at a behaviorally focused private nonprofit group home (Rehabilitation Mental Health Services); and residents of a facility encouraging interpersonal and phenomenological interaction (Soteria).

The National Institute of Mental Health funded an 18-month pilot comparison study of the proposed Soteria model with treatment on the psychiatric wards of a local general hospital; however, it did not approve Len's proposed companion study of a more strictly behavioral program, which he had intended to administratively house in a preexisting community-based setting in San Jose. So Len, who was the original principal investigator, saw his study cut from the research. He soon exited as well, and Alma became his replacement.

Meanwhile, because the Rehabilitation Mental Health Services dropped out, it was necessary to find an existing private nonprofit organization to use as an umbrella for the 18-month pilot grant. Loren and Alma, therefore, sought a working organization to do so. After a series of negotiations, the Mental Research Institute, the Palo Alto-based facility that had been home to luminaries like Gregory Bateson, Donald D. Jackson, Jay Haley, and John H. Weakland (the authors in 1956 of the double-bind hypothesis), agreed to administer the Soteria grant.

The Institute was chosen for three reasons: First, it had the reputation to give the project the legitimacy required to secure grants. Second, the project would have access to its resources—including well-known staff such as Jules F. Riskin and Paul Watzlawick. Third, the Soteria grant, which contributed indirect costs, was in the Institute's economic interest. The Institute was frequently in straitened financial circumstances because of its difficulty in raising funds to cover administrative costs.

Alma (originally as project director, then as principal investigator) and the research staff maintained offices at the Institute. Loren remained in Washington, D.C., as research director and collaborator. Alma had worked as a social worker and therapist on the Rappaport-Silverman ward at Agnews and was, therefore, qualified to find and staff a community-based facility without the constraints imposed by the hospital. Her ideas about facilitative relationships and the social contexts necessary to deal with psychosis were often similar to Loren's, who was exultant that, after nearly a decade of gestation, some of his notions about how to deal with psychotic individuals appeared close to a reasonable test. His and Alma's enthusiasm and optimism were transmitted to the staff they selected.

But the National Institute of Mental Health reviewers drastically changed the original proposal: They pruned Loren's three-way comparison to two, deleting Len's behavioral project and reducing the requested 5-year pilot study to 18 months. Omission of the second community setting made the study unable to determine the relative healing power of two community settings whose differing theoretical bases generated different milieus. So it cannot be said with certainty that the environment flowing from Soteria's interpersonal phenomenology was specific to its effectiveness. Indeed, it could be argued that the normalization inherent in taking care of psychotics in a small home in a conventional community was its most important contribution. Without a second residence in a functioning community but with a different philosophy for comparison, the effectiveness of the Soteria model's practices and milieu remains an open scientific question.

Because of the time required for grant review, it was necessary to begin a new grant proposal after only six months of Soteria's actual operation—hardly enough time to collect meaningful data. The unfriendly initial review predicted the tenor of the following seven evaluations, and Soteria never received either as much time or money as it requested. Part of the government's hesitance may have been rooted in its nervousness about California ecology: As respectable and traditional as the senior officials at the National Institute of Mental Health were, the Northern California landscape was not. This was a time, everywhere in the United States, but particularly on the West Coast, when counterculture flourished. California was where the hippies thrived, the Grateful Dead played, the Free Speech movement raged, the Black Panthers stalked, and Patty Hurst underwent her ordeal and metamorphosis.

For all these reasons, the result—for those seeking funds for Soteria, working at Soteria, and living at Soteria—was a deserved sense of insecurity.

Basing Soteria in the community raised two significant questions: Since the Mental Research Institute was not located in a neighborhood appropriate for a Soteria-style experiment,

- In *what* community should Soteria be set?
- How should a relationship be established with the community?

The question of *where* to base the project was difficult to resolve. At the time Soteria was conceived, many large homes, primarily unused fraternity and sorority houses, were available in the downtown area near the campus of San Jose State College. Because of its proximity to Agnews, a state hospital being phased out, San Jose was a prime spot for halfway houses. The city was also convenient because the control group would be chosen and housed nearby at the Valley Medical Center.

The implications of community basing were complex: How would Soteria become a part of the neighborhood, and how should a healthy relationship with it be fostered?

Getting It All Together

Once federal funding was in place, several other people besides Loren and Alma became important participants in the Soteria project. For example, Stanley Mayerson, who was first responsible for screening at the local inpatient unit, played in addition a major role in setting up the early structure of Soteria. Another central figure was Stan

Redd, the first house psychiatrist, who trained the staff in clinical issues as well as found the property and the house that became Soteria.

Also contributing in unofficial capacities during the early stages of Soteria were Silverman, Perry, and the Esalen Institute, all of whom helped with training.

The next step was to hire a staff. (For further details, see pages 242-244). The first on board was Daniel, a psychiatric technician who worked on the experimental ward at Agnews State Hospital. Next was Voyce, also a psychiatric technician at Agnews State Hospital, who had served on a traditional ward. Susannah, a volunteer on the experimental ward, was the last full-time staff member hired at this time. Three part-timers also joined the project: Tara and a couple, Tom and Kim.

The couple was originally supposed to be responsible for the house during nights and weekends, leaving the other staff in charge during the active part of the day, but this pattern never worked.

Establishing a Program

There were no funds for furniture, but the Mental Research Institute received generous donations of household appliances and other necessities from board members and other friends of the Institute. Some Institute members were also helpful with training.

On Monday, April 3, 1971, Project 37 (the grant name for the project that eventually became Soteria) began operation. The staff spent the first few weeks trying to establish the general program and purpose of the house, offering no treatment at this point. They cleaned and painted the house, fixed the yard, set up a training schedule, looked for places to buy food, and established the responsibilities of staff members. Project mainstays found out, subsequently, that the exterior improvements made to an until-then rundown property were critical to Soteria's acceptance in the community. Finally, the staff tried to give the project a name. The last task was particularly difficult.

After hours of discussion, the staff decided on "Together House," a name that lasted for three weeks, until Loren made his next trip to the project from Washington. He suggested that naming be postponed until someone came up with a name with larger connotations. Eventually, Alma uncovered *Soteria* in a dictionary of proper names.

Staff and administrators spent many hours training. Alma talked to the staff about treatment issues. All staff members had participated in a vigil at the experimental ward at Agnews and in subsequent follow-up discussions. Voyce offered some training on how to deal with violent patients. Loren and the staff also spent a weekend at the Esalen Institute learning alternative methods of dealing with madness. Stan provided information about and did some training on use of medications: How to administer them and what to look for when someone has difficulty with them. In addition, Stan trained the staff in a variety of interpersonal techniques for use with regressed residents, and Loren discussed his notions about the efficacy of using interpersonal phenomenology with psychotics.

A Year-Long Honeymoon

When Soteria began, for about a year staff members experienced no conflicts that couldn't be resolved by discussion. They were all generous with their time and relaxed about compensation.

About three weeks after the house opened, treatment began for the residents. By design, no specific staffing pattern was set at this time; the staff were permitted to organize their time any way they chose, so long as two people were *always* on duty. The staff decided to wait to see what developed before implementing a structure. This freedom was possible because five of the seven staff members—all but Susannah and Voyce—lived at Soteria. The scheduleless period preceding the arrival of the residents posed no problem for the staff. But when the residents began coming into the house for treatment, people found it hard to leave without feeling guilty, and it became clear that burnout was a danger.

At this point, the staff tried to set a schedule that would both meet the needs of the house and maintain a loose structure within the program. In addition, staff were encouraged to take time off. It proved difficult to both live and work at Soteria; hence, the staff gradually began to move out. This process of moving out of the house developed into a tradition—in particular, residents and staff helped members of the Soteria community move; writ large, this meant that people remained a part of the Soteria family even after they left the program. When Susannah moved out of Soteria and into her new house, remembered Tara,

> everybody got involved. One of the residents who was having profound difficulties two weeks ago seemed transformed into a completely different person during this period. It took most of the week to get all of Susannah's things moved. She rewarded us for our help with a party for us in her new home.

From Honeymoon to Crisis

Two factors precipitated Soteria's first crisis: Alma began to spend most of her time at Mental Research Institute, rewriting the grant continuation, and, simultaneously, the staff overextended.

At the beginning of the program, Alma spent four days a week at Soteria and one day a week at the Mental Research Institute. After the first year, this pattern reversed—one day at Soteria for every four at the Institute. Alma's reallocation of time became necessary because the grant had to be renewed if Soteria was to continue to operate. In addition, Soteria had to make contacts within the community mental health system to maintain its position in the network. But the house clearly needed more administration as well. When Alma left a void, it became necessary for someone to fill the position she was no longer able to occupy. The staff's attempt to do so ended the honeymoon.

Another issue that contributed to stress was staff burnout. The grant funded only four full-time staff positions of the eight requested (another example of the National Institute of Mental Health's ambivalence). Because there was essential work for about eight to do, the staff operated under severe strain. The "solution": Staffers on part-time salaries worked a number of 40-hour shifts; full-time staff, as much as 60 hours a week. One staff member remembered his schedule during a summer when two employees were gone for a month: "Besides doing my 60-hour-a-week shift, I was at Soteria almost every day (for some period of time) for at least two months." Furthermore, if called when off duty, staff members commonly responded to emergencies. Exhausted and overworked, the staff began to split over personal issues. There's a lesson in this, Voyce and Loren, note ruefully: Exploitation, no matter how worthy the cause, has severe consequences.

Besides the problem that arose over the vacuum caused by Alma's departure, another erupted over hiring a woman staff member. The job candidate was promising but headstrong; eventually, the community decided not to invite her to join it. The other controversy arose over Daniel's attempt to take Alma's place. Daniel thought his original position included the agreement that he would later become the house manager. Without the strong presence of Alma, a struggle ensued between Daniel and members of the community who did not want to be responsible to him. At this point, Daniel oversaw volunteer scheduling, food money, and weekend shifts. A major difficulty arose when he decided that he should be responsible for staff schedules and for the residents, too. His attempt to take on these jobs led to a major division within the staff that ultimately resulted in two separate shifts—one on the weekends and one during the week.

This issue was finally resolved when Daniel went to Dallas with Alma to do a presentation on Soteria. When most of the staff told Alma that, if Daniel returned to Soteria after his six-week leave of absence, they would quit, he was asked to leave.

From Crisis to Jung

Influenced by the opening of Diabasis, a new establishment in San Francisco, much treatment at Soteria next evolved into Jungian orientation. For example, see the discussion of the "birth" and "rebirths" of Chuck Starr (pages 171–194). Like *soteria, diabasis* is a Greek word, this one meaning "crossing over."[13] Organized in 1974 by Perry, who had consulted on the Silverman-Rappaport drug/nondrug experiment at Agnews, Diabasis replicated Soteria in general but added the requirements that residents work with Jungian therapists and that staff members receive individual Jungian supervision. Several of Soteria's staff members worked there briefly: A number of Diabasis volunteers trained with Della at Soteria, while Ed and Susannah helped out at Diabasis. Perry's program had a significant impact on the program at Soteria, causing both its Jungian phase and its rebirth from the chaos of the first crisis.

The Soteria community talked frequently during this period about archetypes, rebirth, death trips, and the like; they stopped doing so abruptly when, six months later, all the Jungians left to work at the other facility.

Curry Days

Dramatically and suddenly, Soteria turned from West to East. As the Jungians left, the gurus took their places. Within three months, Soteria hired three people who had traveled a month or more in India; another staff member was doing his graduate thesis on Jung and transcendental meditation. Three new volunteers who had spent time in India joined the community. One staff member was married to an Indian. A new resident had been to India within less than a year. The only two staff members remaining from the original staff were Tara and Voyce, both of whom hated to cook. Lots of curry was the result.

Most of the community became vegetarians—although meat was served on Monday when Voyce worked alone. (Tara had decided that her health would only allow her to work 9 to 5, Tuesdays through

---

[13] Crossing Place (English) is the name of a residential alternative to hospitalization based on Soteria's model that Loren helped found in Washington, D.C., in 1979 (See page 2.)

Fridays.) Fortunately, a volunteer interested in cooking began working at Soteria, and Voyce took care to schedule her when the non-cooks were in charge.

The Indian period was fundamentally unstructured. Alma had retreated to the Mental Research Institute, and Daniel was gone, leaving Soteria loosely supervised by Voyce and Tara, each with the title of senior staff. Due to the particular personalities of staff members and the diffusion of power between Voyce and Tara, no one was really in control. These conditions were ideal for growing gurus.

During this period, the program at Soteria was influenced more by internal factors than external ones. The few demands for change coming without were met only if the members of the community thought them useful. In order to effectively administer Soteria, a staff member had to be there; the more any one person was present, the more he or she influenced the direction of the program.

The problematic issue was authority. Tara and Voyce seemed to have it, but in fact the staff looked for direction from Alma. Another complicating factor was Tara's health; most of the time, she was either asleep, at the doctor's office, or at home, sick. This left most of the burden on Voyce, already working a 72-hour shift (24 of them as the sole staff member in the house).

But although Voyce was almost always there, he was not truly in charge. As a result, there were no real lines of authority. This decentralization made positive communication between staff and administration impossible. Voyce's stress began to show as he tried to control what he couldn't. He wrote,

> I can recall one period when I had to go to so many meetings that I was almost never at the house. I was always afraid to return to Soteria, because I was worried that some horrible disaster awaited me. Considering that, during this time, there were only three residents, who never caused any problems, this was clearly an unreasonable reaction.
>
> At one of the house meetings, staff and residents criticized my authoritarian behavior. They complained that I phoned the house and told people how to make every move

and also criticized my harsh way of handling people who made decisions that I didn't agree with. One of the residents complained that I was pressuring the staff to treat him like a child.

It was apparent to me that I was trying to control *Soteria* in order to control my anxiety. Simply by spending more time at the house, I could make a significant change in my behavior. Therefore, I made it a policy to have as much contact as possible with the house members, to be there as often and I could.

The effect of the lack of structure on the residents was both good and bad. On the one hand, it had a negative impact on actively psychotic residents and those going through major crises, which seemed to escalate at this stage of Soteria's growth. The rule against violence had to be explicitly reintroduced at this point, because several residents had been verbally threatening. (On earlier occasions, Alma had suggested that residents exhibiting violent behavior be expelled, but until now, when the members of the house saw the need to make such a rule, serious violence had not happened.) In fact, of course, a rule against violence had been in place since the project's inception; however, almost everyone (with the possible exception of Loren, Voyce, and Alma), had chosen to forget about it.

On the other hand, Soteria's loose structure benefitted other residents, because at this time the staff and the residents participated more in the social network that encompassed the house as well as the community. Participation beyond group boundaries was more common. That most members of the community came to Soteria from far away, however, was a factor that made long-term involvement difficult. Staff both arrived from afar and departed the area: One man left to buy a boat to sail over the world for several years; a woman moved to London to set up a program with Laing's Philadelphia Association. Such distances posed major problems for keeping in contact, even though there was a great deal of communication by mail. The residents dispersed as well, but not as far or as often as staff.

Insufficient funds made this era of Soteria hard on everyone. With a new staffing grant from the San Jose-based Community Mental Health

Center, however, future personnel were better able to provide administrative support to the house, to participate in day-to-day administration, and to frame a definite structure to the program.

Centralizing Authority

The crisis of decentralization in the "Indian" period was resolved by hiring a house director and a mediator to work with staff. In the summer of 1974, a new period dawned in Soteria history led by Voyce as program director.

Hiring a house director was now possible because of funding provided by the new staffing grant. Soteria was at the same time in the process of negotiating with Marin County about funding a similar program. Voyce was slated to become the director of the new Marin program; Tara, to direct Soteria. When the Marin experiment failed to materialize, Tara decided to quit Soteria, and Voyce was the logical choice to replace Alma as program director.

Because of the conflict that had developed when Alma turned to other preoccupations, decentralizing authority, a facilitator was called in to try to alleviate some of the troubles. He also provided Voyce and Alma with a forum to clarify their new roles and relationships to the staff. This mediation, which lasted a week, had a dramatic and positive effect on Soteria's program. Although not all of the negative feelings from the previous period dissipated, mediation helped open the lines of communication necessary for Voyce to regroup the staff positively for meaningful future action.

Soteria Comes of Age

As the smell of curry faded, the graduate student phase began, when Soteria organized a program with the California School of Professional Psychology. Through this arrangement, graduate students could earn credit by volunteering at the house for 20 hours a week and attending a class once a week. For all their difficulties, these four years were

Soteria's halcyon days—enough money, staff, volunteers, and residents and, overall, a calm and united community.

Several staff members were eventually hired as a result of the California School—House cooperation, and the staff became disproportionately composed of graduate students. Soteria already had on staff Keith, a graduate student from the University of California at Santa Cruz, and at one point 14 regular volunteers from the California School helped at the house. The students made another startling change in the type of staff at Soteria and also created some new problems. The graduate student as staff member was not always flawless.

One serious problem that surfaced during this period concerned the students' attitudes towards their work. Most were studying psychology to become professionals; consequently, they sometimes spent more time reading articles about Soteria than attending to the residents. By the end of the 1970s, there were at least 16 papers in print; today, they could have perused more than three times that many. Another indication of the graduate students' view of their work as preprofessional preparation for their careers became evident after they left Soteria. Whereas only one member of the "guru" staff stayed in the field of mental health after departing from Soteria, all of the graduate students continued their field work, and most became mental health professionals.

Many of the students tried to separate themselves from the previous staff (whom they saw as *un*—rather than *non*—[or Voyce's *para*-professional). Two students from the California School volunteering at the end of the "guru" period were particularly certain of their superior understanding of what was therapeutic and what was not. When this group played the dominant role at Soteria, many people became obsessively concerned with "finding their identity."

The notion of *being with* (see pages 169–201) and the vigil still remained the most vital foundation of the program, however. Both graduate student and regular Soteria staff were generally in unison about the important of *being with*, frowning on therapeutic techniques that diverged from that approach. In fact, when a student from Santa Cruz used the hypnotic techniques (which he had learned from a professor there) to treat an unconsenting resident, the volunteer was promptly thrown out as intrusive. He was not simply *being with* the resident. Commented another volunteer,

> It was really spooky being around him. He told me that he used his training at Santa Cruz on one of the residents. I think it is irresponsible to hypnotize someone without telling that person what you are doing. I always had the feeling that he was hypnotizing me, but I was never sure. I'm glad we got rid of him.

A positive development of this period was more interaction with the Mental Research Institute. Staff members attended workshops and participated in weekly staff meetings. Another plus was the Soteria community's initiation of involving and welcoming the families of residents in the process of their offspring's healing.

This middle era, which lasted roughly from the summer of 1974 to the summer of 1978, was the most stable period in Soteria history: Funding was consistent; volunteers were plentiful; and communication between the house staff and the administration was working. Out of the stability marking Soteria's middle years came Emanon, the Soteria clone in San Mateo, which like its parent was supported by a National Institute of Mental Health grant. Taking advantage of Soteria's lessons, Emanon got off to a smoother start than its parent, both financially and administratively. Emanon lasted from 1974 until the early 1980s, when both refuges foundered. Diabasis had already gone under in 1979.

A series of successful grant applications written by Loren and Alma made this period of growth and security possible. Unfortunately, while funding a proposal in 1975, the federal review committee mandated that project data analysis be moved from Loren's Washington, D.C.-area office to the Mental Research Institute in Palo Alto. It also called for replacing Loren as research director with a California-based administrator connected to the latter institution. When this requirement went into effect, Soteria's research contributions dwindled, and only the pre-1976 data analyzed in

Loren's office have been published and made widely available. Working in the last decade with Bob Vallone, Loren gathered some of the disorganized and incomplete second-cohort data and, insofar as it was possible, analyzed them. Much later, social worker John R. Bola joined him to analyze data from both cohorts (Bola & Mosher, 2002, 2003). See below, *Learning from Soteria* (pages 247–279), particularly *Why Soteria Worked* (pages 266–270).

Rationalized as a more efficient arrangement, removing someone from leadership of the scientific project he had designed and implemented is actually an extremely rare occurrence. Far from increasing Soteria's effectiveness, this step considerably muted its scientific impact. (See also pages 303–305.)

From Grad School to Job Training: The Years with CETA—The Comprehensive Employment and Training Act

The CETA period overlapped the graduate student phase, starting in 1976. Its initial impact was not great; both new and existing staff were young and well educated. The Mental Research Institute allotted one of its six CETA positions to Soteria. Although never so formally defined, CETA's soon became the screening process for staff positions at Soteria.

Unlike the original staff, the "Indians," and the students, CETA staffers were all local residents as required by the terms of the Act. Soon residents, staff, and volunteers lived in the same neighborhood, a striking difference from the previous situation, when most of the staff lived over 40 miles away.

The metamorphosis from graduate-student stage to CETA stage happened so gradually that it was almost imperceptible. But in two smooth years, the preprofessional group was gone. During this transition Soteria added another tier of administration: Voyce filled the new post of clinical director, another program director took over at Emanon.

At this time, it became clear that Soteria needed to think about some form of long-term funding other than that provided by the

National Institute of Mental Health. To find such money, Soteria administrators involved themselves in local politics and with groups like the California Association of Social Rehabilitation Agencies. It became difficult both to supervise Soteria and to attend such meetings. More time was eaten up in fund-raising and in submitting proposals in response to counties' requests. Finally, administrators developed a grant proposal for a study to submit to the National Institute of Mental Health—*Soteria Alternative Family Education (SAFE)*.

This activity required still more staff involvement with the Mental Research Institute but of a different sort than that which had recruited the graduate students. The former involvement with the Institute worked to the students' benefit; now, the CETA group sought money for Soteria's survival under pressure of the program's closing for lack of funds. The CETA group had to match state, local, and private funds with the federal monies, which were declining annually.

During this period, the Valley Medical Center stopped admitting clients to Soteria in response to several lawsuits raised by incidents at their own facility. Because of the violence on one of *its* wards, Valley concluded that it was too risky to send patients to *other* programs that weren't tightly secured.

This loss presented a major problem. A diminishing subject flow for the experimental group was not conducive to research, and the clinical program was also at a disadvantage. Most of the residents, often ones who were unwelcome at other programs, now came from private referrals. Another disadvantage: More time was necessary to look for sources of new clients. Finally, it was difficult to deal with the reality that, when residents left, the program was approaching a zero census, and, without residents, obviously, Soteria would be history.

This presented the biggest dilemma for the group, one that was never resolved and only grew. In order to maintain the program at Soteria, people needed to have a long-term sense of involvement. One of the problems with a high number of private referrals was that the residents, who often came from distant places, had been not only sent away from home but also from community and friends. Making such isolates part of the network was difficult, sometimes impossible.

Thus closed the middle phase in Soteria's history. While usually fairly stable in funding and in program, unresolved issues shaped the character of its last stage.

The Sense of an Ending

During December of 1980, Emanon died. Voyce sadly described its final days. Shutting down Soteria's clone was, he wrote,

> one of the most difficult things that I have ever had to do. We held a house meeting that had been called especially for the purpose of laying off staff members. The meeting took place in the basement, where the staff usually had their meetings. I made the announcement and then handed everyone his or her notice. After a long silence, a former resident asked, "Would it be possible to keep Emanon open if everyone volunteered?"
>
> Volunteers were in fact necessary but only to place the remaining residents in appropriate settings. Our years of struggle with inadequate funding did not make the Emanon graduate's question less touching, but they did make it impossible to answer affirmatively.
>
> Everyone agreed to help resettle the remnant.
>
> Then, we spent two hours dealing with our feelings about what had just occurred.
>
> The next day we met again to discuss what still had to be done. Some of the staff helped place clients; some, including Emanon's house director, did not. He left the entire responsibility to me. I spent the two weeks before Christmas working three-day shifts—including 48 hours on December 24 and 25.
>
> Clients needed to be placed.
>
> Emanon's program director, a Soteria graduate named Stephen, and I moved all of the Emanon furniture to Soteria on the 28th of December.

Then we had a party at a staff member's house. We all
brought food and drink and sat around and talked about "the
good old days."

The closing of Emanon had a profound effect on Soteria. Many
times in the past there had been talk about closing both Emanon and
Soteria because of lack of funds. When Emanon actually closed, it
became increasingly difficult to believe that something would come
along at the last minute—as it always had—to save Soteria.

Emanon's demise also brought some of its staff members to
Soteria—primarily to fill a few vacancies. In retrospect, Voyce thought
this policy a mistake, since Emanon staff traveled carrying some
resentment. Several conflicts developed during this time, and new
problems surfaced. Soteria staff were also angry that Voyce, *their* clinical
director, had previously spent so much time at Emanon, and hostilities
arose.

Soteria staff felt they needed more of Voyce's attention, and
arguments flared as the senior staff members struggled to fill the
hole Voyce had left. During this period, two female staff members
banded together against one male staff member. Others briefly took
sides. Nonetheless, this conflict eventually escalated into a major crisis
needing drastic intervention. (See below.)

Cracks in the Foundation

*In the early summer, when Soteria was having trouble with state licensing, the
conflict among the three staff members erupted again. Something had to be
done. Voyce's solution:*

> *The problem revolved around three people, but to some degree,
> everyone played a role. In better times, I would have preferred to
> resolve it by intervening without laying anyone off. But, because of
> the degree of conflict at a time when the state licensing department
> could shut down the house, the problem demanded immediate
> resolution.*
>
> *I called the group together and informed them that I would be
> getting information about the conflict from as many points of view*

as possible for one week, and then I would make a decision from that information. I informed everyone that I would listen to anything that anyone wanted to say, but that I was not going to bring it back to the group until I had decided what to do.

It became clear to me that in order to end this conflict I was going to have to fire someone. It was also clear that firing just one person would not resolve the conflict but would just change its nature. Therefore, the only fair and effective way I saw to end this difficulty was to fire all three individuals at once. I called a meeting of the three, informed them of my decision, and gave them their notices.

Then, I called a meeting of the house to tell the community what had transpired. One of the messages I wanted to relay was that no one's comments got anyone fired—it was the three's unwillingness to compromise that made my decision necessary.

The biggest remaining problem was that the three fired staff members were significantly involved with other members of the community. Hence, the sudden disconnection could present difficulties for some of the residents. To minimize the rupture, I suggested that the three stay in contact with the community (if they wished) but not come to the house for at least two months. This proved to be a good solution because they did keep in touch with the Soteria community and did not cause any more conflict.

To save Soteria from Emanon's fate, the staff started to take preventive measures. They discussed dismissing staff and recruiting more residents, among other methods. By the middle of the spring of 1981, it was clear that some cost-cutting moves were necessary. Reducing the staff wasn't going to help, because staff members were essential for the residents, and CETA no longer supplemented the existing staff. The community decided that Voyce, the clinical director, should replace the house director—and do both jobs, saving Soteria the money that went into the clinical director's salary. Thus, Voyce became not only the staff's immediate supervisor but also the individual responsible for the overall running of the program.

In the early fall of 1981, an influx of private referrals seemed to bring more energy to the program. This lasted through early January of the next year, when Soteria again slowly began to empty. The end of the staffing grant (to occur in August 1982) loomed. Some difficult residents, who did not respond well to Soteria's mode, made it even more difficult to sustain morale. (The original model was developed to respond to the needs of newly identified psychotics, but Soteria now housed primarily long-term treatment failures grasping for yet another straw.)

Departing staff members were not replaced. Thus, Voyce was not only recruiting clients but also administering, and working shifts. He had time to perform none of these duties effectively. In early June of 1982, when it became clear that everyone was going to be laid off, notices were given, and, on June 30, Soteria was scheduled to close because of insufficient funds. Several members of the community—both staff and residents—responded as did the Emanon graduate: "Keep the house open, even if we have to work without pay."

There was another reason to keep Soteria open: Staff feared that two of the residents would be severely damaged if required to go to *any* other treatment center; worse yet, staff thought, if these two couldn't get into another residential refuge, they would be sent back to locked hospital wards. The community thought that there was a good chance of finding more private residents in the fall and decided to stay open.

This decision meant that at least four staff members would have to work for nothing. Two people living in the house volunteered—one former resident and one volunteer who had recently moved to California. Voyce and three other staff members also agreed to volunteer. This arrangement gave minimal coverage and allowed staff to continue working with residents.

This shaky pattern continued for eight months (at which time a small amount of funds to pay Voyce and two other staff members became available). Slight progress was also being made in procuring state funds, and the world really looked brighter when David L. Rosenhan, a board member and professor of psychology and law at Stanford University, well known for a 1973 study called "On Being Sane in Insane Places," offered to help Voyce seek funds to buy the house. Wrote Voyce,

I can recall that before David got involved, I was beginning to burn out and I was trying to think of how to close Soteria in the least destructive way possible. But when he got involved, it was like a shot in the arm. I'm not sure if it was the possibility of getting funds or the fun of working with David; both probably played a role.

Working with someone as aware as David made going to work exciting. Again, I felt that there was a good possibility of connecting with some funding source. Another part of the elation had to do with David's outlook on house maintenance; he also felt that the house should be kept in at least decent condition—an unpopular view among some staff members and residents.

This partnership came to an abrupt end when the owner of the house sold it in August after promising David and Voyce that they had until December to secure the funds Soteria needed to buy the house. This betrayal was especially painful to Voyce, who learned the news just after he had gotten back from a meeting with the county, where he had been told that money would shortly become available.

The sale finished Soteria's clinical program, and the house officially closed on September 30, 1983.

The community had one last get-together that November.

Here, after 12 years of struggle, ended Soteria's active service to its disturbed and disturbing residents. But its data, its techniques, its understanding—its message—survive.

Some Problems and Some Solutions

P HYSICAL VIOLENCE IS of enormous concern in a residential psychiatric setting, a concern of both the program and the community in which it exists. Unfortunately, the violent patient has received a great deal of attention through books, TV, and other media. Although violent acts are frequently portrayed, understanding for the motivation behind them is rare, except, occasionally, with respect to suicide. For some, the psychotic personality is synonymous with violence. Although violent criminal acts are not more common among psychotics than in the general population, there is good clinical evidence that, for many mad people, dealing with anger and aggression is particularly troublesome.

Aggression

In many cases at Soteria, it was helpful for residents to locate the objects of their anger, to learn why that anger existed, and to find safe outlets for releasing the hostility generated. Soteria staff, therefore, allowed individuals in their altered states of consciousness as much expression of anger as possible. Staff tolerated substantial property damage—property is expendable and its protection, secondary—and tried to tune into people's feelings of aggression rather than encouraging repression. Staff also discussed techniques for dealing with their own fears of violence, acknowledged individual differences in ability to tolerate it, and identified those best able to deal with it. Staffer Della described her belief that understanding was the best way to handle fears about violence:

> I guess one of the things that would screw up your being able to handle really aggressive behavior is if you were to show to the person who is really angry and violent that you're terrified of what physically might happen to you. Being aware of the person's space, what's going on inside, helps me. It makes me feel more competent to deal with it because I figure, "I'm not like that right now. I'm together enough so that I'm not in a rage, so I can be of some help." It's kind of hard to explain. If I met somebody just off the street, and they came up and just started being violent, I'm sure I would react very differently. Maybe I would show my fear; maybe I'd run like hell; probably I would scream, but that doesn't happen here. Part of it is because you know the people. It's not like strangers' violence or rage that you don't understand. I think it's the *not understanding* that scares you.

The early days at Soteria saw many discussions of violence, which, it became apparent, takes various forms as well as has different impacts. Several of the staff members, for example, believed that a certain level of aggressiveness was desirable because it gave them material for therapeutic encounters. Others disagreed, finding all forms of violence unacceptable. Many hours of discussion produced no answer; however, for a number of years, uncontrollable violence presented no major problems because of the adequate support always available—at various times, staff and volunteers lived in the house, and both paid and unpaid helpers were willing to come to the house at a moment's notice. This was a positive aspect of the project's countercultural notoriety. In addition, and probably more significantly, staff were actively and continuously involved with clients on a one-to-one or a two-to-one basis for the duration of any difficulty, and in Soteria's 12 years, violent residents caused fewer than 10 injuries, almost all minor.

Still, Soteria recognized an obligation to provide a safe environment for everyone at the house and therefore developed some general precautions. The staff also tried to curb aggression when they thought it might become dangerous. Staff learned to pick up clues from residents in a destructive mood and, by anticipating violence, sometimes prevented its occurrence. For example, Geoff noted,

> Naomi played the Rolling Stones when she was angry. When they came on, you knew that Naomi was going to come out and stomp around and maybe try to break a window or something. The Stones were a signal. Now she'll go back to her room and put on that goddamned "Squeaky Fingers" or whatever the name of it is. She turns it up full blast, and everyone will know that Naomi's angry. Then somebody will go back and *be with* her. That's all she plays right now. That's the message: "Goddamn it, you've got to pay attention to me because I'm pissed off, and I'm going to break walls, etc . . . ." And you go back and that's exactly the mood she's in.

Said Susannah, one of Soteria's original staff members,

> When Tracy was angry she started talking about burning. She'd say she wanted to burn the house down or wanted to see flames or talk about the flames of hell or whatever. Flames, fire, burning would come into conversation. It might be an hour or two beforehand. She'd let you know, generally.

Another check on violence was Soteria's high tolerance of deviant behavior. Staff actively intervened to control only when clients were dangerous to themselves or others. When aggression reached a point that it threatened the initiator, staff, other residents, or the program, it was halted. In one such situation, staffer Kay explained the limitations on violence to a resident and then helped her deal with those limits.

> After she had broken one of the big windows, Kelly was just sitting on the floor in the living room, fairly frightened. I sat

next to her on the floor and said, "You know, if you keep on breaking the windows, which could hurt you or cut others, you won't be able to stay here. Also, we can't have the house destroyed." She said "OK, I'll leave." I said, "That's not what I'm saying. I don't want you to leave. I want you to stay. I want you to be able to stay, but to stay is not to break windows." At the same time I said, "You're free to leave. It's your choice. I'm not going to keep you here if you want to go." Kelly seemed relieved that she didn't need to leave but said, "But I need to break windows."

I said, "When you're going to break a window, or when you're going to start a fire or anything like that, just tell me you're going to do it, and I'll take the responsibility from then on in." I said, "Will you do that? Will you tell me?" She answered that she would. So we just talked. About an hour later, she'd gone upstairs and then came back down and walked casually by—very fast—and said, "I feel like breaking a window."

So I got up and went with her right away. She went into her room, into the bathroom—I guess to break a window—and I just held her there, and she turned around smiling and said, "Well you told me to tell you, and I told you." I said, "Well that's all right; now I've got the responsibility for you, and you didn't break it. It's OK."

And that worked out. After that, she was much more explicit and told me ahead of time. Not way ahead of time: She wouldn't come up and say, "Hey, I want to break a window. Stop me." She'd make you pick up on it. She'd throw it out in the middle of a conversation or, offhandedly as she walked by: "I feel like breaking a window. I feel like lighting a fire."

Even that didn't work forever, however. It worked for a while though.

No one was forced to take medication. In fact, as noted already, during residents' first six weeks at Soteria, the research design forbade drug therapy, except under highly unusual circumstances. If an emergency situation seemed to require medication, staff or the attending psychiatrist *persuaded* the resident to take it. Soteria had no syringes or needles with which to forcibly administer drugs. Voyce, who had worked with violent patients and trained staff at the local state hospital wrote, retrospectively, that

> as a member of the admissions team, I was available at all times for backup anywhere in the hospital. As a consequence, I became one of the staff who trained new employees to deal with hostile patients. What I found most unusual at Soteria (as compared to the situation in the hospital) was the residents' infrequent aggressive behavior.
>
> Not for a year did I understand some of the reasons for the difference between the hospitals' psychiatric patients and Soteria's residents. First, at Soteria clients were not forced to do what they didn't want to do or what they didn't believe was in their best interest. They didn't *have* to take medication or be secluded, for instance. Nor were they prevented from flight—Soteria's doors were not locked.
>
> The third difference was more subtle. I felt as if I never *really* knew any patient at the hospital; the reverse was true at Soteria, where it was difficult not to know people who stayed for more than two or three weeks because of the way you interacted with them. Put another way, there were no interpersonal consequences when I dealt with patients at the hospital. On the contrary, I suspect that the residents at Soteria—depending on the amount of time spent in the house—found it difficult to breach the barrier between verbal and physical violence. The personal consequences could have been too great.

But, although violence at Soteria—to others, to self, and to property—was unusual, it did occur and had to be dealt with.

And, noted Loren, deal with it the community did in a nondoctrinaire, practical, and effective manner.

Violence Towards Others—The Reasons

Violence, especially that directed at others, is a major source of anxiety for the staff in most treatment settings that help acutely psychologically distressed individuals. Physical aggression exhibited at Soteria was a result of anger, panic, loss, and/or frustration, emotions that often stemmed, paradoxically, from a desire to save others.

Frustration

While violence usually took the form of verbal aggression—that is, threats—there were occasions when it went beyond the verbal to the physical. When this happened, it usually turned inward. When violence erupted against others, it often did so because someone was prevented from taking a desired action. For instance, one new resident, Alfred, became so obsessed with his need to leave Soteria in order to board a spaceship to prevent its landing, dangerously, in Rio de Janeiro, that it took six members of the community—staff, residents, and volunteers—to hold him down. Eventually, he accepted a bag of popcorn in place of his journey and calmed down. Whether Alfred's expression of violence came because the community was in his way or because it wouldn't help him get to his destination was never clear.

Panic

Panic could also trigger violence towards others. The most unpredictable and the least understood form of physical violence, panic was usually directed against the person closest to the sufferer. After suddenly hitting a friend, a resident commented, "I don't know what came over me. My voices told me she was going to kill me." Even such "explanations" like this one were rare, however, and usually unrelated to the events that led to the violent act.

The most common episodes of panic violence occurred when clients were either entering or emerging from regressive states. Male clients not infrequently struck at women staff in such panics. For instance, Kevin, a resident who had just been readmitted to Soteria because he felt that he was "going crazy again," was sitting in his room when a female staff member to whom he had been close came in to say hello. Kevin suddenly became verbally threatening and then chased her into the kitchen, where other members of the community were eating breakfast. The group subdued him. Several minutes of talk between Kevin and his would-be victim—with others present— defused the tension. This was atypical behavior for Kevin, who had no history of violence before or after this incident. Although he never said why he suddenly attacked someone to whom he normally felt close, he reestablished and maintained a close relationship with her after the incident.

Anger

More than three fourths of the violent episodes at Soteria stemmed from anger—usually consequent to rejection by someone close. It also resulted from intrusions into someone's "space"—real or imagined. Finally, residents' feeling deprived of something or of someone on occasion produced outbursts. Voyce's memories of the frequently violent results of compelling patients in the hospital rather than persuading them encouraged Soteria staff to use force as infrequently as possible. Sometimes, however, residents had to be made to stop actions that could hurt themselves or others or do serious damage to property. For instance, wrote Hal, a 21-year-old resident named Thomas

> had decided to go over to our favorite restaurant, the Harvest Inn, to get a milk shake. He became confused and began shouting. At that point, a waitress called Soteria and asked for assistance, so she wouldn't have to call the police. Two members of the staff and a resident who were close to Thomas drove over and tried to talk him into coming home.
>
> We had made an agreement with Thomas that, on the one hand, we would do whatever we could to get him back to Soteria and avoid situations that might get him hospitalized. On the other hand, we promised that he only had to say,

"Stop," and we would let him go, unless there were danger of injury to him or someone else.

When we arrived, Thomas refused to leave and became upset with the manager, who was asking him to leave. When it became clear that Thomas's behavior was going to warrant a call to the police, we said we were going to take him back home, and if he wanted us not to, he would have to say, "Stop." One staff member took him by the hand and led him out the door. As soon as the door closed, Thomas decided that he was going to run back in and do *something—what* wasn't clear to us—but something we felt would make the situation worse. The three of us grabbed him and put him in the car—with Thomas attempting to hit and otherwise trying to escape—but he never said, "Stop."

When we returned to Soteria, Thomas became remorseful and apologetic. Within two hours he went over to a fast food restaurant and ordered a milk shake without any problem. The difference this time—a former resident went along.

Examining this episode makes it evident how difficult it is to determine who is the aggressor and who is the respondent. We assumed Thomas was going back into the restaurant to misbehave. But he may have wanted to go in to apologize to the manager.

The question here: Did Thomas throw the first blow, or did the three members of the community who restrained him? This issue is important (see below). Residents justifying their violent behavior raised just such questions, even though, unlike at many other treatment facilities, Soteria staff made every effort to preserve freedom. Voyce recalled a similar struggle, with different results, at a state hospital where he had worked earlier.

The Use of Force

Voyce Remembers

The last incident with which I was involved at the job I had prior to Soteria involved a young man admitted to the hospital sometime before the day shift arrived on the ward. During the change of shift,

I first noticed him sitting in a corner of the ward, making gestures with his hand in front of his face, smiling, and talking to himself continuously.

The ward was over-full, and the night shift had had a difficult time. Several new patients had come on the ward, and several "incidents" had occurred during the night. In addition, we were understaffed by two, which made it even more of a problem trying to deal with over 40 potentially violent or unknown (recently admitted) patients. At that time, the maximum-security patients and the new ones were on the same ward.

During the change of shifts, I noticed that the head nurse was looking upset about the smiling patient's behavior. She asked the night-charge psychiatric technician if the patient had taken any medication. "No," said the technician, "he just arrived on the ward." We stopped the meeting to confirm that medications had been ordered. A nurse was told to give the new patient his medications.

As the nurse approached, the patient stopped smiling and gesturing and began to act "weird." Before the nurse said anything, he warned, "I'm allergic to that stuff." She checked his chart for an allergy to Thorazine (the most common tranquilizer at the time). Because there was none mentioned, she obtained an order for an injection. The patient refused to submit, suggesting that she give the shot to the head nurse instead.

She returned with five of the staff, including me, to make sure he cooperated.

When he saw us coming, he began to run. We were, of course, able to subdue him—he was restrained in a locked room—but he resisted violently.

As a result, he was secluded, and his chart annotated his hostility and aggression towards the staff. While he was in the seclusion room, he bit off a chunk of his arm.

Later, it was discovered that he was allergic to the medication.

As a member of the treatment team, I felt we had followed the right processes. Not until months later, when I was working at Soteria, did I realize that the incident would not have occurred here. In this case, the patient was defending himself against what he rightly identified as a violent act. The staff was wrong to give him

*medication to which he was allergic. But further, I wondered, was it
actually necessary to medicate the patient? If so, need it have been
done so disruptively?*

*My perspective, from the staff's point of view, before starting to
work at Soteria, suggested affirmative answers to both questions:*

*Upsetting the ward, especially given its overpopulation and
staff shortage, was to be avoided.*

*The patient was behaving psychotically, which called for
"treatment," and medication is treatment.*

*But when I came to bring my Soteria experience to bear, I came
to some different conclusions. Someone was upset, and the nurse
thought that someone was the patient. But, on closer observation,
someone else was upset as well—the head nurse. Her solution was
to cure the patient's upset with medication (which seemed
counterproductive because he became even more upset). His solution—
to give her medication instead—might have worked if, as they both
believed, medication had the power to calm people. In addition, his
solution would have allowed the patient to continue enjoying himself,
to keep smiling, thus avoiding a crisis for the patient and the rest of
the ward.*

*The patient's solution, though probably flawed by the limitations
of the medication, certainly was better than the nurse's.*

Due to Soteria's philosophy, violent episodes resulting from the
staff's compelling client behaviors were comparatively uncommon
and usually mild.

Violence spawned by feelings of rejection was more common,
happening occasionally when residents felt they were not receiving
appropriate attention. Rarely did clients hit or become violent with
the person by whom they felt rejected. Their ire usually fell upon a
rival for his/her attention. Although caused by rejection, such violence
took the form of anger. A resident, Toni, followed this pattern. Wrote
a staff member,

> Toni had been out shopping and returned to find that the
> staff member she called "Mother" had gone to a film with a
> male resident she disliked. When the two returned, Toni was
> eating dinner in the kitchen. When "Mother" and her
> companion walked into the kitchen, Toni accused—"Mother,
> I thought you couldn't leave the house today because there
> wasn't enough help?"—and poured hot coffee on the other
> resident.

In this case, although the moviegoer had not provoked Toni
directly, he was the victim of her misplaced anger.

An even more common form of such unprovoked violence
occurred as a result of something that happened before clients came
to Soteria. Thus residents sometimes struck out at staff members who
reminded them of their parents. Other forms of free-floating anger
that sometimes led to violence at Soteria occurred when clients
aggressively protected what they called their "space" against intruders.
Residents hit, kicked, or bit, because they felt cheated, defrauded,
robbed, or otherwise treated unfairly.

Such perceptions could, of course, elicit aggressive responses in
normal people. Residents at Soteria responded to frustrating
situations that would anger almost anyone but often in exaggerated,
dramatic ways. The difference in degree was a function of the
residents' level of crisis, which was often exaggerated by the fact that
they had been taken out of their normal environments—most often
against their will—and housed with a group of people whom they saw
as alien. Soteria's residents' violent acts were similar to those of the
general public but more extreme.

Violence Towards Self

Staff members found it more painful to deal with self-destructive
impulses than with aggression directed towards other people or
property. Hurting oneself in its broadest sense is a more common

form of violence than violence towards others. Aggression in this area culminates in suicide, true, and other obvious forms of self-destructiveness. But there are more insidious self-destructive behaviors—for example, that of the person who smokes unceasingly from the time of rising in the morning until retiring at night; that of the person who stays awake for three days; that of the person who eats nonstop or not at all. Self-directed traumas like these can be more detrimental in the long run than a single, failed suicidal gesture.

The motivating factors behind self-directed violence were unresolved anger and the need to attract attention and/or reduce anxiety. Staff felt an awful (sometimes unwarranted) responsibility for residents threatening to hurt themselves. The following dialogue between Alma, Soteria's social worker/administrator, and Tara O'Neill, one of the house's original staff members, demonstrates the impact of work with acutely suicidal residents.

> ALMA. Did you ever find yourself catching someone's fear?
> TARA. I did once. It was with Iris, and I really picked up on her fear. Iris, you know, is never really physically violent, but one night she was very angry about something that was going on downstairs, so we two had gone upstairs together. I had a sense that I didn't want to leave her alone. I went into her room, and she started throwing things, picking things up, and throwing them at the window. The more frustrated she became, the more impotent she felt, the more enraged she became, flinging stuff, yelling, and swearing. She was talking about how she wanted to kill herself and wished she were dead. I really picked up on her fear because she was much more angry than she was scared. I was scared to leave her: I was scared to take my eyes off her. I don't think I dealt with her as well as I could have, or had before, when I hadn't been that emotionally involved with her, feeling so much what she was feeling.
> ALMA. How long did this go on?
> TARA. The throwing things and the swearing combined lasted an hour, maybe a little bit longer, and then I took her

for a ride. Getting away from the house calmed her down somewhat. She was still very angry and seemed very withdrawn. At one point during the drive, she talked again about killing herself, about different ways she could do so. I started to get scared again and felt the responsibility, thinking maybe it was a really dumb thing to take her out for a ride. So I turned the car around and came back; however, that made her even madder. She wanted to drive around forever. I told her why I had stopped driving—because I was scared that she would try to jump out of the car. So then she just went upstairs. I went up too and stayed with her all night. She hardly slept at all.

ALMA. You didn't sleep either?

TARA. Not that night. Usually when I stayed up with somebody who needed me—somebody who was too scared, too angry, too violent, took watching, or whatever—I'd fall asleep for a little bit from sheer exhaustion. That night my fear kept me awake. That's the only incident that I can recall that I was so touched by what was happening with a person that I caught the fear or the anger or whatever. I really, really felt it, and that scared me.

ALMA. You weren't really afraid she would do something to you?

TARA. I was afraid she would kill herself if I took my eyes off her and didn't watch her every second. I had a feeling she was scared enough, angry enough, even strong enough to do it. So I wasn't about to let her out of my sight.

Violence Inward—>Losing (1)

It is sometimes hard to see suicide purely as *self*-destructive, because— "successful" or not—it is also abusive to others. The suicide of Evan, a former resident enrolled in another psychiatric program, who killed himself when visiting at Soteria, exemplifies this double thrust. In contrast, Tammy's suicide seemed more purely self-focused. She killed herself several months after leaving Soteria in a city some 300 miles away. While Evan's act was the result of a complex and unclear series of events and emotions, Tammy's motivation was simpler—she shot herself after discovering her former lover in bed with another woman. (See below.) Perhaps the sad lesson from Tammy's act is that it is impossible to prevent a well-organized person bent on self-destruction from doing so.

No suicides took place among the 200 or so residents while they lived at Soteria.

EVAN. Voyce summarized Evan's background:

> Evan's difficulties apparently began when he lived in Idaho. There, he said, he began experiencing difficulty after a "bad LSD trip." One staff member said that Evan told her that "I was at the end of a cycle of good times and was about to begin a period of bad times." Between the LSD trip and Soteria, Evan had made numerous suicide attempts and had been hospitalized on several occasions, primarily because of them.
>
> He showed a few other overt signs of psychosis. For example, one staff member reported that "Evan also complained of hearing voices (female) that instructed him in various ways." Evan was otherwise fairly reasonably behaved, however, expressing his depression only through his suicidal gestures. "His character can best be described as intensely mellow," observed one former resident.
>
> After several pseudo suicide attempts, Evan was admitted to the local county crisis unit, with the recommendation that he be kept in a secure place. Soteria staff feared that if left alone, Evan would succeed in his quest to commit suicide. After a week, Evan was admitted to a local community psychiatric hospital where he obtained day passes for short periods of time.
>
> He began coming to Soteria, asking to be readmitted, but because there was no apparent change in his attitude towards self-abuse, he was refused. The house had dealt unsuccessfully with Evan's suicidal behavior, which did not

abate, for several months. The Soteria community reached consensus that its best efforts had made no headway with Evan and that, therefore, unless he could offer some assurance that he would not kill himself, readmission to Soteria would be pointless and useless. Such decisions were not made lightly or frequently, and suicidal tendencies were never, in themselves, a reason to refuse anyone a place at the house.

Several days later, Evan was out on a day pass from the long-term "locked" (L) facility where he was a resident. Believing him to be ready for discharge as soon as a place in the community opened up, L facility staff issued Evan passes on request. This time, however, Evan went to a local gas station and bought a can of gas. Without anyone noticing, he slipped into Soteria's backyard, laid several books and different types of fruit on a blanket, sat down on it himself, poured the gas over everything, and lit it.

A few minutes later, one of the residents discovered the pyre and shouted for help. As the rest of the community came out to put out the fire, the fire department and ambulances arrived. In the middle, Evan, fatally burned, protested, on the one hand, "I did it because of you," and pleaded, on the other, "Please don't hate me for this."

Evan presented himself as concerned with the state of the world; however, he believed that he was the cause of the world's conflicts and, as such, had to do something to alleviate them. His method of suicide also probably had international motivation: The Soteria community hypothesized that Evan chose self-immolation because of a recent widely publicized suicide by burning taking place in India.

A year before coming to Soteria, Evan seemed fundamentally sane. An above-average student, he had attended a local university and had a successful work history. His family apparently provided a good social environment. Then something went terribly wrong, something that led to hospitalization, to residence at Soteria, to institutionalization at two other facilities, and finally to death by fire.

What happened?

Evan's case presented many difficulties both for members of the Soteria community and for his parents. First, how could someone who less than a year earlier seemed to be living the American dream have committed suicide? Second, why did he use Soteria as the stage for his statement? Third, why did the community feel at once angry at Evan and hurt and sad? One fundamental problem shared by Soteria and by Evan's parents, who participated in the community meetings after his suicide, was that they were almost as victimized by his act as he.

A few thought that Evan committed suicide not because he believed that life wasn't worth living but because he wanted to make a statement. They remembered comments such as "If only people could understand what I'm trying to say." Or his apology to Voyce, who finally managed to extinguish the fire: "I did it for you."

The implication here was that his apparently successful earlier life experiences were not inconsistent with the final act, but a precondition that gave more impetus to his "statement." This view was most strongly held by a former resident, who saw Evan not as "psychotic" but as someone willing to pursue an idea to its conclusion at any cost. This attempt to find something positive in Evan's suicide was unusual, however; most took a different view.

The most negative view of Evan's act was that of the staff member closest to him. She thought Evan's act was directed at Soteria in general and her in particular, because he was refused readmittance unless he promised that he would stop his self-destructive behavior, and she had been most adamantly opposed to his return.

Evan's parents took opposite positions in this painful debate. His father, like the former resident, saw Evan's act as a positive statement. His mother saw it as supremely negative, a blow to all who cared for him. While the community's discussions served, eventually, to alleviate somewhat the pain, grief, and anger Evan's suicide left in its wake, the sense of loss persisted among the members of Soteria who were there during Evan's short and dramatic stay and during his horrific final visit.

Violence Inward—>Losing (2)

TAMMY, age 23, was admitted to Soteria two days after Thanksgiving. She had attempted suicide by ingesting paint thinner, following an argument with her uncle at Thanksgiving dinner.

On admission, she had great difficulty speaking (sometimes called "blocking"), showed thought disorder, was mostly without affect, and exhibited catatonic motor behavior. She was convinced that she was the devil incarnate. Auditory hallucinations told her of her "badness."

The preceding May, she had returned home following an auto accident in the metropolitan area to which she recently moved. Although she had not been badly injured, escaping only by a lucky chance, she felt she "ought to have been killed" and decided to change her lifestyle to "find Jesus." She moved in with the Catholic aunt and uncle who had raised her and worked as a full-time volunteer in a fundamentalist religious mission.

Nonetheless, in the two or three months prior to admission, she began to believe she was "Lucifer" and was responsible for evil. She thought that by killing herself she would "rid the world of evil."

History

Tammy, the youngest in the family, lived in the East with her mother, father, sister, and brother until she was five years old. At that time, her father died of a heart attack and a maternal uncle committed suicide. One year later, her mother was hospitalized in a state institution because of "her inability to cope with the death of her husband and the raising of three small children on her own." Diagnosed as schizophrenic, Tammy's mother was never discharged.

At that point, Tammy and her older sister and brother were sent to live on a farm with an aunt, an uncle, and their nine children. All were raised in a strict Catholic environment and attended parochial schools. In 1967, the entire family moved to California, when her uncle took a job with an electronics firm.

In high school, Tammy was a good student, well-behaved, and her uncle's favorite. But shortly after Tammy left for college, her older sister died of asthma in the state hospital to which she had been sent because of her "extremely withdrawn behavior." Tammy did not know her sister very well because "she was very quiet and hid in corners a lot."

Tammy stayed in college for three quarters, did poorly, and dropped out without finishing her first year. After that, she lived communally in a variety of hippie environments, became sexually involved with many men, and at one point lived alone in a tent for several months. Because she did not conceal her promiscuous behavior from her aunt and uncle, Tammy was unwelcome in their home. During this period, she became pregnant and went to New York for an abortion. She returned and adjusted, marginally, to her lifestyle until the auto accident.

At Soteria

At first, Tammy remained quiet, withdrawn, without affect, and preoccupied with her role as the devil. About a month after admission, she attempted suicide with rat poison because she felt responsible for an outburst of violence by another client. She improved gradually over the next several months but remained impassive and preoccupied with the devil. She had great difficulty sleeping when it was dark and occasionally took neuroleptics to help.

In April, some six months later, three days of intensive staff work occurred that seemed to be pivotal for her recovery. Loren and Katy summarized the process.

> Everyone was drinking wine until 3:00 or 4:00 AM, Tammy remaining impassive.
>
> Finally her facade broke down, and she began to express crazy sentiments, again believing she was the devil and should die. She sobbed and sobbed—angry, upset, and nervous.
>
> Katy and I held her for a long time, saying little except to comfort her and support her. Later Tammy went to bed, Katy with her. I joined them, sat by the bed, and held her hand.

She continued to talk about being the devil. She wanted to die: "I should be killed because I am so bad." I asked her who in her life was the devil, and she responded immediately, "My uncle." "He raised people in a warped way," she continued, "treating them like flowers and bushes. He said that they should grow straight as he wanted them to."

She went on to say how her behavior for the past several years had been her way of showing him that she didn't like his ways, but that then she felt bad and that she should die. I pointed out that she was wanting to kill her uncle in her. She picked that up and began to focus on how angry she was with him for what he'd done to her.

She also said he had caused her sister's death from asthma because he had made it so that her sister no longer cared to live. At that point, Tammy began to wheeze, which she continued to do as we talked about her sister—how she'd liked her but hadn't really known her. Tammy felt bad that she'd been stoned when she found out about her sister's death. She had gone to the funeral but hadn't been to the grave since.

She then focused her anger at her uncle in a very real way. She ought to tell him she wanted little to do with him, she said, and with this connection of her negative feelings to him, her mood lightened, she was much less depressed, and she could even laugh. By sunup she was very much together: She was relaxed and her asthma had gone.

She went to sleep peacefully.

The next day, Loren found Tammy sitting quietly and asked how she was. She talked about being angry at everything and everyone but explained how difficult it was for her to be angry. At that point she went into her devil trip and said she wanted to get $89 and go to Hawaii. Loren pointed out that, since the devil was part of her, he'd make it to Hawaii also.

Suddenly, she became sad and was about to cry but wouldn't really let herself. Loren indicated that being sad was "OK" and offered to *be with* her. Tammy decided against a possibly intense experience because she said she was "numb," she "felt nothing," which Loren said might be easier than being sad. She heartily agreed.

Then, Katy, Tammy, and Loren shared some of their early life experiences. Tammy and Loren had both been raised as Catholics and had both left the church, stands that were, unfortunately, accompanied by considerable guilt.

Without much further brooding, Tammy then talked for about an hour, almost nonstop, about her losses: father, mother, sister, cousin—in that order. When talking about her sister's death, Tammy slipped back into her conviction that she was the devil and again asserted that she needed to die. Loren gently redirected her to her sister's death, and she continued to unburden herself.

Sadly, poignantly, she talked about her mother. She'd resented her sister telling Tammy she'd be her mother, when Tammy felt no one other than her mother could fulfill that role. Tammy's feelings about and recollections of her mother are all positive. For example, "She made me feel safe and good when I went to bed." She was similarly warm about her father.

And her brother, she said, was "always there when I needed him." During this monologue her affect was always appropriate: sad about her losses, angry and somewhat sympathetic about her uncle, who has alienated the children he hoped would take care of him late in life.

Loren and Katy's major efforts were to take Tammy back to the stimulus which spun her off into madness. They also acknowledged the incredible number of losses she'd suffered, pointed out that putting them into perspective did not necessarily mean blaming anyone but did help sort them out.

There was an immense sadness in her that made Loren sad himself. He acknowledged and supported her efforts to keep in touch with her feelings and pointed out again and again that it was avoiding them that had led her to feel like the devil with all his "badness."

Finally, Katy and Loren and Tammy spoke about her fear of losing people, a fear that prevented her from letting people get close. Katy said it was hard for Tammy to acknowledge closeness to her: "I will go off duty in two days," Katy warned, "but I'll be back, and I'll miss you."

Tammy, now quite calm and at peace, went to sleep readily.

Katy and Loren were the staff combination one more night during Tammy's stay. As Tammy and others were sitting round the table, Katy noticed that Tammy was behaving differently than previously: She was acting silly rather than either being down or feeling good. Loren conjectured that this mood was related to the staff change coming the next morning, and Tammy agreed.

Over the next several hours the three discussed this issue, including relating it to her many other losses. Occasionally she slipped away from the pain and acted silly—but in the context of the relationship with Katy and Loren seemed able to return to it, tolerate it, and come to terms with it.

Again, a natural resolution of her pain allowed her to go comfortably to sleep. In the course of the discussion, Loren, Katy, and Tammy acknowledged their regard for each other, a regard Tammy noted that she didn't hold for many people.

Following this evening, Tammy improved dramatically and began to make plans for herself. For the next two months, there were few signs of continuing psychosis. The weaving she had begun in a desultory way she now pursued with great care and attention.

First Leave-taking

Tammy arranged to live with a staff couple in a nearby city and left Soteria after a stay of nearly eight months. For the next two years, Tammy remained well, living communally with the staff couple for nearly a year and then moving to her own apartment. She worked full-time as a waitress and continued weaving.

A year after leaving Soteria, she met a man she liked very much and, two months later, moved with him to a farm in a nearby state. But after nine months, the relationship broke up, and Tammy began to go downhill.

Having received no formal treatment or medication during her two years in the community, Tammy was readmitted to Soteria in a state very similar to her original. She was suicidal and preoccupied with her "badness."

But this time she stayed at Soteria only six weeks. She chose to take neuroleptics for a month of this stay but discontinued them two weeks before leaving. She reorganized rapidly and arranged a job and living situation for herself in the same area of the nearby state from whence she'd just come. As before, she left the program unpsychotic.

Last Leave-taking

"Everyone was pleased," remembered Katy, "that Tammy had gotten better so much more rapidly this time. We thought her quick recovery portended well for the long term."

Five days after resettling near the farm, however, Tammy made an unannounced visit to her friend. She found him in bed with a woman, took his gun off the wall, stepped outside, and shot herself through the head. She died instantly.

Violence Inward—>Winning

KELLY. Responsibility for dealing with dangerous, self-destructive behavior could continue even when a staff member was off duty and away from the house. For example, Loren recalled Susannah's effective intervention:

> I found Hal with Kelly sitting beside the front room heater. She had blindfolded herself and then poked holes in her right wrist, lacerating it superficially. She was clutching pieces of broken glass in her left hand. I told her that I wouldn't let her hurt herself and that I wanted her to give the shards to me—she grasped them tighter. Hal made the same request with the same result.
>
> Luckily Susannah (who was not working) called back to see if she was needed. Hal and I tried to persuade Kelly to talk to Susannah. She said yes by allowing us to lead her (still blindfolded) to the phone, but she said nothing. Susannah spoke to her, and in a couple of minutes she gave Hal the large pieces of water glass. Her hand was uncut.

> Susannah had told Kelly that she loved her and accepted
> her but didn't want her to hurt herself anymore—Kelly hurt
> enough inside without having to hurt her wrists.
>
> Without ever saying a word on the telephone, Kelly
> followed Susannah's request and handed Hal the rest of the
> glass.

Why did Kelly resist help from men, wondered Loren. She needed and wanted women's acceptance, something she never had from her mother, who had consistently rejected her. The question is, he continued, why did Kelly think only women can tolerate and accept her "badness"? When she felt a woman (i.e., Susannah) could, Kelly reverted into an infantile, within-the-womb state of blindness (even to a blindfold), into silence, and into a need to be cared for. Her experience with her mother led Kelly to predict rejection by females, especially if she were to do something "bad." Not finding this to be the case, Kelly was able to stop mutilating herself.

Interpersonally Problematic Responses

Soteria residents expressed themselves in a number of bizarre ways. Staff members learned to respect these statements where appropriate, to alter them where useful, and—on occasion—to halt them altogether. Three particular responses had to be handled frequently—residents exhibiting withdrawn, infantile, and sexual behaviors. Staff dealt with each situation uniquely; however, certain community members had better tolerance for certain behaviors than others. Sometimes, it was possible to "specialize" and assign particular individuals to deal with the behaviors with which they felt most comfortable.

Withdrawn Behavior

Staff members dealt with withdrawn persons idiosyncratically; a number of approaches seemed often to work. Tara's and Ed's responses, for example, were restrained. Tara explained,

I left Tamara pretty much to herself when she was in that withdrawn stage. I wouldn't try to force her. I remember the first time I met her. She was lying on the couch, and I went up, leaned over the couch, and said, "Welcome, my name is Tara."

She barely looked at me and said "Hi" in a very quiet voice, not responding at all otherwise. I don't remember how long she was like that. I would sit with her. I would tell her that it was time for dinner and sometimes bring her food to her, but usually she ate with everybody else. I'd keep an eye on her, but I never pressed her, like "Let's get to know each other." I just didn't think that kind of pressure was indicated or right.

Ed related to a withdrawn resident named Leo similarly.

For the first couple of weeks, Leo must have spent close to 20 hours a day in his room. He'd come down for lunch, dinner, and a cup of coffee late at night. I would go up and talk to him in his room and ask him if he really wanted to stay there when he was welcome anywhere in the house. I reassured him, however, that this was his room, and if he didn't want me or anybody else in there, "Just say so, and I'll leave." But I'd invite him to come down for a cup of coffee and stuff like that. He'd just kind of work into it.

Another staff member, Susannah, found nonverbal means to forge a relationship with Leo, who was still withdrawn.

For some reason, it was very difficult for Leo to use words to communicate. So, when you sat down and tried to have a conversation with him, you were unwittingly threatening him, putting him on the defensive, rather than building your relationship.

So I guessed we should think about activities in which we might engage Leo where he wouldn't be obliged to talk.

One night I remember, he wanted a beer, so I took him to a liquor store to get one. I didn't know the way, so he was giving me signals with his hands—which way to turn and so forth. When we got there, Leo didn't have money or identification, so I paid for the beer, and then we came home. There was no conversation either way.

After we walked in, I was really tired, so I lay down on the living room sofa to rest for a minute. I suddenly became aware that it was very cold in the room. Then I looked up and Leo was standing there, putting his jacket over my shoulders to keep me warm. And then he just walked away. I guess you could interpret that in a lot of ways, but to me it seemed he was telling me "thank you" for the beer by returning a favor.

But it was a mind-blowing experience, because it was all nonverbal. And doubly mind-blowing because I think we all saw Leo as absorbed in his own fantasy world, as comparatively unaware of other people's needs. And yet that night he knew what I wanted—a coat—without my even saying so.

Still another staff member, Geoff, expressed to Alma his serious doubts about whether such gradual methods of building a relationship were valid:

> GEOFF. My first reaction to that really heavy withdrawal is to give Leo a kick in the ass. At first, I thought of almost forcing myself into that space. Forcing myself into it with him; or forcing him to come out to me—one of the two. The other one would be just to stay with him for 3 weeks for 24 hours a day, for as long as it took, but I don't think I've got the energy to do that.
>
> Sometimes I have the fantasy of going in and dropping a bomb—a really very aggressive kind of "Goddamn it, relate to me!" That's what we did in the psychodrama groups with which I worked before, and usually it worked. You dropped the bomb and then went around and picked up the pieces and put them back

together and held the person. And, there's a really heavy aversion, which at times really upsets me, against that approach around this house. It's almost like saying, "That's the space he's in, and don't do anything with it."

ALMA. But sometimes I think there is also the part, that you are OK, no matter what you do. And I really think the only thing that will make you understand is to, some day, watch them wake up from that withdrawal and tell you what's been going on. And then you will be less likely to want to intrude.

GEOFF. Yeah.

ALMA. There can be a great deal of work going on.

GEOFF. The thing that worries me—my main worry—is that it doesn't put any faith in Leo. Because what if he stays there? What if everybody gets used to that, and says OK, that's where Leo's at. We'll let him stay there. And, three years later, he still hasn't come out. You know, how do you then do something about it? By then, the pattern is established. What can you do then besides just putting him on a ward somewhere, because somebody didn't do something at the right time, or the environment wasn't right, and the person just didn't come back.

Infantile Behavior

With severely regressed residents, Soteria staff found the simple reassurance imparted by physical contact to be particularly important. (Although traditional modes of therapy often caution against touching a "schizophrenic" person, staff found that physical contact was a significant means of expressing warmth and concern.) Touching was thus an important form of communication at Soteria, and staff member Ed found it natural to hold and rock Kris, a young man regressing to infancy:

I think I'd been here a week. I put Kris in my lap, and he accepted the gesture completely, lying there for about an hour and a half. Then I stayed with him all night. He'd get a little sick once in a while and spit into a pan that we had there. I'd be washing his face off with a wet cloth; then he finally sat up, and I just gave him a back rub. I stayed with him the rest of the night. When someone's regressed down, and you're nursing him, there are no sexual feelings. You have the feeling that the person is two years old, no matter how big they are. With both Kris and Chuck—I didn't see Kris as 20 or Chuck as 18. I felt as if I were holding two-year-old boys in my hands, in my arms.

With Kris, it was the first time I'd done it, and I was sort of watching myself doing it and saying, "My god, he's two years old; that's all he is." I was like a father and a mother together. You're not aloof from the experience thinking, "Now this person s regressing, and I have to hold him." You're just doing it instinctively.

Sometimes a regression to infancy includes a desire to nurse. Staff member Kay described such an event when she was tending to Tamara:

I had had three hours of sleep, and even that had been broken sleep. Sleeping with and guarding Tamara is not especially conducive to good resting. I was sleeping on the floor by the door, so I would wake up, if she tried to leave. She awakened at 6 o'clock, demanding food. I got up and started to fix her breakfast. She was sitting at the table, waiting most impatiently and then urinating on the bench. I took her to the bathroom and changed her pants; then we went back to the kitchen. I fed her at the table. She finished and sat quietly for about two minutes. Then she looked at me with a fearful expression on her face and asked me what day it was.

I told her it was Sunday.

"No, I mean what day is it *really?* You know what I mean!"

"Sunday, September 5th."

I knew that this was Tamara's birthday, but I just didn't want to deal with it then. I was tired. I was sad. Here it was, Tamara's 16th Birthday—"Sweet 16"—her special day to celebrate, and there she sat in Soteria, soiling herself, terrified of dying, of being alone, of *being with* people, of spiders, of noises, of being loved, of being unloved.

"Happy Birthday, Tamara"—it was so goddamned sad.

When I told her the date, she was stunned. She sat completely still and stared at me. Then came the change— fear, anxiety, joy, little-girl pleasure, sorrow, and pain all flashed over her face. Then she started to cry, a slow, sad, and painful cry. And then she said, "It's my birthday. Say `Happy Birthday' to me." And I did. Then she got up and came over to me and sat down. She took my hand in both of hers and said, "Hold me!" I held her, while she cried for a few minutes.

Then she sat up and said, "Give me a present. Give me something. Give me anything. Give me something you don't want anymore. Give me something you hate. Just give me anything of yours, and I'll love it forever." I told her that she would be getting birthday presents later in the day—that we hadn't forgotten her.

I was wearing a T-shirt that morning, one that Tamara liked. She asked me then if I would wear her shirt and could she wear mine, just for her birthday. No one else in the house was awake—it was early, and it was Tamara's birthday— so we exchanged shirts.

When I took my shirt off, Tamara stared at my breasts and seemed to freeze for a few seconds. I can't describe even to myself the expression that was on her face, so I won't try here. She collapsed into my chest with her eyes closed, completely limp. I almost fell under her weight. Her face was towards my chest, and she moved it a little and started sucking my breast. For a very brief moment I panicked, afraid of being bitten and wanting to pull away. But that feeling passed quickly, and I didn't withdraw.

Maybe it was instinctive. It just all felt so *right* to me then. Without thinking of appropriate therapeutic moves or words, I held her, cuddled her, nursed her, cooed to her—all very freely and naturally—and it ended.

Suddenly, Tamara moved away from me and said, "I'm not your baby: You're mine." She then ignored the episode and went on to deal with the rest of the day. She seemed much more in touch with her environment for the next 24 hours, and the staff guessed that this episode may have been in part responsible.

As usual, however, there was not one answer, one cure. Such temporary periods of recovery were characteristic of residents emerging from deep regressions.

Regression, while never induced at Soteria, was allowed when it happened naturally. It often seemed to be an important step towards reintegration. Soteria staff dealt not infrequently with incontinence and permitted messing about with food and/or paint. When staff member Keith realized how helpful smearing was to Tracy in expressing her emotions, he thus encouraged her:

Tracy had been working for weeks, 6 to 10 hours a day, on a big oil painting "by numbers" to give to her mother. When her mother finally told Tracy that she could not come home for Easter, Tracy was really angry. She took the paints and started with the brush to make wider sweeps, finally using her hand, mixing all the paints together and smearing them on the painting until the original design was practically obliterated. But she was smearing with style.

She was creating another kind of painting. At one point, she stopped and looked at it and said, "What do you think?" I said, "It's the best painting you've ever done." I really liked it. There was anger in it the way she was using the colors. This one had meaning, whereas the painting by numbers didn't have much. She kept on working and finished it up. At the same time, she was getting back at her mother.

When she finally finished the picture, she started painting on the wall, drawing figures, writing the names of people in her family . . . . She looked around to see if it was all right, and I thought, well, she had half the wall already done—she might as well keep going on this section.

Finishing that wall, she left the art room and was starting to splotch paint around the house.

"Let's stick to paper," I suggested. "I don't know if that stuff will come off or not. I think it will, but I'm not sure." There was paper on the walls for painting and I said, "Use the paper." She did. But when she was done, she dumped the whole pan on the living room carpeting as a finishing touch.

She was writing members of her family's names over pictures of things like cats and dogs, mixing people in the house with her biological family. The result was really good, both as smearing and as a real expression of herself, something she hadn't been able to do for a long time.

During the painting, I talked to her about what I saw in it and what she saw in it. I sometimes asked her, "Who's this? Who's that?" She'd say, "That's the girlfriend I had in high school. That's my younger sister. That's my mother. That's my uncle . . ." She was writing "cat" and "dog" and "witch" and stuff like that. We just talked about what they were. One of the reasons why it was effective was that it wasn't done as therapy, as *me* helping *her* see what she was creating.

I was curious as to who they were. I didn't know.

Keith's spontaneous interaction with Tracy, combining his genuine interest in her with a responsible attitude towards the house as a whole, was typical of Soteria's approach at its most successful.

Sexual Behavior

Original fears that staff and residents might engage sexually—despite the extant incest taboo—proved exaggerated, and staff members quickly learned to deal with sexual expressions with relative ease. Susannah explained,

> Ike was, I guess, seemingly much more together than most of the other residents we've had, and Ike got a crush on everybody as far as I can remember. He'd want to go for walks with you and put his arms around you, and, you know, act the way a little 16-year-old would act with his girlfriend. You had to let him know that, although you weren't his girlfriend and weren't going to become his girlfriend, this didn't mean that you didn't like him and didn't care about him—he was manly, exciting, and so on and so forth. But he's the only one that I've ever had to deal with on that kind of level, because most of the others were too spaced out to ever do much with their crush.

Staff members usually found it easy to distract acutely disturbed persons acting sexually, simply by paying attention and calmly discouraging overtures. Keith remembered,

> Tamara would come up—This was the time she was running around naked, and she would come up and jump at you and wrap her legs around your hips, and she would start jumping up and down and say, "Let's fuck." I didn't feel at all threatened. It was always hard to keep myself from laughing. Maybe that's some kind of a nervous reaction. I would just always unwrap her arms from around my neck and try to get her legs off and sit her down, and I would stay with her.

Staff members recognized that sometimes sexual expressions actually expressed anger or worked out conflicts. Ed saw Iris's performance, framed into a "safe" game, as more a result of anger than lust:

> Iris would play at being the sexy southern belle, and she was really good at it. One night she put on a big, round,

broad-rimmed hat, tied her blouse up, and was swinging her hips all over the place seductively. "Hi, boys, how ya'all doing," she drawled. That it was a game made it safe, allowed her feelings to come out. Sometimes she'd get into a kind of sly viciousness. One night, for instance, she was playing a heavy come-on. But when we responded, she'd cut off fast. She'd call you in and then slap your face and then start again.

At one point, she offered—seductively—to make me some coffee. So I said, "Sure, go ahead." It was in the game. She went and got the coffee and filled it full of hot sauce. Returning, with a changed expression, she very sweetly gave me the coffee.

The first drink burned the shit out of my mouth. She made this into a game too: "You burned yourself, boy? Gettin' hot now, boy?" It was all in play, so it was all right, safe.

There was anger in there too, though. My burned mouth testified that she had been able to express it.

Many times, because residents were afraid of their sexuality, they were scrupulously careful not to engage in sexual expression. Others tried to defuse their fears with lascivious talk. Wrote Tara,

I know that right now Naomi is very uncomfortable about the homosexual thing and gets paranoid about the whole question of massage. I try to be really careful with her, not careful because I'm afraid that she's going to try to make love to me or whatever, but careful because she's so scared: She's thinking, "If you give me a little back rub, does that mean you're hot for my body?" I know that she's thinking that, so I'm very careful. Naomi's also going through a stage where she's thinking about sex all the time. She talks to me about her sexual fears. She also likes to talk to Susannah about them, and she talks about how all she thinks about is sex, orgasm, and fucking—and not just with men but with women and dogs and clothes and walls and everything. It's a real scary preoccupation with her now.

Susannah recognized and helped defuse lesbian fears in another resident, Tracy:

> That one weekend when I was watching Tracy very closely, I'd been with her during the day, and if she'd want to take a nap or something, I'd sit on the floor. At night, when she wanted to go to sleep, she didn't want me to be in there. I still wanted to watch her closely, but she was getting really up tight and couldn't sleep—she was staying awake, watching me.
>
> So I finally said, "I'm going to sit on the floor outside your door. I'm going to sleep here tonight, so if you need anything just let me know." She said, "OK. Thanks."
>
> This promise let her know that she was both private and safe.

Fighting Fighting—Soteria Style

Sometimes an effective technique was to fight violence with violence. When a resident, terrified by his/her aggressive impulses, was afraid that others could not stop him/her from destroying people or property, sometimes a staff member returned the aggression to show control, to demonstrate competence in dealing with others' aggression.

Kris's Case

For example, at one point Kris, a resident, began to go on a rampage, breaking things and verbally assaulting others. At this point, a staff member, Daniel, followed Kris into the living room and physically subdued him. As they wrestled, Daniel in control, this dialogue occurred:

> KRIS. Let me go. *(Almost crying.)* You are humiliating me.
> DANIEL. So what. You humiliated me. You've been humiliating me all night, doing all that stuff.

KRIS. I know it.

DANIEL. That's right, you know it, so don't bullshit me.

KRIS. Fuck you, queer.

DANIEL. I'm not going to let you fuck me.

Daniel allowed the struggle to become more even and then took solid control again, repeating the process several times. When neither was winning, Daniel called Kris the same names Kris called Daniel, giving some credence or validation to Kris's phase of fear and anger. The situations of equality-in-struggle and Kris-under-control balanced; Daniel and Kris thus stayed in touch emotionally and verbally.

At this point, the two remained at almost equal position in struggle, Daniel having gained a slight advantage. Encouraged and expecting momentarily to have Kris under control, Daniel explained, "When you get outa hand, I just have to show ya." When Daniel took control, the weight of responsibility lifted off Kris, but the struggle acknowledged and validated that Kris was a young man testing his strength.

Shortly, Daniel released Kris, who sat in the living room for a few moments and then went into the kitchen where, mad at the world in general, he threw a cup on the floor. His rage built, seeming to focus on *everyone* in the house (instead of just the girls, as it had earlier). When Kris noisily continued breaking things, Daniel again confronted Kris with the ready-to-fight affect in physical carriage, tone of voice, and expression.

> DANIEL (*about a foot and a half away*). Well, what are you
> doing?
> KRIS (*straightforwardly, not angry, not afraid*). Well, you sure
> are angry.
> DANIEL. Well, so are you, so what!
> KRIS. Well, so what!
> DANIEL. Yeah, so what.

The tone of their dialogue modulated between anger and rough play. The mood of the two admitted the emotion and tried to figure it out a little—but more simply experienced it. Kris's fear of Daniel, so evident earlier, disappeared; at times, they seemed like two angry comrades stomping around and trying to figure out what to do next. Eventually, Daniel succeeded not only in subduing Kris's aggression but also showing that it is okay to be angry, that anger is safe when it can be controlled and subdued by others.

Another staff member, Kay, used a diversionary technique with Kris. She reported,

> On one of those afternoons, Voyce had taken somebody out for a ride, and I was the only staff person in the house— this was rare. We were all in the living room. All of a sudden, doors started slamming upstairs, and Kris was carrying on and going into his usual "fucking slut" routine. He came downstairs and opened up the door of the room and just slammed it as hard as he could and stomped out, kicking, yelling, and demanding, "Where's the food? Where's the goddamned lunch?"
>
> I thought that he was really starting to get into one of his rages, and I had a moment of panic and I thought, "Oh damn it, I can't handle Kris when he starts to get physical." Then I just got pissed off, because I felt he was taking advantage of there being nobody in the house but four women. So I went into the kitchen.
>
> Kris was standing there glaring at me. He called me a slut or something, so *I* started banging cupboard doors and going on about how there was never anything to eat in the house.
>
> "I'm so sick of this mess! Nobody ever cleans up the kitchen!" I continued, going into a phony rage about the mess.
>
> I slammed the back door and went out into the backyard.
>
> With a smile, Kris looked at me in a surprised way and went upstairs to his room. He didn't make any more noise. I felt proud of myself, but I didn't know what else to do. I knew I couldn't handle him if he got into a rage.

Tracy's Case

Finally, staff sometimes used acts of aggression as therapeutic tools. By staying with residents in crisis states as long as necessary, staff members sometimes were able to uncover troubling things still fresh in mind. (See further *Getting It Together*, pages 165–201.) In this case, a resident named Tracy had early one morning set her bed on fire, hoping, she said, to cremate herself. At about 6:00 AM, after the fire was extinguished, she and Loren began to talk. He recalled,

> I asked her what was happening with her; she sat quietly and without any show of emotion told me she was the devil and that the radio and TV had been giving her messages to "burn, baby burn," to feel the fire of hell. She said subsequently that later she'd gone to a Puritan[14] gas station. Her logic: The Puritans burned witches, and she was a witch; therefore, because Halloween was coming, she would burn.
>
> I told Tracy that it seemed to me she was saying she was bad in some sense, that she'd done something wrong, and her way of handling these very painful feelings was to see herself as the devil. I then inquired about recent life events that might have resulted in her feeling a "bad person."
>
> She related, at first in a very disorganized way, something about having had a fight with her sister in L.A. I asked again about recent events of note; she gave me, in a much more organized way and with some real sadness, the story of how she'd not gone to her maternal grandfather's funeral last May, although her sister had called and asked her to. She said she'd not gone because she was afraid of funerals, she didn't want to see her grandmother hurt and crying, and she was afraid to try to deal with her mother and sister.
>
> Both descriptions were punctuated by occasional silly giggles, questions as to whether I thought she was the devil, and assertions that she, in fact, *was*. I said it seemed to me

---

14   There actually *was* a company with this name.

she talked about being the devil whenever she began to experience the pain of her sadness and "badness." In time we agreed that her irrational, but firmly held, beliefs (delusions) and her notions that many events going on around her were intended to have special meaning for her (ideas of reference) came to the forefront when she was confronting the pain of her life. Later, we agreed that her belief that she was the devil might be her way of avoiding that pain.

I went into some detail with her about her relationship with her grandfather and how she'd lived with her grandparents when things were bad for her at home. We also talked about the funeral she hadn't attended; she knew her grandfather had wanted to be cremated and wondered what in fact had happened to him.

She said then that morning's fire was no accident. Intending to cremate herself, she had placed a lit cigarette in the mattress, watched it catch fire, and allowed it to burn her hair before deciding that burning the place up would be unfair to *everyone else* there, so she went to get Hal.

Our chat then returned to her sister. The story unfolded—complete with photos and a heart-rending letter about her sister's complete hysterectomy. The sister's letter described how empty, depressed, unfeminine, and hopeless she'd felt. Several remarks Tracy made about her sister made me think that theirs was a self-destructive, competitive sexual relationship in which Tracy was always the "bad one," the "irresponsible one," the loser in the eyes of her mother and sister. I thought that Tracy's burning herself might also be an attempt to destroy her femininity. At this point, she unraveled a tale of nearly lifelong sexual promiscuity. Since her sister's surgery, however, she had for the first time gotten into a variety of homosexual relations and into kinky heterosexual ones.

Around 9:00 AM, we switched to the living room couch, and, as we focused on these events, she began to cry quietly. When I got inattentive or sleepy, she would bring up the radio and TV messages "addressed to me." (They told her how bad she was.) I suggested that maybe they were Tracy talking to Tracy and brought up some of the situations we'd discussed about which she felt so guilty. She really delighted in those notions and brought them up many times over the next several days.

During our time together, I often told her I thought she was really all right but recognized how bad a person she felt she was. When she asked me what was good about her, I told her I thought she was bright, competent, and pretty—each of which she was. I held her hand, stroked her burnt hair, and made small talk. Often I found myself reaching out to her, because she was so sad, and I wanted to comfort her and let her know that I could stand to share it with her.

When I tired, Voyce moved quite comfortably in to *be with* her. Earlier Tara had taken care of brushing out Tracy's hair and tying it back so it didn't look bad. Everyone involved performed a role—changing places as necessary over the six-hour span. I was not "the designated therapist," with others subservient. Several of us shared this *being with*: Immediately after the fire, I was primary, but later Tara, Voyce, and Daniel were very much involved with Tracy.

By noon, Loren concluded Tracy's short-term outcome was positive. She was in touch with her feelings, both pleasant and not. Her face was now mobile and appropriately expressive. Her psychotic disorganization, delusions, and ideas of reference had receded almost completely. While Tracy could by no means be called happy, she was responsive, having lost the deadened, zombie-like appearance that characterized her between 6:00 and 9:00 that morning.

Softening the Blow

Violence of any sort affected all of Soteria, and the staff learned to be particularly conscious of the fears violent actions frequently generated. Often, cooperative action resolved the situation—while some staff members provided support and control for a resident in acute crisis, others dealt with the remaining residents' fears regarding the crisis. For example, Tara recounted the effect of Kris's violence on another resident, Katherine. The team approach was vital:

> Kris would usually flare up and then it would be all right for a day, maybe. He'd go to bed. He'd control himself. (He couldn't do "it" that night, he'd explain.)
>
> But one night, he was throwing things and talking about wanting to get knives. He picked up an ashtray and threw it at Katherine. Kris was just all over the place, rolling on the floor, bumping into things.
>
> I'm quite sure that if Daniel hadn't been there to handle him, Kris would have come even more unstrung. I, myself, was scared, but Katherine was flipping out. Her eyes were rolling around in her head, and she was just holding on to me and not wanting to move. I was trying to get her up to my room, because at that time my room was the only one that had a lock on it. I finally got her back to the bedroom and she was really scared. She was trembling and started to cry, though she tried not to. Part of her was concerned for Kris, wondering, "why is he like this?" But his violence also brought out all her fears.
>
> To help calm her and because she was hungry—during these days she was always hungry, I made a little tea party. I got crackers and cheese and tea, and we just locked ourselves in the room for quite a long time.

Susannah recalled another of Soteria's peacemaking ventures. A fire of uncertain origin had just flared upstairs. She remembered,

> Once we got the fire out, Naomi, Chuck, and Leo were all still here. Both Naomi and Leo got really frightened by it. At one point, Naomi darted out of the house and ran down the street and around the corner. I went off looking for her, but she came back on her own. Shortly after that, Katy spent a lot of time with her.

Then Leo was going to leave. Evidently he had walked out on the porch and asked Katy where to rent a room. So I went out and talked to him. I asked him if he wanted to move out, and he made no response. He said he had his check and wanted to cash it. On Sunday night there was no place he could, so I offered to lock it up in the box upstairs. He was talking about how he needed a gun to protect himself and his check.

We just talked about how he could leave if he wanted to leave but how also he could stay and still be protected if he were feeling that he couldn't hold on any longer. He could stay here and let go, and there would be people here to protect him at all times. The gun wouldn't be necessary. We talked like this for pretty close to 45 minutes, after which he turned around, came back in the house, gave me the check, and told me to lock it up. There was no more talk of a gun. He had been scared, and the gun symbolized the protection that Soteria wasn't giving—at that point. Once the house protected him again, the gun wasn't necessary. Nor was he leaving. He felt safe again.

Getting It Together

More than anything else, they [schizophrenics] are simply
human.

—*Harry Stack Sullivan*

SOME MEMBERS OF Soteria's founding group had worked on the
rather similar Silverman-Rappaport study based in San Jose in
the late 1960s and early 1970s where unmedicated "schizophrenics"
on a special unit had been treated in a large state hospital setting.
(See page 46 and pages 103–111.) This experience helped staff
associated with that project predict and deal with certain problems
arising as Soteria was established. Many of the attitudes and techniques
important to the earlier study, however, were dissonant to Soteria's
interpersonal and phenomenological theoretical orientation; thus,
the only major technique from that research incorporated into Soteria
was the *vigil*.

The vigil was both intervention and training. As an interpersonal
approach, it seemed to offer a way to intercede in the psychotic process
and have an impact on its course. As training, it gave staff members
experience in *being with* someone in psychosis both as observers and
as participants, a concept Sullivan pioneered.

Because of the variety of demands and the large number of
disturbed people on the small psychiatric ward at Agnews State
Hospital in San Jose, administrators for the special ward defined and
allotted extra staff to deal with severely disturbed persons in order to
avoid medicating them. Paired male and female staff and volunteers

stayed with the person in crisis in consecutive shifts of from four to eight hours in a medium-sized, comfortable room designated as the "vigil room." In this way, attendants were able to provide continuous individual help for four or five days at a time. During the vigils, the staff members involved had no duties and were expected only to *be with* the person in crisis in any way that seemed to make sense from the client's perspective. Other personnel took care of necessary functions such as meals. While the acutely ill person was encouraged to remain in the room, the staff did not prevent exits and could, if indicated, use all of the hospital grounds as an arena for *being with*.

To train staff for the Agnews vigils, a mock vigil took place without a person in crisis. Assigned pairs simply remained in a room with nothing to do for extended periods of time. During group meetings held after each vigil—real or feigned—all staff and volunteers discussed their experiences in detail.

The vigils were successful. One patient who fought six times and broke four windows on the ward the day preceding his vigil, was not violent either during his vigil (four and a half days and nights) or— towards people—after it. He went through an acute "schizophrenic" crisis to full reintegration in three months. Not only did all patients given vigils improve, but also there was much lighter property damage, less emergency medication, no injuries, and fewer transfers to the maximum security ward.

Soteria Staff on Agnews's Vigils

Soteria theoreticians originally thought vigil-like experiences would be the most efficient way of helping staff learn to relate to a person in crisis. Some found this kind of preparation useful. Said Daniel,

> I think the most time I spent was 12 hours. I think that if
> you'd done 24 with one person, you could build a kind of
> comfortable feeling. I learned about my patients [the
> hospital's label] and about my own talents. I learned that I
> have a lot and can take a lot. It was a really good place to learn

how to let be, that I didn't need to interfere. I like the vigils.
I can really stay on an unthinking level in them. It's a comfort
to just be there, and I think it's comfortable for the patient
with me to just be there like that.

Others had less meaningful experiences. Tara wrote, for example,

The vigil went on . . . for a hunk of time, and then you'd
come back. I didn't spend a whole lot of time at Agnews,
maybe a couple of weeks. The vigil wasn't that exciting or
interesting. We would sit in the hospital's vigil room. The
patient was able to do whatever he wanted—like he talked. I
had it all built up in my mind that the vigil was going to be a
really mind-blowing experience, and it wasn't. My idea of
what a vigil should be was to give somebody who was in really
heavy space a good time to zero in and get some good stuff
done with them. Well, my patient wasn't like that.
He wasn't really needing a vigil.

The original preconceptions of Soteria's staff called for providing
a vigil similar to that at Agnews for every new resident shortly after
his/her arrival. They therefore designated and equipped a "vigil
room." The first residents taught staff, however, that newcomers usually
do not wish to leave the central part of the house. Further, in Soteria's
open framework, it was unnecessary to set up a formal structure to
allow a few staff to devote full attention to a person in crisis for
prolonged periods. As one staff member put it: "The whole house is
one constant vigil."

From the Vigil to *Being With*

Prior to the arrival of the first resident at Soteria House, staff
participated in a series of vigils at the state hospital. The hospital-type
vigil, however, proved unnecessary at Soteria and was used with but
two clients, the first two, who spent short periods of time in the house's

designated vigil room (see below). One of them, Bonnie, resident at Soteria for only a week, had returned from running away the day before.

Wrote staff member Katy,

> We felt that a good way to get to know her better would be to spend intense time with her. Bonnie was exhibiting very regressed behavior, spending a great deal of time curled up in the fetal position. She had chosen not to speak and communicated only occasionally by gesturing. We described to her what we wanted to do, and she gave her consent by nodding her head affirmatively. The room was set up to start the vigil.
>
> At this time the staff was not yet working on assigned schedules; thus, members of the group who were closest to Bonnie covered her vigil, which could have lasted for up to two weeks if necessary.
>
> What we discovered was that, unlike the vigil at the hospital, we could get the same effect almost anywhere in the house. All it took was a quiet room with the door shut and one or more persons she felt close to. We also found that the vigil didn't have to be continuous. It could last for three hours in the morning and six hours at night or go on without stopping for as long as 48 hours.
>
> Bonnie's vigil went off and on for three- to six-hour sessions, two or three times a day, for a week and a half. During this time, she changed dramatically from a mute, regressed infant to a person who appeared nearly normal: She talked in a rational way and participated in the activities at the house.
>
> During this process, Bonnie took no medication.

The Vigil Room

Approximately 12 by 15 feet, the vigil room off the kitchen contained no hard furniture except for a stereo set. The carpeted floor was covered with an old, well-preserved Persian rug. Scattered around the floor were several large and small pillows. A set of lights with multicolored bulbs could be moved around to give various effects.

The central location was deliberate to avoid relegating those in acute crisis to a position out of the mainstream and to encourage the rest of the community to be part of the process. (Something potentially frightening can become even more so when hidden.)

At the same time, the vigil room had to be a safe, low-stimulation, comfortable place where people could regress with minimal intrusion. This goal required everyone's cooperation because not only the kitchen but also the living room and the art room were nearby.

Staff members and a resident used the vigil room formally only once more, because the process didn't seem to demand the well-defined space that it did in the hospital ward. In fact, the prescribed vigil seemed too confining and structured a process for Soteria: In the summer, for example, the process worked better in the backyard. The room became only one of many possible refuges. In retrospect, what evolved was in keeping with an interpersonal phenomenological perspective; community members met residents wherever necessary without regard to preconceived notions of what individuals' processes would be.

Commented Loren: The differences in the "vigils" at the hospital and Soteria offer good examples of the importance of context to what actually happens—despite the same label.

The Soteria Process—
Early Stages of *Being With*

Out of the concept of the vigil grew *being with,* the basic mode of the Soteria process. What started as a specific technique eventually developed into a much broader concept.

It was not uncommon for an individual staff member to spend entire shifts for weeks on end with one resident, often even sleeping in the same room. Tara recalled,

For a long time, Monday through Wednesday was my shift, and I'd spend the whole time with Iris when she wasn't asleep. She went through a long period where she just didn't sleep at all at night, like, you know, we'd watch the sun come up every morning, talking. Iris was an all-nighter, all right, one of Soteria's most famous all-nighters.

Iris was "consumed by the devil" in the beginning, but she wouldn't talk about this as much after a while because she knew that people would try to talk her out of it. Then, she really started to believe that there was something inside her beside the devil, and the closer she would come to figuring out things for herself, the more she would talk back to you, really getting a lot of garbage out. She needed a sounding board.

She'd suddenly become more and more rational. She would talk about how she really knew she wasn't the devil, yet inside, she felt so awful. Sometimes I argued with her about it. She would talk about how she was the devil; then, together, we would find coincidences that could prove that *anybody* was the devil or that she *wasn't* the devil. After a while, when she really became aware that nobody in the house believed that she was the devil, she was sort of pissed off and would, again, try hard to prove she *was*.

Sometimes I'd get angry at her if she was really carrying on trying to prove she was the devil. I'd tell her about the parts of her that weren't the devil.

While Tara's extended contact with Iris was regarded as a typical daily occurrence in the house, on certain occasions residents were isolated and the prolonged and intense involvement they underwent was close to the hospital's vigil, as in the experience with Chuck Starr, described in the next section. As the staff gained experience in understanding the needs of people in crisis, their comfort levels increased, and their reactions became more spontaneous.

Soteria's *Being With* Chuck: His Vigil

The following section documents one resident's first week at Soteria and offers a brief follow-up. Neither this interchange—mostly originally from taped discussions by staff members—nor the situation was particularly unusual. Administrators quoted include Loren, Voyce, Alma, and consulting psychiatrist Stan; Soteria staff Ed and Susannah provided notes and oral recollections. Present at the first vigil, but not contributing directly to the record below were the following volunteers and staff members: Della, Hal, Geoff, Nelly, Katy, and Bart.

Following Soteria procedures Voyce, who had picked up Chuck Starr from the emergency service, stayed with the new resident he had retrieved.

Background

Chuck's father took his son, 16, to the hospital after finding him lying, dazed and confused, at 6:00 AM in an apple orchard. Over the previous week, Chuck had stopped sleeping and going to school and was generally behaving inappropriately. Over the preceding month, he had broken up with a girlfriend, had several dissociative episodes, and believed he could control everything and foretell the future. Before that, however, he had been his father's favorite—a good son, a good student, a good athlete— and had many friends.

The child of divorced parents, both of whom had been psychiatrically hospitalized as schizophrenics, Chuck had lived with his father and three younger siblings (the older children lived with their mother, who had remarried, in the Midwest). About a year before Chuck came to Soteria, Chuck's father had also remarried. Chuck was torn by loyalty to his siblings and his mother, but he was a responsible member of his father's family, working part-time and helping with child care.

He was diagnosed upon admission as "confused, over-talkative, severely thought-disordered, with grandiose and controlling delusions, auditory hallucinations, and exhibiting bizarre behavior— schizophrenic."

First Encounter

VOYCE. I went to pick up Chuck in the early afternoon. I was surprised at how he looked—a blue-eyed, blond young man with a short haircut who looked very straight. The other thing I noticed about him, however, was the fact that he never stopped talking. The first thing he asked was whether I could be his "voice." I agreed, "Sure," but at that point he certainly didn't need another.

So Chuck and I got in my car and drove over to Soteria. All the way back, it was pretty much him talking, talking about his world. (We would later discover that Chuck would alternate periods of talking with ones of total silence.) I stayed with him— as was usual—continually for the first eight hours. (The duration depends, of course, on how the person adapts to the house. Sometimes I stayed with the person much longer.) I showed Chuck around the house and introduced him to the people there. He seemed to settle in quite easily, so after eight hours, I planned to trade off with Ed. But before I did so, Chuck and I went together through a crawling episode that briefly showed his other side, providing a mini-version of what would eventually prove to be a critical experience for him.

We sat in the living room for a few hours. Then Chuck said he was tired and wanted to go to his room. As he was going up the stairs, he went limp, and I had to carry him. When we got to his room he lay on his bed and appeared to sleep, but I got the feeling that actually he really wasn't asleep.

He stayed that way for half an hour or so; then he began to make motions like curling up, rolling over, lifting a leg up. I sat beside him on the couch to keep him from falling on the floor. His body actions became so violent that I actually helped him down on the floor where he wouldn't fall. This went on for approximately 20 minutes.

A couple of times I asked him questions to get him to communicate but received no verbal response, although he seemed aware that I was talking to him. After that, he began to make movements, crawling or scooting on his stomach around the room. No direction to it at all. Then the motion became a more definite circular crawl. While he was crawling around me, I was standing with one arm or hand on him. He started getting up on his knees; each time it was a little higher. He reached out, and I held on to his hand. When he stood up, he continued going around with his head usually back, hanging back, all the time his eyes were closed, never opening his eyes. I continued to hold his hand, and he continued to go around me, head twitching, arms swinging back and forth in sort of a slow motion.

My impression was that he was going through some kind of birth ritual. I didn't become aware of it as such, however, until he started crawling around. (Afterwards, we talked together about being "born again." Sometimes, he seemed to mean this figuratively—his family were fundamentalist Christians. Other times, he meant that he literally wanted to emerge from the womb as a baby. And sometimes, he seemed to mean both religiously and physiologically.)

The whole episode upstairs gave me the feeling that he wanted me to take care of him, that he was reassured that I was there with him. Whenever something happened to make me take my hand off him, he did something to make me touch him.

He seemed so into his world that he was not really clear about things going on around him, but afterwards, he said he was not only aware but felt that he was controlling everything around him. That was one way for him to make his surroundings familiar—to control them himself. After circling about an hour, he suddenly stopped and opened his eyes, apparently back in the state before we'd come to his room some two hours earlier. He indicated he wanted to go back downstairs and meet some more people. We went downstairs, and he started talking to one of the residents in the kitchen.

With hindsight, I realize that this episode was a prelude to the critical week-long interaction—"rebirth"—occurring about six weeks later. Between these two episodes, his behavior was fairly uneventful.

STAN. Voyce, you were Chuck's first contact when he came to the house and spent several hours with him. When he started walking around with his eyes closed, you were with him, following him around. He then started to talk in a steady stream, fragmented, bouncing from one subject to another, but buried in some of the content was his view of you as his mother.

VOYCE. Well, he talked about me "being his voice," my speaking for him, his talking through me. And, as I said, I got the feeling that he wanted me to take care of him, to hold his hand. A couple of times I actually physically held him. For the first few hours, he seemed to be getting acquainted with me—going upstairs, for example, he gave himself over to me to be put to bed. At first, it felt as if Chuck were just talking—if nobody were there, it wouldn't have made any difference. Later, he was looking for somebody to grab onto.

STAN. One kind of psychosis occurs with the fragmenting, the breaking down of the bridge between the subjective inner world and the objective outer world. Chuck was trying to attach that bridge to some objective outer world formed from his own inner experiences. He referred to you as parts of people, as parts of people's functions, as a brother, as a mother.

VOYCE. You're right; he was saying that he and I were brothers, and he did say that I was his mother. He went through some thought that he was actually black like me.

STAN. In your role, Voyce, you made very few comments. You were present—a real, close presence—and you maintained steady contact to help him from feeling angry and unsafe.

VOYCE. Yes, I got the feeling that he wanted to be close all the time. He talked a lot.

STAN. Apart from the content of what was said, if he had made a comment like, "You're my voice," you didn't contradict him, making comments like "No, that's not true, I'm not your voice." You'd agree with him.

VOYCE. Yeah.

Being With *Continues*

ALMA. Ed, you were on duty six weeks later when Chuck again attempted a birth passage, and you stayed with him exclusively?

ED. Yes.

ALMA. Do you remember why you did this?

ED. Because Chuck was in no state to be alone. Most of what went on took place after people had gone to bed. All that night he referred to me as "dad" or "father." When we were up in the room, he talked about Howard Hughes, the Lear jet, "Harley Bird,"[15] Steve McQueen, Raquel Welch—the whole bit. One time he said Steve McQueen was his backbone.

VOYCE. And Harley Bird would become Steve McQueen, and then Chuck would become Steve McQueen.

ED. They would be separate, and then they'd be the same again, yeah. He kept talking about how his father was Howard Hughes. At this point he was lying on the bed, and I think I was sitting on the floor next to him. And he was saying he had to find out where his Lear jet was parked. I asked him why he wanted it, and he said he had to get back to Nevada to see his mother. He was complaining that his back was very sore, so I gave him a back massage. He talked more about his mother. He wanted to see his mother and bring her back here. He'd start crying a little bit. This went on for pretty close to an hour. Afterwards he said his back felt better.

He said he could wait to go see his mother, but he still wanted to find his Lear jet. He thought it was parked on the driveway. We went out to the driveway, but it wasn't there. He said it must be at the airport. We came back in the house and went to his room again. He was talking about things that happened in the war between him and Harley Bird.

I wanted some coffee, so we went over to Spivey's [a nearby restaurant], and I bought him a hamburger. He told me all about

---

[15]   Harley Bird was an imaginary person/alter ego Chuck made up. His choice of first name was perhaps influenced by his fascination with Hal's motorcycle, which *was* a Harley Davidson.

when he was a kid—about his childhood and his paper routes and his school. Every two or three minutes he'd stop and laugh, "Well, this is silly for me to tell you; you're my father; you already know all this." As we were coming back, he stopped and said "That was really nice. I knew you were going to take me out to dinner some night, Dad. And now we've done it."

When we got back to the house, he told me the Venusians were going to come down and visit him that night. So we went out on the back porch where he could stare at Venus. "I can see them coming down now," he observed. "They are going to be waiting for us." Next, we went across the street under the stoplights, because he had to see the sun, which was just coming up over the side of the house, at the same time he saw Venus. (He had to be between Venus and the Sun for the Venusians to be able to find him.) We waited there for maybe a half hour or 45 minutes. Then, because it was getting light and Venus was disappearing from the sky, he figured, "Well, they aren't going to come today, after all."

We came back to his room around 5:30 or 6 in the morning. He was talking about a belt given him by Harley Bird that allowed him to go through space and time (it was also a seat belt for the Lear jet).

Somewhere thereabouts he fell asleep, and I fell asleep too.

ALMA. Why did you take him outside and to the restaurant?

ED. To the restaurant, because I wanted some coffee—There wasn't any made downstairs, and he was hungry too. And outside because that's what he wanted. He did most of the directing, as to what he wanted to do. I felt comfortable about his actions.

STAN. When he told you you were his father, what did you do?

ED. I didn't say either yes I am, or no I'm not. At that point I was generally just listening. He wasn't asking *whether* I was, he was saying *that* I was.

ALMA. Did you feel uncomfortable with that?

ED. No. *(Changes subject.)* He slept until about two the next afternoon— in his assigned room—for the first and last time in a long while. I slept with him.

STAN. About then, Chuck started to repress a lot of the free thought and the reactions to it; he became a little more appropriate, a lot more concrete. Certainly the free flow was shut down, and he ceased some of the kind of events taking place in the preceding

24 hours. As I remember, the repression didn't last, and he went right back into action.

VOYCE. That day we didn't talk too much. He was pretty coherent. We went for a walk, and ate lunch out at Spivey's, and he wanted a newspaper.

SUSANNAH. I remember I was coming up from the basement from doing the laundry, and he was going down the stairs. We bumped into each other and then I got into the process. Chuck was trying to get on Hal's motorcycle. (Now Hal was his brother.)

Because we were worried that Chuck might take off on the motorcycle, we went with him to the back lawn and lay on the grass, keeping him between the three of us. We followed him through a number of different activities—climbing on the motorcycle, coming into the house, walking up and down the stairs, crawling—sometimes backwards—up and down the stairs, being carried up and down the stairs, going out on the back lawn. He'd climb on the motorcycle, and I'd sit behind him.

Then he went to my car parked on the street. I sat behind him in the car, and he climbed in the driver's seat. Ed sat next to him. He wanted to start the car and drive away. I told him to listen, and he'd hear the engine start. He got into that fantasy and decided that he could hear the motor running and feel the car moving. Eventually, we talked him into coming in to get something to drink.

He was wearing the motorcycle helmet and sunglasses all of this time, Though sweating profusely, he didn't want to be without his helmet.

ED. He did go for a ride with Hal on the motorcycle around the block.

First Rebirth—Á la Jung

SUSANNAH. Chuck, Hal, Ed, and I ended up in the back bedroom. Chuck was talking about wanting to be reborn, because he had been a blue baby and had come out wrong and wanted to be born right.

So we put him between us on the bed and then he would push down from our chests' level, and then he'd turn over and try it again, keeping his eyes closed all of the time. He was up on the big double bed where he could crawl up to the window and look out—like he was coming up for air or coming up for light. He was lying between Ed and me; Hal would be either on top of him or partially across all three of us, almost surrounding us. He pushed out from among us a number of times, each time saying, "It's not quite right." We kept telling him what he was doing was OK.

But we had to stop him when, a couple of times, he tried to crawl out the second floor window. We'd let him put his head out the window and look at the moon, the stars. He would leave the window, crawl to us on his back, head first, and then come back up and lie kind of sandwiched between us. He said he needed to be surrounded—I guess in a womb-like situation, in kind of a family situation. He didn't get into a sexual thing with me but stayed childlike, making us into mother and father figures.

After about five hours, he started out to the lawn, crawling down the steps, sliding, so we tried to carry and support him as much as possible.

ED. Lying between us, he said that he had to be the result of my and Susannah's love. He said that we had to make love and that he between us would be the result.

SUSANNAH. During that time, I was his mother at times; I was Raquel Welch at times; I was Mother Earth at times. I was the opposite of what Ed was at times. I was the result of his love at times, and the three of us were the result of each other. We said very little. He just kept talking, and he didn't ask questions, and we simply affirmed whatever he was saying by occasionally nodding or smiling. Sometimes I'd say, "Yes, I'm your mother," or "Yes, you're being reborn," but mostly he did the talking.

ALMA. And then how did this whole thing end?

ED. It didn't! It went right on through the night!

Labor Continues

VOYCE. Then I came back, and we went through the same things Ed and Susannah described.

SUSANNAH. We eventually ended up in the next room.

ED. He moved with slow, fluid motions.

SUSANNAH. He knew what he was doing and was quick to find out what he needed to do and what he needed from us.

ED. His actions were deliberate, as if part of a dance or a ritual.

SUSANNAH. About 11 or 12 o'clock, Ed was sleeping in the living room and Voyce on the couch in the same room. I was sitting, back against the wall, legs spread, and he was lying between them, against my chest. I held him for a while, that way. Then he wanted to sit back up and have me move into a variety of positions so that he could move back and forth between my legs. At times he'd begin to get sexual: I'd say he wanted to come out again; he wanted to be born again; then, he would revert back into moving in and out between my legs.

Next, he wanted to exchange jeans. I went into the bathroom, took mine off, and put on my spare pair. He put my jeans on and seemed satisfied to be wearing my clothes for a while. That morning he started getting into boy/girl stuff, becoming more sexual—wanting me to be in high school, wanting me to be his girlfriend and talking about other girlfriends, wanting to kiss and hold me . . . Later, he got out of that.

VOYCE. Sometime after I awoke, he started walking around and went downstairs. He was still talking, more like the day before. He talked a lot about Bangladesh.

ED. When I came back, he was between the mattress and the wall. He said he was in outer space. Once in a while we'd go downstairs. He was exploring the house, making sure where everybody was.

Expanding Theater

VOYCE. Later, we went out for a walk and then sat in the backyard. He was going to look at the sun. He "looked" at the sun with his eyes closed for quite a while.

ED. Still later that day, he tried to crawl out a window on the first floor. He had to get out on the ground. He wouldn't go out the door; he had to go out the window.

Hal and I held him there at the window, so he couldn't crawl out, because he wanted to just drop down on his head. I got someone else to hold him, and then I went outside and caught him as he came out.

SUSANNAH. I was up by that time. And I saw Chuck going out the window.

ED. He had such a need to get to the ground. We were on the first floor, and he must have known that it was safer, that he wouldn't hurt himself. But he mentioned later that he felt frightened. That was the first time he felt frightened.

SUSANNAH. He was wearing Hal's motorcycle helmet then too, wasn't he? Yeah. Then, he wanted to get in my car. He crawled into the back seat, then moved up to the driver's seat. We stayed with him in the car for awhile. He was sweating, dripping, shifting the gears, wanting to drive, but I wouldn't give him the keys. He kept repeating "I want the keys; I have to have my keys."

We finally got him out by telling him we would get him something to drink. After he stuck a Kleenex in his mouth and ate it, we persuaded him to return to the house. It took about 20 minutes to get him out of the car. We wanted to get him back into the house.

ED. He and Hal slept outside that night. He *did* sleep that night; he went to bed very early. Eight or nine, before dark. He was up with the sun the next morning. Most of the day on Saturday he spent with Hal, just sitting out there talking with him. He was drinking a lot of milk, but he kept saying that he had to eat mercury. He was eating toothpaste, too.

Connecting, or No More Peter Pan

ED. Chuck and Naomi [another resident] had gotten into a quarrel— he was telling her to "think happy thoughts," and she was angrily saying how shitty she felt:

"Who are you to tell me what to think? I'm not thinking 'happy thoughts.' I'm not happy; why should I think happy thoughts?"

"When I have bad thoughts," answered Chuck, "I don't think about them. I think nice happy thoughts. That's why I am wearing these colored glasses—things look pretty when I wear them."

"If I commit suicide," countered Naomi furiously, "will I go to hell?"

"What do you want to commit suicide for?" Chuck questioned.

Naomi gave him these reasons: She was hallucinating; she didn't feel good; she had a stomachache and a headache. "That's why!"

"Well," said Chuck agreeably, "go ahead and do it. I'll get you a knife and cut your throat."

"Who are you to tell me to commit suicide? Who are you to give me a knife to cut my own throat?" she shouted, throwing a glass, really hard, against the wall. Chuck was lying on the couch; she was sitting in the rocking chair; she threw it on the wall between them, really smashed it, and got up and walked into her room.

That scared the shit out of Chuck, who went outside and wouldn't come back in. Hal went with him and comforted him as he cried. He came back in temporarily, but wouldn't take off the glasses or the helmet. Then he and Hal went out on the back porch for a while. Then I joined them.

Chuck was crying and angry—angry at Nixon at this point, for taking over the world, for lying, for using money. A huge tirade, delivered as he clung to the post on the stairs really hard, screaming anger at Nixon, "the totality of evil," or something like that. Chuck was really hurting, sobbing with anger.

Tending to Necessities

ALMA. I would like to get a little bit of information back from the people involved as to what their subjective experiences were after so prolonged a period of time spent in very intensive contact. How did you feel during and after?

SUSANNAH. I really got turned on by it; I was really impressed with Chuck's being in touch with what he needed and what he wanted—his deciding and choosing and making the rebirth happen and, if it wasn't right, making it happen again. Insisting on its being right. I was really impressed by that. I didn't get tired as I expected I would. I was with Chuck from dusk of Thursday night until noon on Friday—about 15 hours straight.

Chuck had a good sense of humor and that would come out quite often. It was just a delight, very refreshing. By the time I did finish I was tired, and yet it didn't seem to me to be too long.

ALMA. You weren't bored.

SUSANNAH. Oh, no.

ALMA. What about taking care of yourself? Did you eat and bathe?

SUSANNAH. I don't remember!

ED. Chuck took a shower about midnight. That's when we went down and got some coffee and took a break. While he was in the shower, I went in and talked to him.

VOYCE. Chuck took a shower that morning, too.

ED. That was about his third shower of the day. I remember him as having a fourth one as well.

Meaningful Work

ALMA. Can we hear about how you felt about participating in the whole thing?

VOYCE. I remember the feeling I had when I was going to pick Chuck up. A lot of anxiety—what's it going to be like? When I saw him, though, all of a sudden I was relieved—my mental picture of him was all wrong. I didn't expect Chuck: I expected somebody quite different. He was a pleasant surprise. Talking to him was easy, kind of a relief. Later, during the long hours with him, I would get a lot of real comfortable feelings; I felt really good. I can remember at times that night I was very sleepy but really not wanting to quit.

ALMA. How did you feel when you returned from sleeping? I can fantasize that I might think, "Well, Jesus Christ, it's still going on, not more of that."

VOYCE. No, I didn't feel like that. I remember on the way over here that it was easy to return. I didn't feel put out.

ALMA. Certainly, no one seemed to feel put out by the end.

VOYCE. My impression of the rest of the staff was that there was really a good feeling there, even though everybody was tired. I was surprised that they all kept going.

SUSANNAH. I was tremendously impressed by the whole staff operation. Everybody was taken care of without having to talk about it.

ALMA. Anything more you had to say, Ed, about your subjective reaction to the whole thing? This was a new kind of person coming into the house for you, wasn't it?

ED. I never saw anybody come in this intense.

VOYCE. I remember Susannah was tired, but she was really having good contact. Everything was working beautifully.

ALMA. It sounds like everything did. The whole thing went on for about a week?

ED. It ended about 7:00 Wednesday, when Chuck did his final birth and "came out right."

ALMA. How did you keep the house running? At that time we had how many other residents here?

SUSANNAH. Four others. But somehow everybody pulled together without talking about it and took care of everybody else. The meals got cooked, and most of the dishes got done.

Naomi was frightened, I remember, when Chuck first came. I spent time with her. Somebody was here to take over when I was not with her. The same happened with Iris and Kelly. There was a continual flow of people to pick up when others would tire.

ALMA. Do you know how that happened?

VOYCE. It wasn't planned . . .

ED. It had to be done.

ALMA. Susannah, I know that when you're here, you usually take a lot of responsibility for the meals. Did you verbally communicate with anybody to say "Hey"? . . .

SUSANNAH. I didn't . . .

VOYCE. All I can remember is Chuck.

SUSANNAH. I can remember feeling okay about working with him— I felt very safe. Everything was being taken care of. I didn't worry about everybody else.

ALMA. Who was taking care of the rest of the house during that time?

ED. Nelly was here at that point; Katy was here; Geoff was here; Hal was here; Bart was here. Whoever wasn't with Chuck would be downstairs with someone else. He also wasn't into the thing the whole time that intensely. Friday he went to bed. Saturday he went out in the backyard with Hal and watched the tennis tournament on TV.

ALMA. How was he talking at that time?

ED. Pretty straight, at that point. He just wasn't into any kind of ritualistic talking at that point. He was still talking about Harley Bird off and on and about Howard Hughes. He and Hal had a real thing going. Hal watched the tennis tournament too.

VOYCE. Usually, if Chuck wants to do something, he does it. He initiates things himself.

ALMA. Did he eat Saturday?

ED. Saturday he was eating a lot of salad and a lot of liquids—milk, water, juice, whatever.

SUSANNAH. During his heavy time we gave him milk out of the baby bottle. He would drink it out of the bottle but without the nipple. He would take the top off and just drink it down that way. That was fine. He had two or three bottles like that right in a row.

ALMA. Were you concerned about his not eating?

SUSANNAH. None of us ate. Forgot about food.

ED. Saturday and Sunday, he didn't seem to be that heavy. Seemed like he broke it off for a couple of days.

ALMA. Did you provide close supervision for him during that period?

VOYCE. Somebody was with him all the time. I played Frisbee with him for a while, and Geoff did too.

ED. We all played badminton.

ALMA. Did he talk about what had happened to him?

ED. Yeah, off and on he would talk about his rebirth. Very matter-of-factly, just saying that it happened. The feeling was that this was the intermission, that it hadn't been completed yet, that he was just taking a rest.

VOYCE. Sunday he talked a lot about the hospital.

Analyzed Loren later: Chuck's behavior just described offers a particularly good example of the episodic recovery process. He alternated between periods of quiet near-sanity and silence and highly energetic times of psychosis.

The Last Push

ED. Sunday night and Monday there was a lot of pathological talk. Mercury, Venus, the moon, the hospital talk, Bangladesh.

VOYCE. The hospital took away his powers.

ED. There was a dynamo somewhere and he could hear it running in the hospital where they were programming him. That's how he explained lots of things—by saying he was programmed to do all this stuff by a big machine in the hospital.

Right around dinnertime Monday he had been lying for a couple of hours on the couch in the living room with a big pillow over his head. Geoff in the rocking chair was next to him. All of a sudden, he crawled off the couch. Geoff called, so I went in. Chuck was crawling towards the door on all fours, flat on his stomach. He was pulling himself and pushing with his legs, and he started crawling up the steps. Geoff got behind him, keeping a hand on his leg. I was in front of him. I would just touch his hand. He didn't want me to pull him; he wanted to do it himself. He was sweating really profusely and really straining.

He crawled all the way up the stairs, turned in the right direction, and crawled all the way back to the back room. His eyes were closed all the time, but he knew exactly where he was going—into the back room and towards the window. He started crawling up the window up to reach out of it. Geoff and I both grabbed him around the waist. He said "I'm not going to jump; I just have to see the sun." We said "OK," and he leaned against the window sill, his eyes still closed. He breathed deeply for maybe 5 or 10 minutes, as we repeated, "There's the heat of the sun; you can feel it on your eyes. You can feel the heat of it on your face."

When he lay back down, we put him in my lap. He lay there for maybe 10 minutes. I had to go fix dinner, so I gave him to Geoff. Then Della came upstairs too. Lying in Geoff's lap, he had his arms resting on Della. Then he made motions that he wanted to lie in Della's lap. When I got back, he was in Della's lap. There he stayed for maybe an hour. We brought up his milk in his bottle.

It was pretty hot. He'd use a towel to wipe the sweat off of him, then Della would wipe it off for him, then he would take the towel and do it himself again. They were lying there for close to an hour, Della talking to him softly and breathing very deeply, so he could feel her body breathing.

All of a sudden he got rigid and turned around and doubled up into a ball, a fetus, and crawled out from between her legs and got up on his knees. He opened his eyes with an amazed expression and asked "Where am I?" Della said, "You were just born" and gave him a big hug. And he got just this big smile—a really broad grin on his face and gave her a big hug back. They sat there for a while and talked about it. He was lucid again at that point. He described it as he was in a dark pit and crawling out through this channel . . . the canal . . . up some steps. He said he felt as if he were being reborn at that point and that he came out right. After that, he didn't have any more rebirths.

He became quiet then and was calm for an hour or so, then became overactive. He didn't want any dinner. He was talking fast.

The Journey After Birth

ED. Stan came in at about this point and said, "You're hungry." So Chuck came to the dinner table. He talked about his rebirth, his "mothers," and then again started saying he had to go to Bangladesh. He ate a little and then became really vehement.

He had to go to Bangladesh.

There was just no way out of it.

He had to call the hospital and find out where "they" were hiding his jet.

He had to get to Bangladesh for an eclipse at noon the following day.

Then, he would get his total power.

He couldn't go in a fantasy anymore; he had to go physically.

Up to this point we had been encouraging him to go on his journeys in his head. Said Susannah, "You've managed to stay in the house and go to Venus and the moon, and you've been reborn all while being in the house."

"I can't do that anymore," he said. "I have to go there physically" and went to get his jacket.

"It's a physical impossibility," I said.

"There's no way to go," Geoff said.

Chuck yelled, really angry, that he couldn't go there in his head. We shouted back that he had to stay. At that point he had his jacket on.

ALMA. Did you try to initiate the fantasy?

ED. Yeah, the same way that we had worked the ones about the motorcycle: "Feel yourself moving."

He got really pissed off, saying, "I can't do it that way this time; I have to go there."

He shouted that he had to go there to get his total powers, to see the eclipse, to watch the world being totally dark, totally black at Bangladesh at noon on Tuesday. He had to be there for that. The sun, symbolically, had been his father—that his last name was "Starr" may have played into all this somehow. The eclipse of the sun would be his mother. And he had been born.

Actually, he was talking about Venus and the moon and the sun throughout his time at Soteria. When he went into the process after feeling the heat of the sun—when he lay back on Della— the sun was out. An hour later, when he had had his birth, there was a half or quarter moon out, with Venus about four degrees from it: The only two "stars" in the sky were the moon and Venus. The last thing he had seen before birth was the sun at the window; the next time he was at the window, after birth, the moon and Venus were up. It fit psychologically.

He returned to the eclipse. His father was the sun, light. His mother was darkness. The two opposites. He was experiencing this; he wasn't talking about it symbolically.

Different Reactions

ED. Geoff tried to explain the symbolism to Chuck, who got very angry: "I don't want to hear that." Della and Bart were into astrology and were saying that Venus means one thing, the sun another. Chuck would pick up what he agreed. To what he didn't, he'd say "I'm not talking about that." There was a straight conversation running through all of this.

ALMA. Della and Geoff were a different kind of team?

ED. The birth thing was the same with all of the staff—it had the same kind of intensity. Everyone knew exactly what to do and was sure it was the right thing. Each had the same feeling of total confidence, without doubts. And the *actions* different people tried were a lot the same. Chuck lay in Della's lap in the same way he had in Susannah's.

ALMA. But the *responses* were different?

ED. Yeah. The people working on weekends were into astrology. Also Chuck was conversing by then; he wasn't just laying out what had to be done. He wasn't acting; he wanted to talk.

ALMA. Do you think that had anything to do with the expectations of the people around him?

ED. There weren't many expectations, if any. One was that he would get a good birth. I was really glad to see it; I was awful surprised. Just the one was enough at that time.

ALMA. This was what I wondered. How would you explain the different quality of the interaction?

ED. Just different personalities.

ALMA. Let's get back to the description of what went on. You decided that he couldn't go to Bangladesh. What happened then?

ED. At that point I was physically holding him. So was Geoff. We both pulled him. "No, you can't go."

This was the first time since he had been here that he didn't feel believed; therefore, he couldn't trust us back. The fact that we were going to physically hold him here—he was frightened by that. He was also angered and was laying out some pretty effective guilt trips—"Everything was nice until *you* tried to ruin everything by not letting me go to Bangladesh."

ALMA. And you felt bad.

ED. Yeah, I felt guilty about it. I felt we didn't do it right. We should have let him go out of the house and walked with him at that point . . .

ALMA. Was there any physical reason why you didn't want to do that?

ED. I was really exhausted. This was Monday; I'd been here since Wednesday. I was really tired.

> *Looking back, Loren noted that the staff's theorizing created a disjunction between them and Chuck. Loren also pointed out that the staff's exhaustion made them try to put limits on Chuck's behavior and the result was that he became afraid, frustrated, and then angry in the space of under an hour. A worn-out staff, Loren pointed out, is, obviously, less tolerant than a fresh one.*

Encouraging Fantasy

ED. I was also angry at him for saying that he couldn't go to Bangladesh in a fantasy, when he had done everything else with fantasies, and for setting up a situation where I had no choices.

There was also our fear that he would go out into the street and get hurt.

ALMA. What made you feel differently about taking him out? You'd taken him out before in the middle of the night.

ED. Yeah, he was more lucid at this point. He wasn't spaced out. He was using logical arguments, explaining, for example, "No, I can't do it that way. Before I did things in fantasy, and I know they were in fantasy. This time has to be physical. The other things were all right; they were good; they were necessary; they were in my head. This one I have to do with my body." Those are logical arguments, and he set up an impossible demand on me.

ALMA. How did he plan to get there?

ED. He was going to get money from the people at the hospital. They were going to pay for his trip. He wanted to call them and find out where Harley Bird was. Howard Hughes had his jet waiting for him at the airport. He was going to go to the hospital first, get the money, and then fly to Bangladesh.

ALMA. You were going to drive him to the hospital?

ED. No, that was what I wouldn't do.

ALMA. I mean, if you had been willing . . . that's what he wanted you to do?

ED. Yeah, if I had been willing, that would have been fine. Otherwise, he'd find some other way to get there. But this time was a physical thing that had to be done in reality.

ALMA. I wonder what would have happened if you had just walked out into the street with him.

ED. That was my qualm. That we would have handled it better if I had just asked, "Where are we going to go?" and stayed with him. This was the first time that I hadn't been with him in an experiential way. And that stopped the trip he was on.

ALMA. That decision might have come from your own exhaustion or something, because you let him climb out the window, let him get in the car, let him take the risks.

ED. They weren't felt risks. This was a *real* felt risk.

ALMA. So what happened then?

ED. One reason I was pissed was because I hadn't been with him all the time. During the birth, it was Geoff and Della. Then he came down for dinner afterwards and was telling me that I had to take him to Bangladesh. And I was kind of mad because I was involved with other people at that point, and my inclination was for him to stay with Geoff and Della.

ALMA. And he didn't stay with Geoff and Della. Why not?

ED. Because they also told him, "No."

ALMA. I see.

ED. He was already angry at them when he came down. And he was angry at Stan, at Dr. Redd.

ALMA. So what happened then?

ED. Then we stayed up the rest of the night. We kept explaining why Chuck couldn't go to Bangladesh physically. Then he just started talking and talking. It had kind of worked out before I left around three that morning—He had realized that he couldn't make it there physically, but he still wanted to go sometime, somehow.

By this time he was having a good conversation with Della and Geoff, talking about the whole thing. They got into an exhausting exchange about what was happening. They all went to sleep about four.

That was the last of Chuck's "trips" for two or three weeks.

Commented Loren: Ed's expression of his annoyance with Chuck was consistent with Soteria's philosophy. Staff members were allowed to say what they felt, even if their positions disagreed with others— what was important was that each communicated openly and clearly.

After the Trips

ALMA. So that was the end of it. The next morning he was up at six— two hours after he went to bed—cleaning the kitchen?

ED. Yeah, he had to justify being here. He was very helpful, trying to get the place in shape, make things a little cleaner. He didn't do much sleeping; he went to bed late and got up early. He also didn't eat much at that point. Then he began being a therapist and solving the problems of the other residents. Being helpful and analyzing . . .

ALMA. One other question: How did you feel about the ending of the intensive period?

ED. I didn't like the way it ended; I felt bad about it. I don't know how much of that is my own guilt. I feel that I handled it poorly. I wish I had done it differently. There was an alternative, for example, which at that point didn't occur to me, of walking outdoors with him.

ALMA. I would like to think about that. Perhaps the staff was doing too much interpreting?

ED. How so?

ALMA. Were you expecting him to intellectualize too much at that point? Maybe his press to leave had to do with wanting to get away from the situation. It sounds like there was a burst of interpretation in the end.

ED. No, there was almost no conversation then. Nothing was said. Afterwards he explained it all, what was happening. He said he felt that he had been reborn.

VOYCE. I kept feeling that the Bangladesh thing might have been a way of leaving. So might his wanting to go to the hospital. The first day, he seemed sort of uncomfortable at one point, and, by going back to the hospital, he could get away.

ALMA. The other things he was saying indicated his idea that people were controlling him. By Wednesday he was calling Soteria a hospital and in many ways he was trying to control, to undo what had happened. I think it's really worth thinking about. The possibility is that that was as far as he wanted to go at that time.

But we want to know if there are any things we could do better.

> *Loren's analysis: Here, Alma introduced a supervisory view, correctly bringing attention to the staff's need to interpret, in Jungian terms, what Chuck had experienced. By so doing, she brought them back to interpersonal phenomenology, encouraging them to relate to the experience rather than judging or categorizing it.*

Journey's End

Chuck's psychic journey ended at this point. Six weeks later, he went through a similar acute phase, which lasted four or five days. At that point, Voyce remembered, Chuck was again crawling around, but this time pointing his finger as if it were a "ray gun" with the power to "zap things out of existence" and making humming sounds. Chuck's regression at this point took place when Soteria was short-staffed and serving several other residents in crisis; it was therefore less well-equipped to deal with his needs. This second crisis took place over a three-week period and was resolved after a 24-hour stint—fully clothed—in a warm bath. Finally, he got out, shed his wet clothes, put on dry ones, and appeared finished with his second major regression.

At that point he went back to functioning very well, even doing some work for Stan. After that, he moved gradually towards complete reintegration. Four and a half months after admission, he was a remarkably mature and self-confident young man who lived at Soteria as a volunteer, went to school, and worked at a part-time job.

Later, he moved out to live with his brother, keeping in close touch with Voyce through tennis, visits, and by accompanying Voyce's family on a vacation (see below). Finally, he moved to his mother's in the Midwest, where an older brother's wedding made him the focus of his mother's wrath and led to his rehospitalization. A year and a half after first graduating from Soteria, Chuck was readmitted.

> *Loren summarized: This admission lasted six months with a similar content to the psychosis and similar behavior in the house (i.e., alternate periods of talkativeness and quiet). Staff were not able to contain his destructiveness (he broke several windows and threatened several staff and clients), and he required drug treatment for 10 days. This time his period of manifest psychosis was shorter, less intensive, and the degree of regression less.*

Chuck moved out after six months to live with another former Soteria client, then with a relative, and was not readmitted for almost three years. Over that period, he maintained contact with Voyce. Then, wrote Voyce,

> Chuck was threatening to sue people again, which is an indication that he's beginning to get into his power and control space again. This time when he came to Soteria, he never really got into his verbal or his quiet space in the same way. There was sort of a combination of somewhere in between both of those spaces, but it lasted only for two or three weeks at the most, at which point he came out of it and moved back home with his brother again, after staying only two months.
>
> I haven't been able to locate him since then, but he is probably doing what he normally does—getting a job and making himself busy.
>
> Sometimes I feel as if we have almost a father-son relationship, but in other ways it is more like a peer

relationship. It depends on where Chuck is with it. When he is spaced out, he's quite a heavy person to be around, but when he's out of it and together, he is pleasant and enjoyable.

I see Chuck as going through some type of growth process. He seems to be developing and changing with each experience of psychosis. I feel that at some point he will be able to avoid these episodes completely.

Loren concluded: Chuck's journey is an example of "growth from psychosis," a notion to which a number of writers such as Menninger, Perry, and Laing have referred. Chuck's progress, Loren believes, could not have occurred without the Soteria milieu; instead, "Chuck would probably have remained in hospitals, his growth processes interrupted by neuroleptic drugs." Except for the 10 days noted above, Chuck took no antipsychotic drugs during any of his three stays at Soteria.

Being With Matures

The core concept of the Soteria model gradually shifted from the formal vigil motif into the broader concept of *being with,* which offered more potential for interaction in a variety of social contexts. In the vigil room, both noninvolvement and self-absorption were possible, limited by the confines of the room itself. Only a few activities or stimuli could exist therein.

Staff discovered the *concept* of an enclosed space around an individual worked better at Soteria than *actual confinement* in a specific place. Meaningful interactions among people can close off surrounding distractions, even in a crowd. Staff member Nelly describes such a situation:

Toni was a former Soteria resident who had been hospitalized at the local inpatient ward of a private hospital. She had been isolated as too psychotic to spend time with other patients because of concern that her "crazy" behavior would upset them. When we found out about her situation, we arranged to have her released into our custody. We had decided to go to the beach that morning, however, and it would be difficult to spare a staff member to stay home with Toni, so the trip was canceled.

When the staff member returned with Toni, she was upset because she had been told that the community was going to the beach, and she insisted that she be allowed to go also. After a long group discussion, we decided that we would try to find a quiet beach and make several staff members and residents to whom Toni felt close responsible for *being with* her.

When we arrived at the beach, Toni and four members of the group went down to the water's edge. It was a hot day, and the usually quiet beach was quite crowded. Toni was behaving abnormally: She was making strange, gesturing motions that, on occasion, fit in with others' dancing and, on occasion, did not. She was also talking to herself, as if she were hearing voices, and making disconnected statements and observations. But she appeared to be having fun, and her attention was so caught up with her companions and her inner processes that she didn't seem to be aware of the crowd (nor they of her).

The effect sought from the vigil is the fusing of awareness among individuals by excluding excess stimuli. So more people at the beach had to engage Toni than would have been needed to achieve the same interaction in a quiet room.

Being With in Three Stages

The three stages of *being with*, as the process occurred with most Soteria residents, were

✎ the major crisis, when the client most needed basic care

🖋 the reconstitution, when the client reestablished his/her
personality in relation to the new surroundings

🖋 the extension, when the client began to expand boundaries
of relationships

These stages weren't completely separate; they overlapped, did
not always occur, and were manifest in different sequences.

Stage One

Stage one began when a staff member (usually Voyce) picked up the
client at the screening center. The person who made the first contact
initiated through *being with* the Soteria process of interpersonal
bonding. While relationships generally develop over a long period
of time, some basic ties take less than an hour to develop when the
environment is new and the faces unfamiliar. A friendship an hour
old can seem firm and important, especially if it rescues the sufferer
from a frightening place.

Stage one took advantage of this condition: Thus, the person who
brought the new client home made the introductions to the group
and stayed with him/her continuously for at least eight hours until s/
he connected sufficiently to someone else. Once such a connection
had been established, the vigil could continue to establish the
interpersonal connections that have to develop before meaningful
change can occur. The primary caregiver during stage one, therefore,
had to be the person most able to interact comfortably with the new
resident.

Stage one was the "tight" vigil, as differentiated from the "loose"
vigil of stage two. In most cases, the tight vigil took place in one room—
usually the client's—but on many occasions it happened in other
places in the house or the yard—as in Chuck's case (above).

During stage one, staff tried to make and maintain contact with
the person having difficulty interacting. The tight vigil also initiated
a basic support network. This kind of involvement became the
bonding material for long-term personal relationships. Through
common experience, two individuals can quickly create a closeness

similar to that among family members. These relationships were the building blocks of change at Soteria. And material generated in the tight vigil led to the second stage of *being with*.

> *Loren's comment: Soteria's provision of a low-stimulation, consistent, quiet milieu, which offered interpersonal support, acceptance, and predictability, was especially important for a successful journey through stage one.*

Stage Two

If the first stage of *being with* was bonding, the second stage was development. During this part of the process, a variety of relationships began to form, relationships that became the core of change Soteria-style. Without basic interpersonal relationships to establish supportive networks, clients were unable to develop identities separate from their families of origin. This failure virtually guaranteed another crisis for these young psychotics, who usually came to Soteria fresh from their childhood homes.

The content of *being with* in this process was creating normative interactions. The degree to which the members of Soteria could achieve such relationships was the degree of possible positive change. During the second stage, the content of activities encouraged symmetrical relationships,[16] and residents were allowed a myriad of choices as to how they would spend their time. Staff avoided scheduling too many organized functions for clients in stage two, encouraging residents to take the initiative at this point in organizing their own time in relation to the community's activities.

During stage two, clients began to validate their experiences in the context of a safe, protected environment away from the site where the trouble had its roots. As residents became less disturbed, their socialization and involvement in the Soteria community increased.

---

[16] See *Change Soteria-Style*, pages 24–25, for a discussion of complementary and symmetrical relationships.

Stage Three

The complaint that "I'm bored, and there's nothing to do" often meant that stage two was moving towards stage three. Such a complaint is usually a sign that the client is in fact interested in doing *something*—but something that s/he finds interesting rather than distasteful. Dishwashing, no, for example; a walk or a drive, yes. Having to come up with an alternative rather than simply complaining offers an opportunity for developing internal motivation.

At this point, *all* community members—including but not exclusively the staff—tried especially to reserve time to devote to the client entering stage three. In fact, an important part of this last stage was the breaking of boundaries among groups in community activities and the expanding of relationships within and without the house. In the third stage of *being with*, people at Soteria related to each other as individuals, not as staff, residents, volunteers, and so forth. For example, a former resident remembered a time when she wanted to go skiing and hadn't quite known how to organize the activity. She turned to another resident for help, and he was able to meet her needs:

> You remember that week when we went skiing at Dodge Ridge? I really appreciated Henry [another resident] for going through all that trouble getting everybody to come to the meeting that day. I think that, if he hadn't helped me, I could never gotten the group to go by myself.

On a similar note, Voyce recalled that after Chuck (see above) had entered stage three, his relationships with members of the Soteria community changed dramatically. Rather than having his crisis occupy the house as it did during his first week, he helped the house psychiatrist tend to other residents. His relationship with Voyce changed as well:

> Chuck and I would go play tennis a lot and do things together on a daily basis. In fact, I went to Disneyland that summer

with my kids, and Chuck went along with us and had a good time. It was a lot of fun for all of us.

Of this friendship, Loren wrote, Chuck's very real, down-to-earth relationship with Voyce after his stay at the house is unusual for traditional psychiatric treatment (but not for Soteria). While not defined as psychotherapy, it was clearly therapeutic. Voyce provided Chuck with a model of efficacy and competence (especially self-control) to emulate, and their shared life experiences and positive emotional ties seem to have been critical in Chuck's change over time.

Stage three within the milieu involved extensive collaboration, planning, and negotiation in the context of involvement in a—by then—familiar, trusted, and tightly knit social group whose members played a variety of roles with differing statuses. The third stage was much more complicated than the first.

The Soteria Network

Soteria's maintenance of connection with its former members distinguished it from most other treatment settings, especially from many current community-based programs. The decision to keep in touch with departing staff and clients evolved in response to the feelings aroused in the community when people left—the intensity of involvement by both staff and residents as well as the long hours and the blurred roles led almost to feelings almost like those among family members. "It was like losing a sibling or a roommate when someone moved out," explained one resident.

Early on, Soteria built rituals around leave-takings. There were parties—at Soteria or at the graduate's new home. When clients left, the community (including former residents) helped them to find a place to stay, to deal with landlords, to pack up, and, finally, to go. Often residents moved in with other Soteria graduates. Sometimes a newly departed resident needed a familiar face around to help in the transition. If this were the case, a member of the community stayed with the new graduate temporarily. When staff moved out, either to become day workers or to take another job, the process was formalized to minimize the pain of separation. Sufficient notice was a requirement.

Once no longer in residence, however, both former staff and clients maintained contact with Soteria. Some graduates were frequent visitors at the house, receiving needed support and comfort from familiar friends. Others built networks of Soteria graduates outside the house, keeping in touch by telephone and letter as well as face-to-face. In both cases, the continuing nature of the Soteria experience offered support to fragile people who often still needed help maintaining ongoing relationships.

Later data from the second portion of the Soteria research (1976–1982) affirmed, Loren noted, that it was this peer-based, easily accessible, tolerant, and affirming social network that made the long-term (two-year) outcomes found between the first 1971–1976 cohort of Soteria residents better than those of the second group. The significant difference between the ability to function two years later by members of the 1971–1976 groups—patients at the Community Mental Health Center ward and residents at Soteria—markedly favored Soteria's clients. The latter were better able to survive in the world outside—to take jobs, to go to school, to make and keep friends—than the patients discharged from the Community Mental Health Center. Loren traces this difference to the supportive social networks developed by the first Soteria cohort under the guidance of the staff, who in effect served as benevolent older siblings. This difference was muted in the 1976–1982 data because, Loren thinks, the original Soteria self-help community had already begun to disintegrate in the late 1970s when the project's support dwindled and it was forced to limp along largely with heroic but harassed volunteer help.

Hindsight

In retrospect, wrote Loren, seven ingredients appeared to be essential within the Soteria environment. Interestingly, but not surprisingly, given the community's disinterest in formal procedures of any sort, the seven were never explicitly articulated during the life of the project. These qualities, however, were basic to the ambiance that made Soteria a powerful therapeutic milieu.

1. There was a shared view that psychosis could be a positive learning experience.

2. The presence of multiple, shifting, and often ill-defined roles and relationships created an environment that could respond rapidly and flexibly to changing demands.

3. Clients spent sufficient time at Soteria to imitate and identify with staff members, volunteers, and other residents in ways that allowed mastery of new strategies for coping. Clients had the opportunity to observe, internalize, and practice such skills with the help of people they esteemed.

4. The psychotic experience was accepted for what it was—an unusual state of being that could be understood and have shared meaning when sufficient information became available. Its incomprehensibility was mostly the result of the staff's inability, because of fright, disinterest, fatigue, or other failings, to put themselves into the shoes of the psychotic person, to understand him/her and find meaning, and hence validation, in his/her experience.

5. Staff, not having been specifically charged to *do* anything except prevent harm, saw their primary responsibility to *be with* disorganized residents.

6. Unusual ("crazy") behavior was accepted and acceptable. Controlling such behavior was specifically forbidden unless a situation became dangerous. Staff were instructed to leave events stimulating personal anxiety alone or, if necessary, seek others' help in dealing with them.

7. Staff and residents normalized the experience of psychosis by avoiding jargon when discussing it: Clients were *freaked out* rather than psychotic, *bummed out* rather than depressed, *spacey* rather than autistic.

Structure

Neither Too Big Nor Too Small

SOTERIA'S SMALL SIZE was critical. Most psychiatric hospital wards house about 20 patients, and the combined group of staff *and* patients is likely to fall between 40 and 60 people. Thus, the staff/patient ratio is apt to be between one to one and one to two. (Soteria and Emanon aimed at seven part and full-time staff to six patients; see also pages 6–7.) For severely disorganized persons, however, a social reference group of no more than 8–12 turned out to best. (Interestingly, Soteria's original size was dictated by state licensing laws—group homes with more than six residents were required to have sprinkler systems, an expense that the project could not afford.) Later, staff learned that considerable evidence favored the size group Soteria had stumbled upon accidentally.

A group of 10 to 12 (staff and clients), combined in a homelike atmosphere, maximizes the disorganized person's ability to learn to know and trust a new environment and to find a surrogate family in it; at the same time, this size group minimizes labeling and stigmatization. Eight to 12 people are, interestingly, about the maximum number who normally live in Western households under one roof as an extended family or commune. In addition, most clinicians believe, 10 is about the upper limit for effective group therapy. Finally, experimental psychology's small task groups have been shown to function best with no more than 12 members. Soteria and Emanon were planned to function as homes sleeping 8–10 comfortably—typically, six beds occupied by residents and two by staff—rather than as 20-bed wards attended by 20 hospital personnel.

The houses' social relationships were closely related to their size: To function effectively, every organization, large or small, needs structure. In general, the larger the organization the greater the structure necessary. Unfortunately, organization of elaborate institutions can have consequences that impinge negatively on psychotically disorganized people. Large structures often must be inflexible, must rely on authority, must institutionalize roles, and must rest decision-making power and responsibility in a hierarchy outside the client's control. Those at the bottom of the pyramid—staff and patients—often feel powerless, irresponsible, and dependent.

Soteria was, therefore, as unstructured as commensurate with adequate function. Structures developed to meet functional needs were dissolved if the need for them did. There was no institutionalized method of facing particular occurrences. For example, the house dealt with overt aggressive acts in a variety of ways that depended on a myriad of contextual variables, including physical control (but not seclusion, straitjackets, or forced medication).

But while too big a group made work like that which took place at Soteria out of the question, too few residents and staff could also be problematic. Greater or smaller populations were often therapeutically ineffective—only a limited number of people could interact without creating difficulty for the community. If too many people were involved, the group no longer survived as a whole but split into several parts. Such a breakdown fostered *group* interactions but discouraged *interpersonal* ones. During periods when too many people lived at Soteria, the program experienced its greatest difficulties, difficulties affecting the community as a whole but the staff in particular. Bigness seemed to exacerbate conflicts among staff members. In contrast, established residents in the crowded house seemed able to participate in disputes with little difficulty, making alliances with apparent ease, as their symptoms became less the focus of the group and their support became helpful. For residents in crisis, however, problems resulting when too many were in the community fed their confusion.

Too few people presented a different dilemma for Soteria, fostering isolation. Interpersonal relations, instead of giving way to interactions among groups, were replaced by *intra*personal ones that presented problems for everyone. The resident experiencing psychological distress felt even more out of control. The recovering resident complained of not enough support—or too much. Residents on their way to self-sufficiency, not surprisingly, were not seriously affected.

For the staff, however, a shortage of clients was almost always a problem. If only a few clients, spending most of their time at the house, were in residence, and a couple of them experienced crises, the staff had a very difficult time. When the shortage involved only fairly stable residents, the condition could, briefly, be pleasant. But if it lasted too long, the staff had time to look intensely at *their* own relationships. Ironically, this examination often led to major conflicts, even when Soteria housed fairly calm groups.

What constituted *large* or *small* varied considerably, depending on the demographics and the climate of Soteria at any given time. If most members of the community were experiencing difficulties, large was smaller than when most residents were fairly stable. And in the summer, the environment widened as people spent less time in the house. Private space expanded in the warm months.

Generally, if 12 to 15 people spent more than four or more hours a day at Soteria, conflicts associated with too many people began to arise. On the other hand, if fewer than six people spent under four hours a day at Soteria, flawed interpersonal processes tended to result. So, for Soteria, the numbers were essential.

Soteria Days

Looking in on a typical day at Soteria in the mid-1970s, an observer might find the following interactions and happenings. On this day, two staff members (one male, Adam, and one female, Kimberly) and one volunteer work the shift that begins at noon and lasts through the night. Adam and Kimberly, both of whom began as volunteers, have been working harmoniously together for six months. Adam, who has worked at Soteria for two years, sees himself as an artist and a writer. Kimberly, a five-year veteran of Soteria, has recently finished her baccalaureate in English at a small college in the New England area. They are responsible for six residents. In addition, the house director, Voyce, stops by daily; the house psychiatrist, Ken, drops in once a week. Also spending part of the day at Soteria are several former residents, a friend, and a volunteer named Ned.

On the day in question, one of the six residents, Nicholas, is still having some acute psychotic symptoms but is able to stay alone most of the day with only periodic staff contact. Two residents, about ready to move out, are dealing with separation issues. One of them, Kate, has a job; the other, Thomas, is looking for an apartment. After six years of private treatment, a fourth, Ethan, has been referred to Soteria. Along with the other two residents, Nora and Ben, Ethan is deeply involved in the program.

Business as Usual

On this uneventful day, the Soteria community enjoys a peaceful, orderly interval.

7:00 AM

Kate, the resident who is about to leave Soteria, gets up and goes to work. Since she gets a ride with a volunteer who works near her place of employment, she must leave at 8:30. After she eats cereal for breakfast, she showers downstairs, because one of the residents complains that the shower wakes him up.

Before Kate leaves, she goes upstairs to wake Kimberly as requested. Kimberly is already up talking to Ethan, who is unhappy about being waked by Kimberly's showering next to his room.

KIMBERLY. You never complained before.
ETHAN. I told Kate.
KIMBERLY. If you'd come to the house meetings, you could let
    everybody know that the shower wakes you up in the morning.

ETHAN. They seem so boring. All you guys ever talk about is the house not being clean and who's mad at who today.

KIMBERLY. Well, I suggest you either come to the meeting tomorrow or don't complain when the next person who uses the shower wakes you up. Why don't you ask Kate to change rooms with you since she gets up earlier?

ETHAN. That's a good idea. She said she wished she had my room anyway, because she could grow her plants in it.

8:00 AM

Bob, a volunteer, arrives to pick up Kate. Kimberly fixes breakfast for herself and Nora. While Kimberly is making breakfast, Bob, Nora, and Kate sit around the table and talk about going to see a movie at a local theater.

At 8:30, Kate and Bob leave for work while Kimberly and Nora eat breakfast. Before they finish, another resident comes in and eats some of the bacon and eggs Kimberly cooked. Nora finishes her breakfast and goes upstairs to get ready for her appointment at the office that administers Supplementary Security Income. Kimberly warns her of Ethan's complaint about the shower next to his room. Nora responds: "He should be up anyway. He sleeps too much."

9:00 AM–11:00 AM

Just before Kimberly and Nora leave, Adam gets up and wakes Ben. Both Adam and Ben had decided to go running this morning. Kimberly suggests that they wait until she returns, because Nicholas, who is still experiencing an acute crisis, might get up while they are out running. Kimberly will be back in about 20 minutes, since she just plans to drop Nora off. Nora will return by bus.

Before Kimberly returns, Nicholas and Tom have gotten up, and Adam helps Nicholas cook a cheese omelette. As Kimberly arrives, Adam and Ben are on their way out the door. Nicholas asks if he can join them on their run. Asked if he has run before, Nicholas replies, "Only a little." The three jog around the block twice to check Nicholas's stamina and continue their run with him.

As Adam and Ben are leaving with Nicholas, Voyce arrives and talks with Kimberly and another staff member named Tom about the day's events. Voyce is going a meeting of the California Association of Social Rehabilitation Agencies that will take him away from Soteria from noon until 4:00 PM, but he will then stay until 6:00.

After Nicholas, Adam, and Ben return from running, they join the kitchen cabinet. Nicholas had more stamina than either Adam or Ben and complains because they don't want to run any further. Kimberly and Tom believe that running "isn't always good for you," while Ben and Nicholas claim that it "extends your life and makes you look healthier."

The discussion meanders until Kimberly's discomfort about the runners' odor leads her to recommend showers for all three. When Thomas balks at her suggestion that he do the breakfast dishes, Kimberly agrees to help him.

11:00 AM–2:00 PM

Ethan gets up again and comes downstairs, still complaining about having his sleep interrupted by people taking showers. He asks Kimberly to make breakfast for him, a request she refuses because she has to go shopping for dinner. Next, Ethan travels upstairs to ask Adam to make breakfast, but Adam also tells Ethan to make his own. Angrily, Ethan comes back to the kitchen and begins cooking some eggs, complaining to Voyce: "What are you paying staff for anyway?"

When Ethan's eggs are about half cooked, Ned (a volunteer) arrives. Ethan immediately asks *him* to finish breakfast, claiming that "I don't *know* how to fix eggs." Ned helps.

When Kimberly returns from shopping, she takes Thomas to see an apartment that he found in the want ads, while Adam spends some time with Ethan who has been having trouble with side effects of medications. Since the house psychiatrist is coming at 2:00 PM, Adam suggests that Ethan ask Ken for some medical help in getting rid of the side effects.

Nora returns, upset at her unsuccessful time at the Supplementary Security Income office. She had to wait two hours before seeing anyone, and then she couldn't complete the process because she didn't have her birth certificate along. She will have to go back the following week.

2:00 PM–4:00 PM

When Ken arrives, Adam, Ned, Nicholas, and Ethan are at the kitchen table, drinking the lemonade Nicholas made. Ned plans to get Ethan and Nicholas to help him work in the garden. Ken joins the group for a glass of lemonade, reintroducing himself to Nicholas because he is unsure if Nicholas, who had been very disorganized when originally interviewed, will remember him from the week before. After thinking a minute, Nicholas recalls Ken's face but not his name.

Following Adam's suggestion, Ethan brings up his medications and asks if they can be reduced. Ken reminds Ethan that it was he who wanted the extra medication, that Ken had originally recommended less. The three go upstairs to talk about Ethan's medication problem. Before they go, Ken reminds Nicholas that they will need to talk to further to complete the chart.

4:00 PM–8:00 PM

Ethan and Nicholas being unavailable, Ned goes upstairs and gets Nora to help him work in the garden. Ken leaves at 4:00—about 10 minutes before Voyce returns from his meeting. By then, most of the residents are again in the kitchen with Adam. Kimberly and Ned are discussing the evening meal in the living room. Ned, responsive to Nora's wish to get out of the house because of the hot weather, wants to take the group to Alum Rock Park to have a barbecue but is careful to talk the idea over with a staff member before suggesting it to the rest of the house.

Kimberly okays the idea and invites him to ask other people in the house if they want to go. Everyone (including Kate whom Ned calls at work) is interested except Ethan; however, he gives in to group pressure and finally agrees to go.

The first groups leave in Ned's and in Voyce's cars; the second contingent will take Kimberly's car when Kate gets home. But when Bob and Kate arrive at Soteria, Ethan presents a problem by deciding that he really doesn't want to go. Finally, Kimberly decides to stay at home with Ethan, who seems troubled. Bob takes Kate over to the park and will bring back a load of picnickers later.

By the time Bob and Kate arrive at the park, the first group almost has dinner ready. Nora prepares the meal, while Adam leads an expedition along the trails. Voyce remains, in spite of his plan to leave at 6:00. After eating and playing some volleyball, the picnickers return to Soteria. There, a note from Kimberly explains that she and Ethan had gone for a walk to the local park and to dinner at one of the area's pizza houses. The group discovers Spence, a former resident, waiting in the living room watching television.

8:00 PM–11:00 PM

Nora remembers plans for going to the movies with Bob, who says, however, that he is too tired and needs to go home. Nora asks Ned if he will take her and Kate. Although Ned reluctantly agrees, Kate decides that she's too tired, but Ethan announces that he wants to go. Unfortunately, he doesn't have any money. Ned agrees to lend it to Ethan if Ethan pays him back the following week.

Spence begins to play the piano and sing; Kimberly and Kate join in. Adam and Nicholas go upstairs to talk about Nicholas's concern that Nora hates him because she looks at him in a strange way. Adam suggests that Nicholas should talk to Nora about this feeling when she gets home from the movies, an idea that makes him uncomfortable. Adam refuses Nicholas's request to have the conversation for him but agrees to be there when Nicholas talks to Nora.

After about 45 minutes, the two join the sing-along. At 10:30, Kate announces that she is going to go upstairs to read and get ready for bed. Kimberly suggests that they stop playing the piano in deference to the neighbors' complaints about loud music at night.

Spence tells Thomas there will be a vacancy in his rooming house by that weekend. Spence has asked the manager not to rent it until he has had a chance to talk to Thomas and promises to call the manager on Thomas's behalf in the morning.

> *Loren points out: In clinical terms, an extended peer social network is functioning nicely in this interaction.*

11:00 PM–3:00 AM

Someone turns on the television to watch the news, and most of the people in the house start to watch too. Kimberly and Nicholas are in the kitchen talking about his problem with Nora. Kate has fallen asleep while reading on the bed in the upstairs common room.

When Ethan, Nora, and Ned return from the movies, Nicholas asks Nora if he can talk to her in the kitchen. He has decided to face her alone. In conversation, they realize that they went to the same high school and have had several friends in common.

Nicholas's fear that Nora doesn't like him is never discussed in the two hours that they talk.

At 1:00 AM, Spence goes home, Tom goes to bed, and Kate wakes up and goes to bed. After an hour's talk with Adam, Nicholas goes to bed. But Ethan and Nora again argue, first about the shower, then over other conflicts. Periodically, Adam and Kimberly must mediate until, after an hour of quarreling, the combatants go to their rooms for the night, leaving Ben and Ned watching a late movie.

Kimberly and Adam go upstairs to talk about the day and to exchange back rubs.

A few minutes later, Ned falls asleep on the couch.

Ben snaps the television off and goes to bed.

After making sure that Nicholas is asleep, at 3:00 AM, Kimberly and Adam go to sleep.

Soteria in Crises

During the stress engendered by psychological crises, members of the house try to continue their interactions and to maintain some kind of structure under chaotic circumstances.

6:00 AM–7:00 AM

At 6:00 AM, four of the five clients in residence are asleep—only Charlotte, a long-term resident planning to leave in two weeks, is up. She cooks breakfast for herself and the two full-time staff members on duty—Ophelia, a California School of Professional Psychology graduate and former volunteer, and Keith, a veteran staffer, working on his dissertation.

Ida, who has been awake for 24 hours, is in her second day at Soteria and is still in serious distress. She has just drifted off to sleep on the living room couch. Keith gets up after sleeping four hours in order to relieve Ophelia, who has been with Ida since 2:00 AM. Keith will be off duty in four hours, but Ophelia has another full day ahead.

As Ophelia, Charlotte, and Keith have breakfast, they talk about calling Voyce to set up a vigil for Ida. Ophelia worries that it will be difficult for her to maintain the level of intensity for the remainder of her shift. Charlotte suggests waiting until Ida wakes up to see "what space she's in," and Keith offers to stay until noon, when one of the volunteers is set to arrive. This way, Ophelia can sleep longer while he and Stuart—another veteran staffer who was formerly a psychologist's assistant—take care of the house. Charlotte offers to organize dinner and go shopping if someone drives her to the store.

7:00 AM–10:30 AM

Ophelia goes upstairs to sleep. Fifteen minutes later, Mike, who has been readmitted to Soteria because of a crisis provoked when his woman friend moved out, goes out the front door, whose squeaking hinges alert everyone in the kitchen of his exit. Keith catches up with Mike first and asks where he is going. "Home." Keith reminds him that, because Mike and his father quarrel, his parents told him that he couldn't come home. Keith tells Charlotte, who is standing on the front porch, to wake up Ophelia if Ida gets up because he must *be with* Mike.

Keith and Mike walk towards downtown, talking, among other things, about how scary it is to be away from home. After nearly an hour, the two have walked a circle and are now back in front of the house. Keith asks Mike if he would like some breakfast. Mike says yes, suggesting that Keith cook pancakes. Keith agrees.

When Keith and Mike enter the kitchen, they find Ida, eating eggs and drinking orange juice, sitting at the table with Charlotte. Charlotte is describing how she felt when she first came to Soteria. That Charlotte used to think that Stuart was the devil and could read her mind now seems cause for laughter.

Mike asks Ida if he can have the rest of the eggs still in the frying pan, and Keith suggests that Mike cook bacon to go with the eggs.

At this point, Voyce walks in the door, and Keith invites him to breakfast. Sitting down at the table, Voyce tells Keith that Ophelia called about Ida and Mike. If both these residents stay up all night, Voyce points out, it will be hard for Ophelia and Keith to make it through the next night without help. Voyce says he's "on call," if things become too difficult.

Keith goes up to wake Conrad, another resident, in time to make his 10:30 AM dental appointment. He meets Conrad emerging from the shower, ready to get dressed for his appointment. Elmer, a volunteer who has spent the night, has gotten up and is getting ready to go with Conrad to his appointment (which is just across the street).

When Keith comes back downstairs, Voyce suggests that they try to work out some plan for the day: There may be difficulties if both Mike and Ida start to experience crises. Neither has had much sleep in the last three days, a factor that could exacerbate problems. Keith suggests waiting for Stuart to arrive to participate in the discussion. Voyce also reminds Keith that Ida is scheduled for some psychological testing at 1:00 PM, and that Mike needs to be at the Supplementary Security Income office at 2:00.

Elmer and Conrad leave for the dentist at 10:15, and Stuart arrives at 10:30, late as usual. Five minutes later, Saul arrives and immediately starts to wash dishes (a chore he likes). He claims that it "makes me feel like a part of this place." (Until a month ago, Saul was a Soteria resident. He is now a volunteer.) Saul's shifting roles in the Soteria community are the norm rather than the exception.

10:30 AM–2:00 PM

Ida starts to cry, and Charlotte puts her arm around her and asks, "What's wrong?" Ida doesn't know. She seems to be talking to someone but is not speaking loud enough to be understood. Because Ida seems most comfortable with females, she and Charlotte go into the backyard to talk.

Suddenly, everyone realizes that Mike is not there. Leaving Stuart in the house, Voyce and Keith go looking for Mike, who has managed to get to a local restaurant, where he is arguing loudly with one of the waitresses. He is talking to himself and making other patrons nervous.

Because Mike usually responds to Voyce better than to Keith, Voyce talks to Mike while Keith reassures the waitress. Finally, Voyce and Mike begin to walk back to Soteria. Voyce explains the difficulty that this kind of behavior poses and says Mike should tell the community when he wants to go out "so that we can talk about it."

"Why should I have to tell you that I'm going somewhere?" Mike replies. "You're not my father." Voyce explains that Mike doesn't have to say where he's going but that Voyce would like to know.

As Voyce and Mike walk home, Voyce invites Mike to come along to buy glass to replace a window broken the previous day. Mike accepts. They alert Stuart that they are going and set off.

Ida and Charlotte are still out in the backyard talking. Elmer and Conrad return and join them. Ophelia gets up and, with Stuart and Keith, discusses the change of shifts. Ten minutes later, a former resident named Howard arrives and asks Keith to play basketball. Keith agrees if Howard finds out who else wants to play with them. Elmer, Conrad, Stuart, Charlotte, and Ida are all interested. Ophelia is taking a shower, so the game proceeds with uneven teams.

Voyce and Mike return. By now, Charlotte and Ida are ready for a break from the game, so Voyce and Mike take their places. By the time Ethan gets angry at Howard for accusing him of fouling, everyone is tired and ready to quit.

2:00 PM—4:00 PM

Saul goes over to San Jose State to get an application.

Keith goes home.

Howard asks Stuart for a ride home.

Howard and Stuart leave.

The rest of the group sits down to eat the sandwiches that Ophelia and Ida made. At 2:00, while the group is eating, Leonard arrives. His background is like Ophelia's: He is a graduate student at the California School of Professional Psychology volunteering at Soteria. He greets everyone and hugs Charlotte, Ophelia, and Stuart before sitting down at the table. Charlotte immediately asks him if he will take her shopping for dinner.

"Yes," he promises, but first he wants to learn what has happened since last week. He introduces himself to Ida and explains what he does at Soteria.

Voyce wants to put the window in, so he goes to his van and gets the glass and putty. Mike helps Voyce, Mike quietly talking to himself as he works. Voyce asks if Mike is hearing voices. Mike replies: "Yes, the V-O-Y-C-E type." They both laugh at the joke, and Mike explains that his voices bother him sometimes: "They tell me to do things I know I shouldn't do." After they install the window, the two go back downstairs.

As they enter the living room, Voyce notices Ida asleep on the couch and asks if she should be awakened now so that she will be able to sleep better tonight. Ophelia points out that Ida needs to sleep, because she has had so little since she arrived at Soteria.

As Ophelia speaks, the research assistant walks in, ready to test Ida. He asks where his subject is. Ophelia gently puts her hand on Ida's shoulder. When Ida awakens, Ophelia asks her to help with some necessary paperwork and introduces her to the researcher. She leads Ida and the researcher upstairs to the common room at the end of the hall, informing them that she will be downstairs, and closing the door behind her.

As Ophelia enters the kitchen, the phone rings. On the other end is Howard, upset about his roommate Brett, whom he had met at

Soteria when both were residents there. Howard found Brett sitting in the middle of the floor of their living room, surrounded by strewn clothes and furniture. Howard tried to find out what happened but couldn't get Brett to say anything coherent or do anything but stare blankly at the walls as if he were looking at something outside. Suddenly, before Howard knew what was happening, Brett bolted out the door and down the street. Howard ran after him for a short distance. When he realized that he couldn't keep up, Howard called Soteria.

Because Brett and Howard live only five blocks away, Stuart, Elmer, and Voyce get into the van and to try to find Brett. As they turn the first corner, Elmer spots Brett standing in a vacant lot, staring up at the sky, and talking to himself. From two blocks away, they can see Howard running towards them.

Stuart and Elmer go over to talk to Brett, while Voyce tries to get more background information about Brett from Howard. Pedestrians and drivers stop and try to figure out what is going on, when Brett starts to shout that Howard is trying to kill him. While Stuart and Elmer try to explain to Brett that this is not so, Voyce and Howard stay some distance from Brett. After about 10 minutes, a police car arrives, and Voyce tells the officers what is going on. They ask if they can help. Voyce suggests that, because Brett appeared to become excited when they arrived, it might be a good idea if they stayed out of sight but nearby. They agree to drive down the street, turn the corner, and wait to see what happens.

A few minutes after the officers leave, Brett begins to calm down. Stuart and Elmer start walking Brett to Soteria. Voyce and Howard go over to the officers to thank them and to give them details about Brett and about Soteria's purpose.

On the way back to the house, Voyce and Howard decide that Howard should try to talk to Brett about his delusion about Howard's murderous intentions, but Voyce suggests waiting to see "where Brett is" when they return to Soteria.

Arriving, they find Ophelia and Stuart with Brett in one of the quietest rooms in the house. It was recently vacated by the last resident who left Soteria, and Ophelia had slept in it that morning. Ophelia is sitting on the bed with Brett, holding his hand; Stuart sits on the floor by the bed, resting his head on Brett's knees. Elmer, who has known Brett from previous work at Soteria, remains outside the door until he leaves with Voyce to go into the common room to explain what has been happening.

Brett seems no longer to think that *Howard* is trying to kill him; however, Elmer is afraid that Brett still believes that *someone* is trying to kill him. Elmer says that Brett hasn't been eating for a long time and that he has been afraid to leave his and Howard's apartment for a week but that Charlotte is making food for him now.

4:00 PM–6:00 PM

While Charlotte is getting Brett something to eat, Leonard is making out a shopping list, and Conrad and Ida are suggesting what Charlotte might cook for dinner.

Mike is in the living room, looking depressed. Howard sits down beside Mike and starts talking to him. "I'm nervous," Howard says, "and need to go for a walk." He asks Mike if he would like to come along. Howard tells Leonard and Charlotte that he and Mike are going to Kim's market around the corner to get a soda. Leonard reminds them that dinner will be ready sometime between 6:00 and 7:00.

When she comes downstairs from feeding Brett, Charlotte goes shopping for dinner with Leonard and Ida. In the meantime, Ophelia and Stuart think they would like some backup help tonight. During the last two nights, Mike and Ida had difficult times.

Voyce calls Natalie, a 40-year-old volunteer who lives near Soteria. She offers to arrive at the house around 7:00 PM. If there is an emergency, however, she says that she can get there earlier and can stay until 8:00 the next morning, if she can leave Soteria in time to make a 9:00 appointment.

As Voyce hangs up, Ophelia is waiting to discuss the possibility of readmitting Brett to Soteria. She explains: "Brett is really out of it. He can't keep a thought going for more than one sentence. He also seems afraid of something but can't or won't say what." Voyce asks

Ophelia if she thinks the house could handle another resident at this time. She says it would "not be a problem," if he and Natalie were available when needed. Voyce assures her that both of them would be there all night if necessary.

Voyce calls the house psychiatrist to let him know what's going on and tells Ophelia to have Brett sign an admission form. Voyce also suggests a community discussion at dinner to see if anyone has a problem with Brett's coming back to Soteria. He reassures Ophelia that she need not to worry about dinner or cleaning up—the group will take care of both.

6:00 PM–7:00 PM

Mike and Howard come back from their walk, and Charlotte, Leonard, and Ida return from shopping. Charlotte rounds up everybody (except Brett, Ophelia, and Stuart) to help with dinner. Leonard has already started to make the spaghetti sauce; Mike is cleaning off the table; Ida and Howard are washing lunch and snack dishes; Conrad and Ethan are putting together a salad.

Voyce, who hates to cook, promises to wash the dishes after dinner.

While all this is going on, Natalie walks in through the living room, which wallows in a three-day mess of overflowing ashtrays and other debris, her night bag in one hand and a pillow case full of dirty laundry in the other. She says, "Voyce, you sounded so desperate on the phone that I sent my friend home and brought my laundry with me. I'll go down and put it in the washing machine now, and then I'll clean up the mess in the living room."

Saul walks in the door, and Natalie instantly asks him to help her clean up the living room. She suggests that he start by folding the blankets on the couch where someone had slept the night before.

7:00 PM–9:00 PM

Charlotte and Ida set the table, while Natalie and Ethan put out the food. Leonard asks Conrad to go upstairs to see if Stuart, Ophelia, and Mike want to eat, and, if so, where, but the crash of breaking glass interrupts mealtime progress. Leonard, Voyce, Ethan, and Howard run upstairs to see what is going on. When they arrive, they find Ophelia and Stuart holding Brett down on the bed to keep him away from the window, one pane of which lies in shards on the floor. Brett's right hand appears to be bleeding seriously.

After Voyce looks at the hand more closely, he suggests that someone take Brett to the emergency room. By this time, Brett has calmed down and is sitting on the bed, holding his injured hand. After Leonard and Ethan clean up the glass on the floor, Voyce asks Leonard to get a work glove out of the van so he can remove the remaining glass from the window frame without cutting himself.

Brett wants to see if he needs stitches in his hand, so Stuart and Leonard take him to the emergency room at San Jose Hospital. Ophelia stays and tells Voyce what happened:

> We had been sitting with Brett for an hour, talking about letting him come back to Soteria for a while. For the last ten minutes of our conversation, however, he seemed to be asleep. Stuart and I were talking about working out some kind of sleeping pattern for the night when Brett suddenly jumped off the bed and started to run. He tripped and fell against the window. We weren't sure what was going on with him, so we automatically grabbed him. I don't think he was trying to hurt himself; he just sort of freaked out and accidentally fell into the glass. I think it scared him when he tripped, and we jumped on him. I know it did me.

Voyce and Ophelia go down to the kitchen and join the group eating dinner. Ophelia again explains what just happened upstairs, and a lot of discussion about what to do when Brett gets back from the emergency room follows. Conrad talks about how he felt when he panicked one day and tried to jump out of a moving car. His story precipitates a long discussion about "schizophrenia" that goes on through 8:30 when Voyce begins, as promised, to wash the dinner dishes. Charlotte starts to help, but Voyce tells her, "You've done enough today."

Howard asks Ophelia for a back rub. She says she will give him one if he will reciprocate. Charlotte and Ethan and Ida and Conrad strike the same bargain, so the living room becomes a massage parlor. Everybody participates except, Voyce who is still washing dishes.

9:00 PM–1:00 AM

Stuart and Leonard come back with Brett, laughing about the emergency room nurse who thought that Brett had tried to cut his wrist and missed, even though Stuart assured her that wasn't the case. As soon as they enter the massage parlor, Leonard offers to give Brett a back massage.

Stuart tells Voyce that he is going upstairs to take a nap while things are quiet. Voyce suggests that both he and Ophelia get some sleep. While they sleep upstairs, and Brett dozes on the living room couch, the door bell rings. Suddenly Charlotte remembers that her mother is going to pick her up to spend the night with the family. After introducing everyone to her mother, she goes upstairs, collects some necessities, and leaves.

The rest of the group wanders into the kitchen to watch Voyce finish the dishes and listen to him reminisce about "the good old days" at Soteria, when the community used to stay up three and four days when necessary to get somebody through a "crazy place." He remembers a resident who liked to get him to take a group up to Mount Hamilton to look at the city lights at 2:00 in the morning. Ida says that looking at the city lights sounds fun and wants Voyce to take them up there.

Leonard and Natalie offer to watch Brett in case he wakes up, and Voyce agrees to take the group to Mount Hamilton. He suggests that they get something to drink on the trip. Conrad suggests beer, but Voyce doesn't want them have anything stronger than "coke"—Coca-Cola, that is.

As they get into the van, Mike and Conrad argue about who is going to sit in the front seat. When Conrad wins, Mike decides not to go. Leonard and Natalie feel comfortable with Mike staying behind, knowing Ophelia and Stuart are upstairs if anyone needs help.

Drinks purchased, Voyce starts driving the group to Lick observatory at the top of Mount Hamilton. On the way, they stop at a mountain creek and dance to the music coming from the van radio. They spend an hour in the parking lot of the Observatory, looking at the city lights and talking.

1:00 AM–3:00 AM

The van pulls in to Soteria. Ida sleeps in Howard's lap. Conrad snores in the front seat, his head leaning against the window. Ethan and Saul are talking about going over to Santa Cruz in the morning to look at girls on the beach.

The house seems to begin to shut down. As people get out of the van, Leonard and Brett sit on the front porch, talking. Ida and Conrad say good night; Howard and Saul leave for home; Ethan goes into the kitchen to make himself a sandwich and then goes to bed.

Mike, who was asleep on one of the couches, wakes eager to continue the argument over the front seat. He had talked to Leonard about his concerns while the group was gone, and Leonard suggested that he try to work out the issue with Conrad when he got back. What began as an argument turns into a discussion; then Mike and Conrad sit down to a game of chess.

The voices bring Ophelia and Stuart sleepily downstairs. Leonard tells Ophelia and Stuart that he and Brett, who is getting nervous, are going to go for a walk. He wants somebody to come with them in case he needs help. Ophelia feels like walking and joins them. Stuart goes into the kitchen to get something to eat.

Voyce announces that he is going home. He will be back in the morning with paychecks. "It *is* morning!" someone protests.

Fifteen minutes after Voyce leaves, Ida comes down to the kitchen to tell Stuart about her bad dream. As Conrad and Mike play chess, they listen. When Ida finishes, Stuart begins to interpret. Conrad disagrees with Stuart's interpretation. Then, Mike comes up with his interpretation. Ida dislikes it and tells him to go back to chess. The conversation shifts into a general discussion about dreams.

At 2:30 AM, Leonard, Ophelia, and Brett return. Leonard has some classes tomorrow morning and needs to get some sleep, but Ophelia and Brett continue the discussion in the living room that they began during their walk.

3:00 AM–5:00 AM

Conrad and Mike decide to go to bed while Ida and Stuart continue to talk. Around 3:30, Ophelia and Brett join Stuart and Ida in the kitchen, and the four of them talk there for a half hour before going into the living room. There, Stuart lies on the couch, Ophelia and Ida sit on the floor next to him, and Brett gathers up pillows and lays them across the room. The only lights on in the house are in the kitchen, and in five minutes, Brett is asleep.

After a few minutes, Ida appears to be asleep also. Stuart and Ophelia hope both stay that way so *they* can get some sleep before tomorrow but then notice that Ida is crying softly. When Ophelia asks her what's wrong, Ida doesn't answer and goes back to sleep.

Stuart moves Ida to the couch where he was lying and covers her. Ophelia covers Brett. Stuart plans to sleep on the other couch in the living room. He sends Ophelia upstairs to go to sleep. He will call her if he needs to.

At 5:00 AM, Brett wakes and asks Stuart to tell him in which room to sleep.

"You can sleep in the room where you broke the window or stay here," Stuart says.

"Where are you going to sleep?"

"On the couch where I am."

Brett, who wants to stay with Stuart, turns over and goes back to sleep. Stuart's unpremeditated response is flexible, spontaneous, involved, protective, and of genuine help to Brett. Yet an outsider might be hard put to distinguish staff and volunteers from residents, never, of course, a problem in a psychiatric hospital. A day like the one that has just passed at Soteria would never transpire in a medical setting.

Loren points out: In Soteria's environment, it is truly difficult to tell the players without a program (although there are lists on pages 50-52 and page 66). Reciprocal support is the order of the day, with those in special distress getting extra help when they need it and giving it when they can.

A Quiet Sunday

Quiet days occur when fairly stable residents are becoming independent of Soteria's services. Dramatic but largely nontraumatic shifts in activity often take place when several residents graduate in a short space of time. Since the replacement process can be slow, quiet periods usually last a number of days.

Residents' leave-takings remind the others of their own eventual fate. Those staying on tend to become less dependent on the program and focus more on the time they too will step into the wider community. The difficulty of separation leads to some withdrawal on both the part of the residents and the staff. This withdrawal, which accentuates the quiet, is strongest when the absent resident is active—positively or negatively—in the program.

On this Sunday, no crises erupt, and operations proceed uneventfully. Most of the residents involve themselves in "reentry" activities such as preparing for school or work and seeing friends from outside the house. Three residents remain in the program, and three others have recently moved into the surrounding community. One of the remaining residents is Chip, who has lived at Soteria for two months and is taking a class at the local state college. Christine is the most recently admitted person, and only she still shows signs of having serious difficulties. Orville, the third resident, who came to Soteria as a private referral, has been in residence for six months.

Tabitha and Lewis are the two staff members on duty. Tabitha, a former secretary, now also plays in a local band. Lewis, 35, has recently returned from 10 years' residence in Europe.

Two former residents and a volunteer also make contact with the house during this day. One of the former is Henry, who hasn't been to

Soteria in a year. Luke, the volunteer, is a student at the University of California at Santa Cruz.

Loren notes: The community offers an excellent example of an informally organized open social system.

10:00 AM–12 M

Tabitha is the first person awake. She takes a shower and goes downstairs to read the Sunday morning paper. As she is reading, Hildegaard, a visiting German psychologist towards the end of her two-week stay, and Christine come downstairs. Hildegaard is willing to cook some breakfast if anyone wants some. Tabitha replies affirmatively, but Christine decides that she just wants cold cereal.

Christine gets a bowl of cereal, sits beside Tabitha, and starts to read the comics. While she reads, Chip and Lewis come downstairs and turn the TV on to a football game. Christine complains that that makes it hard for her to read, so Lewis unplugs the TV and takes it into the music room next to the kitchen.

When Hildegaard finishes making breakfast, she joins Chip and Lewis in the music room. Orville is up but is still sitting in his room writing a letter to his sister in Los Angeles. The front door opens, and Henry walks in and asks Tabitha if she knows where the TV is (it's not where it was when he was a resident). Tabitha points to the music room, and Henry hurries through the kitchen to see the game.

While Henry and Chip argue over who is going to win, Hildegaard and Lewis talk about Soteria. Hildegaard asks about incidents that have happened while she has been at Soteria, and Lewis tries to explain why they were handled as they were. Hildegaard also tries to find out about the day's plans.

Hungry, Lewis asks Hildegaard to come in the kitchen, so he can cook breakfast while they talk. Lewis and Hildegaard move into the kitchen, and when Henry decides that he wants to go to Kim's market, Hildegaard suggests that he bring back some orange juice.

Tabitha reminds Christine that her parents are going to pick her up at 11:00 to take her to San Francisco, and Christine goes upstairs to get ready.

After he finishes eating, Lewis returns to the football game, asking Chip for the score and a summary of what he's missed. A big touchdown by the Los Angeles Rams, Chip says facetiously (Lewis is a San Francisco Forty-Niners fan). There actually hasn't been any scoring, so far.

Just before Christine's parents arrive, Hildegaard tells Tabitha that she is going to visit a friend in Berkeley and not to save dinner for her. Christine offers Hildegaard a ride to San Francisco, but Hildegaard says she needs to spend some time alone, so she thanks Christine but prefers the bus.

A few minutes later, Christine's parents arrive, and she leaves. Hildegaard follows shortly afterwards.

Half-time.

The Rams are leading the Forty-Niners 14 to nothing, and Henry, now uninterested in the game, heads back to his apartment, while Chip leaves for the library at San Jose State to study. Lewis turns off the TV and goes into the living room to read the paper, but, instead, begins to talk with Tabitha about how quiet the house is. Tabitha goes up to see if Orville wants something to eat. She finds him asleep.

12:00 M–9:00 PM

Tabitha and Lewis clean the house for about two hours. When Tabitha hears someone taking a shower upstairs, she goes up to check on Orville and finds him, naked and embarrassed, in the hall. After he pulls on some pants, he opens the door and responds with enthusiasm to her invitation to go to a movie with her and Lewis later in the afternoon. He immediately puts in a request to see a popular science fiction film. Not overjoyed, Tabitha suggests that the three negotiate.

In the end, they agree to Orville's choice.

After the movie and dinner at the Spaghetti Factory, they pick up Chip at the library and go by a bar where a former resident is playing in a band.

*Loren's comment: Without thinking about it, the group is negotiating
and networking—casually and vitally.*

9:00 PM–1:00 AM

Back at Soteria, they find Luke, a volunteer whom they had forgotten
was coming, in the living room with Todd, a former resident who
hadn't been back to Soteria in a long time. The two of them have had
several hours to become acquainted.

Tabitha gives Todd a big hug of welcome, but she is the only
person who knows him from his days at Soteria. The group goes into
the kitchen, sits at the kitchen table, and listens to Todd's stories
about Soteria "before their times."

*Loren's comment: Note here the transgenerational transmission of
a unique culture.*

Orville and Lewis start to play poker, using popcorn as money.
After their first game, everybody else joins in. "Soteria Rules" prevail—
it is OK to steal popcorn from the inattentive, but it is also fair to slap
the thief's hand if caught in the act.

The game falls apart when people begin to spend more time
trying to steal popcorn than playing poker. A war with popcorn and
pillows as weapons is followed by a half hour's cleanup time. Todd is
on his way—he has to go to work tomorrow; Chip goes to bed because
of his class in the morning; and Luke leaves for the night.

At about 11:30, Orville brings the TV back into the living room
and turns on the late movie channel. Tabitha and Lewis join him.
Christine calls to say that she is going to stay overnight with her parents.

The movie ends.

Everyone goes to sleep.

*Loren summarizes: Soteria's Sunday could have taken place in a
college dormitory or a group living arrangement—the line between
normal and abnormal is indecipherable to any but the immediate
actors.*

Rules in an Open System

Laing's Kingsley Hall was formally rule-free. In contrast, Soteria's community agreed to certain fundamental controls. Soteria's boundaries—various rules considered necessary—were either *explicitly* set by the community, the staff members, or the administration or *implicitly* transmitted through nonverbal behavior. Everyone understood the implicit rules in spite of the absence of formal agreements.

Soteria enforced two kinds of explicit rules, those affecting everyone at all times—*universal*—and those affecting specific individuals at particular times—*limited.* The former lasted *indefinitely;* the latter for a specified (or *definite)* period of time.

The rule against using illegal drugs—itself a felony—was universal. Obviously, members of the Soteria community were also expected to refrain from other acts forbidden by civil authorities—murder, rape, robbery, etc. The rule requiring that the knife box be locked for a set period after a new resident arrived was limited.

Explicit Indefinite Rules

Early in Soteria's history, the staff tried to figure out how to impose controls without establishing a rigid structure. Although the *administration* had originally embraced three rules—against violence, against uninvited guests, and against illegal drugs, the *staff* defined only two rules whose violation could lead to discharge for any member of the community. Their first, prohibiting illegal drugs, coincided with administration strictures; their second forbade sex between staff and residents.

Staff paid lip service to the administration's regulation against uninvited visitors and embraced their ban on illegal drugs. Although staff at first thought the antiviolence rule unnecessary, it came to find that useful as well. The rule against sex between staff and clients, an incest taboo, was taken seriously as necessary to allow both groups to achieve maximum interpersonal closeness without inappropriate intimacy. Clear boundaries were useful for the staff and clients alike.

Were either of the *community's* rules broken, a group discussion would invariably follow. One possible action was expulsion of the offender, though neither Voyce nor Loren can remember that this option was ever exercised.

Seconding the administration's prohibition, the community also eventually decided to adopt its own third universal rule, against violence—threats or assaults—when the program had been running for three years. The need for more control over some potentially violent residents called for a formal mandate beyond the rule adopted when Soteria opened. It was clear that a rule against dangerous residents wouldn't in itself have a major effect on diminishing violence, but its formulation gave the group something on which to focus as it came to grips with the underlying anxieties that violence produced. An unexpected result of formally prohibiting violence was that some residents began to discuss issues that for others in the group didn't seem to concern violence. For example, while one new resident saw the locked knife box as a violent act against him, most of the others saw it as a preventive measure.

Oddly, the rule against illegal drugs was the most difficult to enforce. Because of the screening process, Soteria rarely housed clients with serious substance abuse problems, but, on occasion, clients would bring street drugs—rarely anything other than marijuana— onto the premises. On the unusual occasions when the community suspected or discovered such drugs, they became a key issue at the next house meeting. "Using" residents justified their behavior as follows: The practice

- helped assert independence from the group
- was a self-medicating process that covered up the voices
- gave pleasure

No matter what the reason, use of illegal drugs was grounds for expulsion. When California decriminalized possession of marijuana, its use became less a focus of attention; at no time, however, was its use permitted in Soteria's public areas.

Explicit Definite Rules

Rules of limited duration, fixed around specific issues or people because of particular problems, usually had greater impact on the program than the universal indefinite ones. Violation of fixed rules could lead to penalties ranging from reprimand to discharge. Failure to participate in housework or gardening could provoke a warning; malicious lying could lead to expulsion.

Limited rules were one of many ways to encourage change in clients at Soteria. Clearly defined boundaries set the structure that guided many members of the community through important changes when a predetermined end had been established. But the rules usually served not to dictate the change to come but to provide tolerable limits within which the residents could choose their own directions towards therapeutic ends.

The rules were successful in direct proportion to the degree that they allowed freedom of interaction. *Unnecessary rules could have been detrimental and are usually unenforceable in any case.*

One effective and necessary rule established around an issue helped Hugh, a Soteria client, control the problem he developed with alcohol. (Prior to the episode of psychological distress that sent him to Soteria, he had not exhibited alcoholic tendencies.) After he was admitted, however, every day about 5:00 PM, he would drink excessively and come home acting in a bizarre way that disrupted normal activities. This pattern went on for two weeks while members of the Soteria community tried by various means to change it. Nothing worked.

Instead of giving Hugh an ultimatum to either desist or leave, the community took a different approach. At a house meeting it was decided to remove the focus from Hugh because, as he put it, "It's not my problem. I'm having fun." No one could reasonably be upset with him, he said, because he "just got a little drunk every now and then." The community disagreed. Hugh's drinking problem had become the house's, and its members and staff decided not to drink for two weeks to break the troublesome pattern.

Everyone agreed to this policy, but many doubted its efficacy. To Soteria's amazement, Hugh stopped drinking, and so did everyone else. After the two weeks were up, the house went back to its normal policy of allowing consumption of alcoholic beverages. At first, Hugh was no less bizarre without alcohol than with it, but gradually his strange behavior ceased.

Soteria faced several issues with its two weeks of abstinence. It acknowledged there was a problem and admitted the failure of solving it by making it Hugh's alone. Because Hugh didn't think he had a problem, this approach gave him no reason to stop drinking. It was the group that had a problem with Hugh's drinking, and the solution had somehow, therefore, to include the group in the process.

Soteria's solution to Hugh's drinking stayed true to its commitment to create as open a system as possible to allow people the opportunity to change in a safe, supportive environment. When rules had to be made, they needed to exist for specific reasons; when the reasons went, so did the rules. Soteria's approach was basic and flexible: It promulgated only useful, enforceable restrictions, which were revoked when no longer necessary.

The Sources of Authority

Soteria maintained a structure with some basic ground rules, defined primarily by the present occupants. Another form of boundaries, however, were traditions, which played a major role in the Soteria process. When former residents returned to Soteria, their memories and progress allowed the program to develop a rich history that influenced its current course.

There was actually considerable structure at Soteria at any given time. Its source, however, rested not in administrative policies and procedures, as in the case of hospitals, but in the behavior of the members of the community as a whole.

Healthy structures, such as those guiding Soteria, are dynamic forces ever changing to fit what is currently happening. Still, certain aspects of Soteria had to fit into larger systems—for example, the mental health community, the public sector, the neighborhood, among others—so it also had to define itself in these contexts.

If Soteria's tradition conflicted with that of the broader society, Soteria's ability to effect change would have been compromised. As an element within society, Soteria had to decide to what degree to conform to its mores. Were Soteria isolated, it could fail in its mission to promote behavior that would assure survival in the world beyond its walls.

For Soteria's process to function as intended, most of its attention had to be directed internally. In concrete terms, the immediate members of the Soteria community—staff, residents, volunteers, and friends—had to be able to interact a great deal and respond to internal pressures with appropriate changes. Attention to this mission, however, could make it difficult to monitor the relationship to the broader community. To avoid potential conflicts, the administrative staff had to represent Soteria to the outside community, to attend to forces that impinged on the program from outside, and to report its findings to clinical groups. This boundary function was essential to the community's survival (see also Wilson's analysis, pages 16–17).

Maintaining Soteria

> In the real world, there's a bunch of people at this house. You know, we all have to eat and keep it clean and stuff like that. I think we always get in touch with the necessities of running a house when we have to—when you run out of peanut butter and jelly, you kind of drop the therapeutic trip, or whatever else is going on, and say, "OK, somebody's got to get it together enough to take the money out, get in a car, go to the grocery store, and buy peanut butter and jelly." There's always somebody together enough to have the energy to go and do that.
>
> —*Geoff, Soteria staff*

Soteria was a home with all of its basic needs and tasks. Staff and
residents did maintenance tasks spontaneously, and the quality of
the cleaning and cooking at any particular time reflected the interests
and needs of the group present. Sometimes individuals had different
opinions as to who should be completing necessary work and how it
should be done. Explained Tara,

> I refuse to cook all the nights I'm here. It's a male-female
> problem with some of the staff members. Often I'll make the
> male staff member cook one night, and I'll cook another
> night. I'll say, "You pick your night, and I'll take the other
> night," and he usually can do that, or else we don't eat.

In addition to the cooking, staff and residents maintained the
lawn, did the laundry, decorated the house, purchased necessary
clothes, sewed and mended, and fixed the plumbing (when
possible).

> *Loren's note: Basic maintenance is vital to every household that
> contains individuals with an interest in the welfare of each other. So
> it was at Soteria.*

Recreation Soteria-Style

Recreational activities were also usually fundamentally unplanned.
Staff member Katy described some of the house activities:

> We've had birthday parties for everybody who's been here.
> Kelly and Iris would bake their own cakes. There's been some
> candle making. We got into tie-dyeing. Kris really got caught
> up in that. The garden, that's been a really good thing for
> Chuck.
>   We've played tennis, and we've gone to the park. We go
> to the beach. I've taken Kelly and Kris ice skating, and Chuck
> goes roller skating once in a while. We go to movies. We've

gone to the Japanese gardens. We've gone to the parks up in San Francisco on the weekends.

We've done some redecorating in the rooms sometimes. Some of the girls have been into sewing. The girls have made some leather things at times. Naomi's talking about making jewelry now. We've done some work with clay. The girls have made mobiles. Kris did a lot of art work. Chuck's done a lot of writing, and so have Naomi, Kelly, and Katherine. There's quite a bit of activity actually. The fellows go and play baseball now, and basketball. We do a lot of walking or sliding, like we rode up to the snow and had snowball fights. We've gone to Mt. Hamilton to see the sun rise when nobody's feeling sleepy. Stuff like that.

Often recreational activities facilitated interaction among house members. Katy continued,

For a while there, we were playing a lot of Casino and cribbage and stuff like that. Especially with Iris, chess gave us a safe structure in which to interact. It became a regular habit every night; we'd play at least one game of chess. It wasn't really important who won, and a lot would happen during that time—you know, you might end up not making a move for 20 minutes, just talking.

Iris would ask if I wanted to play chess, and we would start talking, and she would lay out where she was at on a lot of stuff. (I enjoy playing chess to begin with.) Once we started doing it, we both recognized what it was and said what it was. I'd wait for her to ask me—when she wanted to.

Recreational activities were also helpful at times to release the tension that sometimes built up in the house. Hal recalled several trips that seemed to serve that purpose:

On that night, everyone was really depressed, up tight, so we all kind of agreed to get the hell out of there for a while. We went up on the mountainside. About halfway up, we just sat there and screamed at the top of our lungs—the four of us sitting on the mountainside, arm in arm, screaming. And every once in a while, our screams would all get at the same pitch and just reverberate through our skulls. Kelly would scream out what she was really angry about and call every name. Iris would get into it. Naomi was kind of hesitant, but then so would she, and then so would I. We just sat there and screamed for an hour—really let it out.

And then, we came back down and went over to Spivey's for some coffee. After we had the coffee, I bought them ice cream—banana splits and stuff like that. Everybody was stealing everybody else's stuff—you know, you take a bit of yours and reach over real fast and take somebody else's. When we were done with that, Kelly said she wanted to be alone for a while, and so she walked back. Iris, Naomi, and I rode back afterwards.

Other trips are also really nice. One night we were up all night with Chuck and Iris; no one could sleep. About five in the morning, they asked me if they could go for a ride. So, we went for a ride up to Hamilton again. This was just as the sun was starting to come up, and we stopped five or six places along the way and picked some flowers and watched the deer. And we got to the top just after the sun had risen and sat on the cliff there and watched the whole Bay area. That was really pretty. We were all in good space even before we went up. Iris got up there in the countryside, and she chased the deer through the woods and picked different kinds of flowers and stuff.

Other times I've taken Naomi up when she was really angry, really upset and nervous. Halfway up the mountainside, she has the radio blaring hard rock. As we drive up, she turns it further down and further down and finally off. And she doesn't turn it back on until we hit Alum Rock, coming back down again.

Loren's comment: Soteria's environment adapted itself flexibly and spontaneously to the expressed needs of its inhabitants. There was no procedure manual. When contingencies occurred, the community coped. Activities often took unpredictable turns.

For example, reported staff member Della,

> Kris, Katherine, Kelly, and I were making cupcakes, and I was mixing up some of the frosting, real gummy stuff. I started to put it on the cupcakes, and they grabbed them as soon as I did it. Then Kelly picked up one and just kind of looked at it and looked at me and grinned and went splat right in my face with it.
>
> I stood there for a minute. I could just feel this immediate tension with Katherine, who had her eyes big. Kris was just standing there. I laughed. I grabbed Kelly by the neck and scooped up some icing and rubbed it in her face. Then all of us got into it and messed around with the icing for a while. I guess we did it for about five minutes or so.

One of the most popular activities in the house was massage. Both staff and residents found that massages relaxed tension and helped them get acquainted with their bodies. For residents less able spontaneously to touch and be touched, massage provided a safe structure in which physical contact could occur. Susannah described how massage fostered communication between her and one very withdrawn resident.

> That day, we were having a real massage workshop. There were about 15 of us sitting around the living room, and we began the workshop by giving each other hand massages. My partner was Leo, and I was very unsure as to how he would react to my suddenly taking and manipulating his hands. So I began very gently, putting some lotion on his hands and then spreading it around with very light strokes.

His fingers were just phenomenal . . . incredible tension and rigidity in them. I tried to bend them, ever so slightly, and they fought me like tigers. They were like 10 steel cylinders sticking up in the air. His hands were nearly as bad. The knuckles, bones, and veins just stood out on the surface from tension. There was no flexibility anywhere in his hands. They could have been the hands of an automaton. Touching Leo's hands drew me into what was happening inside of him, and I felt my own body go tense and rigid. For an instant, I wanted to burst into tears . . . just to let all that tension go, in me and in him.

I looked at him and saw an incredible struggle going on. His face was twisted, grimacing, contorted . . . fighting God only knows who or what. I would have to be very gentle, or he would go back inside himself completely.

I began trying to relax just one finger at a time. Stroke it, hold it . . . At length, it did relax, a fraction of an inch, then stiffened back up again immediately. The other fingers followed suit. (God, his hands are as cold as ice!) And his face softened, just a little bit.

This went on for maybe five minutes. I was feeling very much in contact with Leo . . . His hands spoke eloquently of things he is not yet ready to tell us in words. And I was making my hands very soft, gentle, attentive, to tell him it's OK to let go, to relax not to be tense, to tell him I cared for him. And at length those fingers softened a little, his eyes opened, and he smiled a little.

I moved my hands so that his hands could cup around mine and explore them, if he wished. But he was not ready for that yet. We smiled, and I kept on holding his hands. A voice broke in from the outside world . . . The workshop leader was telling us to separate hands. I let go of Leo.

He sat for a moment, then started looking at his own hands as if he'd never seen them before. He stroked one hand, then the other, just as I touched them . . . grinning all the time. I grinned back. I got this message (but in smiles, not words) "Hey! These are my hands! They have feeling in them!"

The massage lady told each pair to talk among themselves about the experience they've just had. A lot of chatter all around us, but Leo and I just sat and grinned at each other. Our communication has been without words. We've said it all without them.

Loren highlights this highly perceptive level of active—involved and involving—empathy.

From time to time, either because of extreme disturbances in the house or to avoid having staff remain beyond their normal shifts, residents were invited to visit with staff at home. Susannah, who had three different residents come home with her, described some of the positive and negative aspects of such visits:

I'm aware that they're there. It isn't that comfortable. I have a feeling of being available to them. One part of me is alert all the time. But it's good for me to take them home. It's good for my kids, because then they see what I'm doing, and it's not so separate from them.

It was very good for Tracy and Iris. I don't know how good it was for Kelly. My kids dividing my attention are hard for her to take.

Susannah's experiments were not routine. They required excellent judgment, trust, common sense, and serious attention to possible impacts on disturbed clients. Because of their attention to context and thrust towards normalization, however, "home visits" were never seriously challenged as a legitimate part of life at Soteria.

Community Relations

Staff members had anticipated that, since Soteria was to be an unlocked facility in the community, they would be dealing with difficult situations involving the larger environment. Such situations arose involving neighbors, a nearby nursing home, shops, medical facilities, and the police.

Such incidents, however, were relatively infrequent; furthermore, they were merely embarrassing rather than dangerous to those involved. In most cases, staff dealt with such situations with a minimum of turmoil. Tara remembered one such time:

> Alma and Tracy and I took Kelly to get her birthday present, and Tracy couldn't keep up or didn't want to and was wandering around. So I stayed with Tracy. She went into Eastridge Imports. There was a card rack of romantic cards with big faces. She set up one of the cards as a kind of altar and knelt down and started saying the rosary in front of it.
>
> There weren't a lot of people in the store, but the lady at the desk was watching. I started to feel uncomfortable, and I didn't know what to do. Finally, I just told Tracy, "Come on, let's go." She was in sort of an ecstacy and wasn't paying any attention to me. She had her face up and her eyes closed, and she was praying. Every once in a while she'd look up at this picture of a woman. For her, it could have been the Virgin Mary or whatever.
>
> Tracy was praying and looking very holy. I figured I should buy the cards, so I paid for a couple. The lady kept looking up, but she didn't say anything, and I didn't say anything. I just went over to Tracy. Tracy started to fall into the card rack, knocking it over. With one arm I was trying to grab Tracy, so she would fall against me, and, with the other, I tried to straighten the card rack, which was very flimsy.
>
> By then, Tracy was crying. I got her up and latched on to her and dragged her out. We went through that a couple more times, just stopping, praying, keeling down . . . I just stayed with her. People were staring, but nobody was coming close enough to laugh at her or say anything. (Of course, she wasn't really disturbing anybody. She wasn't into any kind of destruction. She was just praying.) I stayed with her until we found Alma again.

That was *hours* later, and I was beginning to get very nervous.

At another time, when Tara saw the possibility that a similar excursion could result in real danger both to the residents and to other shoppers, she took firm control of the situation to avert trouble before it began:

There was the time that I took Tracy and Naomi both. At that time, Tracy was no longer into her sweet, prayerful stage. She was into breaking things, burning things, and being very mischievous. Naomi at that time was following the leader. Tracy would break a window; Naomi would break a window. Plus, Naomi was very scared of Tracy.

So, I had Chuck come with me—to keep an eye on Naomi. We got into the shopping center, and Tracy started saying, "All these windows," with a nasty look on her face. Then, Naomi started laughing, "Yeh, that would be fun. Let's break some windows."

I started getting scared. And I thought, "Crap!" I didn't know what I would do if anybody started breaking windows at Eastridge, the biggest shopping center in the world and brand new! Finally, I got pissed off and said, "If either of you break a window, I'm going to beat your butts, and we're leaving here right now!"

That shut them up for long enough to get back to the car. I drove back home where *everybody* could handle them.

Loren comments: Tara's remarkable clinical evaluation and response were possible because of her extensive knowledge of the residents involved. She offered clinical intervention at its finest.

Alma recalled that one of the most serious disturbances in the community involved a severely regressed 16-year-old named Tamara. For about three weeks, Soteria provided two staff members for her at all times. But one afternoon, when left alone for a minute, Tamara climbed out a window and was discovered about 10 minutes later riding, naked, down the street on a bicycle.

During that 10 minutes, Tamara had run to the house next door and, finding the door unlocked, entered, picked up the brand new color TV from the table and placed it gently on the floor, knocked down three vases of plastic flowers, entered the children's room, played with their toys, disrobed, placed her clothes in the washer and pedaled off on the bike she found in the garage.

The neighbor and her children returned home at the end of this caper. "Who's been playing in my house?" the neighbor exclaimed, both furious and frightened. She called the police, her husband, and her parents. For about half an hour she refused to speak with anyone from the house. When we were finally able to talk to her about an hour later, she said she was convinced that our house was ruining the neighborhood and the moral life of her daughters. She told me that Tamara should be locked up forever in the state hospital.

She kept asking me over and over again, "Doesn't she have a mother?" By the time the police arrived, however, the lady was considerably calmer. She seemed especially relieved to learn that Soteria housed emotionally disturbed young people—not drug abusers as she had thought—and with my sincere apologies and reassurance from the police that we were indeed a legitimate facility, she did not press charges against Tamara.

In retrospect, Tamara's adventure may seem humorous, but at the time it was Soteria's most difficult encounter with the community. The worried mother and her young daughters lived next door to Soteria. The patient explanations Voyce and other staff members provided helped her to find *meaning* in this unusual event rather than merely danger.

Loren finds this interaction to be "interpersonal negotiation at its finest. Real people," he comments, "are talking to real people about real events."

Introducing New Members

Staff and clients were recruited differently at Soteria than at other mental health facilities. Soteria tried to bring into its company people who not only would involve themselves in official roles in the program, but who also were comfortable being interpersonally enmeshed in the system beyond the period of critical need. Although residents could not be selected on the basis of extended involvement, most learned from staff members fairly quickly what was expected. New staff had to be compatible with the personalities of established members of the Soteria community. But not until Soteria was two years old did a clear policy begin to emerge on the process of introducing new members into the Soteria community.

The approach that turned out to make the most sense for Soteria's needs was the audition model, some variation of which was used with all persons entering Soteria—residents, staff, volunteers, and administrators. The key ingredient in this process called for newcomers to spend a given amount of time with present members of the Soteria community to allow input from both members and would-be initiates into the acceptance process. This time also gave the potential entrant a chance to see if the Soteria program offered what s/he expected.

Although the house *had* to admit all residents identified and sent by the Mental Research Institute team, Soteria staff instituted a modified audition process for everyone. This procedure reflected the community's perceived need for *everyone* to go through some type of "try out." The process was another way of muting inequalities within the community—thus making role definitions more fluid than in other settings.

So while residents were admitted as required, staff openly discussed with their new clients the two-week courtship period promulgated to fulfill many needs. One such need was the frequent original desire of new residents to leave. During the limited courtship period, reluctant residents often agreed to stay until the community could reach mutual judgment that they were ready to go. Although residents did occasionally leave after two weeks, most eventually returned if they were still dysfunctional enough to need residential care.

The Process for Hiring Staff

The first attempt to use Soteria's audition model to hire staff did not work because of a split opinion within the established group over which of two applicants to hire. The solution to this problem was to modify the consensus process by giving one person the authority to make a final decision. This process still allowed the group input without the same potential for divisiveness. The modified audition took place in a series of six steps.

Hiring

Potential staff was

1. identified
2. screened and scheduled
3. given person-to-person contact with community members
4. evaluated by all affected
5. discussed by all affected
6. hired or not

Volunteers who applied to the program were already familiar with the community, and Soteria recognized donated time as a sign of commitment; therefore, volunteer applicants had an initial advantage over totally unknown ones. Volunteers played a variety of roles at Soteria, in which they were expected to be competent. But not all volunteers were good role models, so volunteering by no means guaranteed future employment. If a volunteer appeared able to function as staff and had been involved long enough to be known by all the members of the Soteria community, only the fifth and sixth steps were necessary. If not, the process would start at the third and fourth steps of the audition process.

Volunteers were given preference in hiring but when no suitable ones were available, the community went through the hiring process in its entirety.

Step One. Everyone in the broader Soteria community would be asked to refer interested applicants to the person designated to screen and schedule. Using word-of-mouth rather than want ads had a number of advantages. It usually produced known applicants who understood the kind of commitment needed to work at Soteria. It also seemed to limit the pool of applicants to a reasonable size.

But word-of-mouth had its disadvantages as well. It tended to produce a homogeneous group while an important quality of Soteria staff was its diversity. The Soteria community included men and women of various ages, cultures, nationalities, lifestyles, and educational levels. Word-of-mouth recruiting also failed to guarantee compliance with equal opportunity responsibilities.

Step Two. Once the applicants called, the screening and scheduling process began. The first appointment weeded out obviously inappropriate candidates and helped applicants get a clearer understanding of the Soteria program.

Steps Three and Four. Once screening was complete, the remaining applicants were given appointments to talk to all Soteria members, in groups if possible or individually if necessary.

Steps three and four both stressed the importance of contact between applicants and members of the Soteria community. They differed, however, in that one focused on individual interactions and the other on group processes. Step three required a significant period of time to make an adequate judgment; step four insured enough input to enrich the next step.

Step Five. The fifth step was a house meeting specifically aimed at gathering input from as many as possible. While Soteria meetings were not mandatory, the importance of bringing a new member into the group led to well-attended sessions. At this meeting, without the candidates present, community members discussed each individual applicant separately at any reasonable length. The final decision, however, was the program director's rather than the result of consensus, as previous attempts to be democratic had led to discord.

Step Six. The final authority was the house director's for a number of reasons: He was intimately involved with the day-to-day processes; he had the authority—by job description—as well as by the respect and trust of the group; he was the natural person to whom the new staff member would be answerable; and he was willing to face the group's anger if necessary. After the hiring meeting was over, therefore, the house director took the group's information, evaluated it, and the next day informed the Soteria community of his choice. Generally his decision merely made the consensus official.

Recruiting Other Groups

After being refined by the process of hiring staff, the audition model proved useful in choosing other members of the community.

Accepting Residents. Once accepted, Soteria's new residents "tried out" for two weeks to allow people in the house the opportunity to make necessary critical assessments. All applicants identified by the Mental Research Institute auditioned, unless for some reason the community immediately thought an individual would get better care elsewhere. This method made the community responsible for persuading the potential resident to want to stay, a task made difficult by the fact that most clients preferred to be at home, which was not usually an option.

The first four steps were skipped over quickly, early in the two-week period. There was no need to recruit, a job taken care of by the research team. Screening and scheduling were also unnecessary because all new residents were asked to spend the first two weeks primarily at the house to give community members ample time to get to know them (steps three and four). Any *critical* information about matters such as aggressiveness towards self or others was disseminated to the group before the prospective residents arrived. *Because psychiatric histories rarely contributed positively to a new resident's reputation, Soteria deliberately withheld information* not *vital to the health of the community or the individuals within it.* This policy, essential to the practice of interpersonal phenomenology, allowed new residents to establish relationships not based on their previous history.

After the two-week audition, Soteria followed steps five and six. The community gathered for its forum, the regular weekly house meeting, and, in the absence of burning issues, decided to invite the new resident to stay. If a problem arose, it was either discussed to resolution or forwarded to the program director, who made the final decision, in consultation with the house psychiatrist if appropriate. But this latter process was rarely necessary—Soteria's auditions usually led to acceptance, with residents who stayed two weeks almost inevitably being invited to remain.

Checking Volunteers. Because of the variety of roles they played at Soteria, volunteers came into the community in many ways. Former residents who became volunteers needed much less investigation than people with no previous knowledge of Soteria. Some volunteers helped without a formal introduction as, for example, in the case of ex-residents, who hung around the house because of their need to participate in some way. Others went through a formal process similar to the staff-hiring procedure. People known by the members of the community—ex-residents, friends of Soteria members who had visited frequently, relatives of community members—generally didn't need the first four steps. In most cases, once someone expressed interest in becoming a volunteer, his or her offer would be brought up in a house meeting. This procedure would complete the audition to step five, leaving only step six, the decision.

The decision process for volunteers partook of elements of both the staff and resident processes. At a regular weekly house meeting, appropriate discussion took place. If there were reservations, the process resulting was like that for controversial new residents. Either the group then decided, or, if they couldn't agree, the decision again was the house director's. Eventually, volunteers were required to offer at least eight hours of service weekly on an as-needed basis. This restriction kept the group to a manageable size, minimized the number of people a resident had to face, and provided Soteria with real, essential help.

> *Loren's comment: So many groups composed of people involved in various and changing relationships led inevitably to blurred roles. Among others, Soteria welcomed former residents, students, friends, family, hangers-on, and so forth.*

Bringing in Friends. Friends of the Soteria community were a diverse group, including a French-Canadian psychiatrist who spent a sabbatical year at the house, a European psychologist who visited for two weeks, and the next-door neighbors who interacted for over a decade. Most of Soteria's friends had a direct personal relationship with one or more members of the Soteria community.

Situations where strangers live together usually necessitate a screening process for new members; however, within such living groups, friends are usually selected much less formally. At Soteria, friends usually visited initially on various errands and then became a part of the group because they and the community found something of mutual benefit or pleasure. For example, one next-door neighbor came over every day after work to play basketball, and a resident's sister became a good friend of several community members. Many friends' interaction with residents was indistinguishable from that of volunteers, and, indeed, friends who sought temporary refuge at Soteria were officially designated as volunteers. Most volunteers came consistently, however, and saw themselves as having official roles.

But friends went through none of the steps in the audition. They were simply friends—an informal and invaluable association that extended the house's network.

Learning from Soteria

FROM THE PERSPECTIVE of public mental health in 2004, the more than three-decade-old Soteria project is a groundbreaking original prototype of a means of providing humane, effective, normalizing residential care to disturbed and disturbing people whose levels of psychological distress would ordinarily have landed them in psychiatric hospitals. Variations on the original Soteria theme appear widely in today's public mental health system; such facilities are generally called crisis houses. Other centers, based either directly or with modifications on Soteria's precedent, flourish both in the United States and abroad (see pages 2–3).

So, despite the controversy Soteria frequently generated—usually because of its stance against neuroleptics—the project is making a reputation. A number of the techniques it elaborated (for example, *being with*) have been incorporated into usual mental health practice. Some of its other specific interactions and techniques, however, do not appear on these pages because no one took them down at the time they happened. Hence, a number of Soteria's (and Emanon's) contributions are unavailable to logical positivist science.

The material making up *Soteria:* Through *Madness to Deliverance* comes from a variety of sources: Audiotapes from staff debriefings, notes in clinical records, psychiatric admission workups, write-ups of particularly significant incidents, and, importantly, retrospective discussions and reconstructions among the individuals involved, particularly those consistently present for the duration of the project.

Soteria also incorporates research obtained through certain formal mechanisms summarized here.

Among *Webster's Third New International Dictionary*'s definitions of *research* is "critical and exhaustive investigation or experimentation having for its aim the discovery of new facts and their correct interpretation, *the revision of accepted conclusions, theories, or laws* in the light of newly discovered facts, or the practical applications of such new or revised conclusions, theories, or laws" (emphasis added). See *Why Soteria Worked*, pages 266–270. Readers wanting more detail should also consult the appendix, especially Mosher and Menn (1978a, 1978b); Mosher, Vallone, Menn, Hendrix, and Fort (1992); Mosher and Vallone (1992); Mosher, Vallone, and Menn (1995); and Bola and Mosher (2002, 2003).

Background and Funding

Soteria was basically federally funded. Its principal support came from a National Institute of Mental Health research grant from 1970 through 1984, save for an 18-month hiatus in the early 1980s. It also received, via the federally funded Community Mental Health Center in San Jose, a modest grant that supported some of its staff between 1974 and 1982. Finally, as part of the involvement of the Mental Research Institute in a federal jobs training program (the Comprehensive Education and Training Act, pages 117–119), Soteria hired several part-time research assistants and one staff member from 1978 to 1980. Soteria also received fees collected on a sliding scale from the residents. No state funds, the usual source of money providing mental health treatment to the uninsured, supported Soteria. Although it received no California dollars, Soteria worked with the kinds of clients seen in public (versus private) mental health systems.

For several reasons, the number of experimental subjects was modest considering the project's 12-year clinical life. Among them:

🖋 A subject could withdraw from the research at any time; however, the project remained responsible for her/his clinical care.

✐ Because the research design called for a *minimum* 28-day stay at Soteria or Emanon, information on subjects who left the experimental setting sooner was omitted from the research data. Some residents left because they had actually recovered, while others left for a variety of reasons: dissatisfaction with the program, family concerns, attempts to cure disorganization by running away, and others.

✐ Because of its chronic funding uncertainty, Soteria regularly took in nonresearch subjects, principally people with extensive histories of prior hospitalization.

These first two factors account for the exclusion of 20 to 30 individuals originally enrolled as research subjects from the final data analyses. Even with a six-month average length of stay, Soteria's six beds should have been able to house about 125 subjects over 10 years with a two-year follow-up. Emanon, open for six years, *should* have been able to work with an additional 75 clients, for a total of about 200 experimental subjects. Because so many spaces were occupied by clients who did not meet research criteria, Soteria and Emanon worked with only 82 subjects who fulfilled the terms of the experiment. After 1978, the former constituted almost all the new admissions to the project, because it seemed clear that funding for the research part of the program would end in 1980 (which it did).

The proportion of private-pay, nonresearch patients varied with the project's perceived need for additional funds. Over the study's life these persons accounted for a third or more of those participating in the program (roughly 70–80 persons). Private-pay referrals became steady as soon as the project received some publicity. Although it is hard to set a firm date for when the sharp increase in private-pay referrals occurred, it was certainly the case by 1973. During the 1971–1976 era, reports from the project appeared regularly on the programs of major national professional meetings, even when there were few outcome data to present. Because Soteria represented a real attempt to, as Webster's puts it, make a "revision of accepted conclusions, theories, or laws in the light of newly discovered facts" about the treatment of persons diagnosed as "schizophrenic," it drew a steady stream of professional visitors, volunteers, students, and trendy psychological groupies. Despite careful guarding of its boundaries (see Wilson's concept of "limiting intrusion," page 17), the project's fame grew rapidly. It was, for example, the subject of a centerpiece article in a 1972 *San Francisco Chronicle* Sunday magazine section.

Soteria's publicity resulted in the project's becoming a 1970s silver bullet aimed at the difficult offspring of wealthy psychiatric cognoscenti. Many of Soteria's private pays had not been "cured" by long stays in the fanciest psychiatric hospitals, or by the latest drugs, or by the latest fad in mental health treatment—then, "orthomolecular psychiatry" (an approach that called mainly for large doses of vitamins but in practice included neuroleptics). Many such admits were failed psychoanalytic patients.

So, for pragmatic fiscal reasons, Soteria accepted the sons and daughters of panacea seekers. Unfortunately, systematic data were not collected about their characteristics and outcomes. Impressionistically, however, while they were usually deeply satisfied to be at Soteria, few experienced dramatic changes. They usually left when their parents failed to observe the wished for and expected cure. Silver bullets are always difficult to aim, but it is especially hard to hit long-term, battle-scarred veterans of high class mental health wars. Despite the high hopes of such youngsters' parents, Soteria was not a psychiatric Lourdes.

The Research Design

Publicly funded trials of new mental health treatments in this country must worship logical positivism. To assure comparability of results, researchers must randomly assign a predefined group of persons (newly diagnosed with "schizophrenia" in this instance) to two different treatment conditions—an experimental setting and a standard one (the control). In actuality, the Soteria project operated between 1971 and 1976 with a minor (to Soteria researchers' minds, if not those of the project's critics) deviation from this practice. Because of limited space at Soteria, research candidates were sought only when there was room available. After an experimental subject had been located, the next person arriving at the referral source who met the research criteria and agreed to participate in the project became a control subject. This design generated comparable groups efficiently by keeping limited space full.

In 1975, federal logical positivists demanded *strict* random assignment. Their process also resulted in exactly comparable groups, but it slowed considerably the acquisition of research subjects. It also institutionalized at Soteria the admission of private-pay subjects in order to keep the facility full. The National Institute of Mental Health's reviewers' rigid application of principle had negative consequences, which they neither foresaw nor had to solve. On the other hand, the lack of strict random assignment has provoked certain critics to dismiss Soteria's results from the 1971–1976 cohort.

Damned if you do; damned if you don't.

Another clinical trial icon is the "double blind." Basically, this principle intends to prevent researchers and clinical personnel from knowing whether a given patient is receiving experimental or control treatment. Most drug protocols follow double-blind procedures; but even under ideal conditions, maintaining a pure double blind is difficult for many reasons. Even "active" placebos (designed to give side effects similar to drugs being investigated) are usually identifiable as being different from drug effects. When staff observe the side effects they have been told to expect, they are no longer blind. So *double blindness*, as opposed to physiological blindness, is at best relative. It sells well to grant reviewers, however.

The Soteria experiment was inherently flawed in this respect. Because two entirely different types of facilities and programs were being compared, the independent research team could not possibly be blind about what kind of therapeutic experience clients were having. Critics point out that the researchers collecting the data could have been biased in favor of the experimental facility, and that results favoring Soteria could have been influenced by such a predilection. Clearly, this is possible. It is also possible, however, that project reviewers were biased against the experimental setting. They weren't blind either.

Because the project's results are based mainly on face-valid outcome measures (that is, questions of fact) about which raters need not exercise any judgment, the chance of bias either way is reduced. Nonetheless, these two design problems—lack of strict random assignment between 1971 and 1976 and nonblindness throughout— have encouraged some critics to dismiss or invalidate all of Soteria's results.

The project's selection criteria were designed to choose a relatively homogeneous group of persons with similar background characteristics who had recently developed, and been labeled by three independent clinicians, as having "schizophrenia."[17]

Because Loren believed a new treatment should be tested on the most problematic clients within this generally heterogeneous diagnostic group—that is, "schizophrenics"—the Soteria project— control and experimental—took in only young, single persons. Psychiatric literature has consistently shown people with these two characteristics—young age at "schizophrenia's" onset and unmarried status—as having *statistically* poor long-term prospects for recovery. (See, for example, Strauss et al., 1977.) Ergo, the Soteria project set itself a challenge—to intervene positively in the lives of young people expected, as a group, to experience long-term disability. The project did not, however, generally have to contend with the phenomenon of *learned patienthood* secondary to frequent or prolonged institutionalization. (For such individuals, effective treatment must distinguish behavior aimed to meet the psychiatric-patient expectations that they have learned to fulfill and behavior sincerely reflective of madness or sanity.)

The data collected at entry, six weeks, six months, and one and two years postadmission were mainly framed by scientific convention and common sense. Researchers collected basic individual and family fact sheet demographic data at entry (for example, age, sex, religion, ethnicity, education, parental occupation, and so forth). Besides diagnoses, at each point in time, researchers recorded basic psychiatric symptom data. At follow-up (6, 12, and 24 months), they noted events

---

[17] See pages 63–64 for the stringent six qualifying criteria.

such as readmission to a mental hospital or other facility, symptom level and change, living arrangements (independent, with family, or in halfway houses), occupation (work, school, unemployment), and friendship patterns.

Every attempt was made to prevent bias. The independent research raters

- rotated between experimental and control subjects
- were trained and retrained to 90-percent agreement among raters on judgment measures (mainly the level of symptoms and degree of change in them)
- solicited objective face-valid information, such as

—Are you working?
—How many hours per week?
—At what hourly wage?
—Where are you living?
—Have you been hospitalized?

The study's basic design characteristics and complete listings of the type of data collected are available in the literature (see especially Mosher & Menn, 1977, 1978a and 1978b; Matthews, Roper, Mosher, & Menn, 1979; Mosher, 1989; Mosher et al., 1995; Bola & Mosher, 2002 and 2003).

Like all productive research, Soteria's science was necessarily subjective, reflecting its carefully examined reality, not what paleontologist Stephen Jay Gould called the "myth"

> that science itself is an objective enterprise, done properly only when scientists can shuck the constraints of their culture and view the world as it really is . . . .
>
> I believe that science must be understood as a social phenomenon, a gutsy, human enterprise, not the work of robots programmed to collect pure information. I also present this view as an upbeat for science, not as a gloomy epitaph for a noble hope sacrificed on the altar of human limitations.

Science, since people must do it, is a socially embedded activity. It progresses by hunch, vision, and intuition. Much of its change through time does not record a closer approach to absolute truth, but the alteration of cultural contexts that influence it so strongly. Facts are not pure and unsullied bits of information; culture also influences what we see and how we see it. The most creative theories are often imaginative visions imposed upon facts; the source of imagination is also strongly cultural.

This argument, although still anathema to many practicing scientists, would, I think, be accepted by nearly every historian of science. (1981, pp. 21–22)

While good science is subjective, its data collection is careful and thorough. Such was the case with the Soteria project's *methods*.

Requiring *three* independent diagnoses of "schizophrenia" for a subject's inclusion in a study was almost unheard of in 1960s clinical research designs. So was requiring that subjects stay at least 7 days in the hospital or 28 at Soteria to be sure they received full treatment. Because the Soteria project's basic hypothesis was that the special social environments established in the house would be the central ingredient facilitating recovery, the study paid careful attention (via the Moos Social Environment Scales)[18] to the nature of the treatment environments, making sure they conformed to theoretical expectations and ensuring that the experimental and control settings differed appropriately and were stable over time.

---

[18] The Moos scales were designed to assess the social environments of psychiatric hospital wards and community-based psychiatric treatment programs, such as group homes and rehabilitation centers. The scales' reliability, validity, and norms have been established through studies in the United States and elsewhere. The instrument, a 100-item, true-false, self-report, generates 10 variables representing how participants perceive their environment. The variables include involvement, support, spontaneity, autonomy, practical orientation, personal-problem orientation, tolerance of anger and aggression, order and organization, program clarity, and staff control. For further information, see Wendt, Mosher, Matthews, and Menn, 1983.

In short, Soteria's detractors to the contrary, its methodology was state of the art, even according to the era's logical-positivist icon. There is no valid reason to mistrust the basic results that emerged from its original common-sense design. The research Tower of Babel demanded by its multitudes of reviewers added only cost, confusion, and complexity. In fact, the project was nearly killed by the kindness of its unusually ambivalent (and mostly unwelcome) consultant-reviewers, all with their own agendas. With friends like these, Soteria needed no enemies. The peer reviewers' willingness to redesign the study according to their own wishes was a source of astonishment and discomfort to project staff. Such intervention probably reflected a combination of the reviewers' anxiety about what they feared was a radical, antipsychiatric, counter-culture project, and project designers' ambivalence about conforming to the tenets of linear causality their evaluators' logical positivism demanded.

Seven Soteria Results

It is difficult to quantify some of Soteria's "results"; other data can be counted. The most important are summarized here; other studies are listed in the appendix.

The present system of psychiatric treatment that relies on hospital beds as the site of interventions for seriously disturbed and disturbing ("psychotic") individuals was created in the United States by reformers at work about a century and a half ago. The original deviance-as-illness metaphor, however, goes back much further. In an attempt to save certain priests' and nuns' lives during the Inquisition, a 16th-century Spanish bishop explained their deviant beliefs as "illness" (to be "treated") rather than "heresy" (to be "punished"). They were "treated" in so-called "mental *hospitals,*" mainly converted, depopulated leprosaria. Hospitals treat sickness, and the social deviants they housed were defined as "ill"; hence, these "patients" were properly "treated" in places that work to "cure" illness. Over time, Western culture has come to accept and expect this intervention, which is generally perceived as humane and civilized. So pleased were people generally with this out-of-sight, out-of-mind solution to the specter of madness and deviance, few noticed how cruel it was for most of the people it was supposed to be helping. Criticism of this form of "treatment"— for example, Albert Deutsch's *Shame of the States* (1948), W. C. Beers's *A Mind That Found Itself* (1939), Goffmann's *Asylums* (1961), and Whitaker's *Mad in America: Bad Science, Bad Medicine, and the Enduring Mistreatment of the Mentally Ill* (2002)—resulted in little actual reform. Hiding egregious practices from public view was apparently easier than changing them. Wilson also reported on what actually happens on psych wards, however (pages 16–17 and 27–30); so does Voyce (*The Use of Force*, pages 132–134).

The Soteria Project thrust itself—willy-nilly—into an adversarial position against the dominant view of madness as illness needing cure in mental hospitals with drugs prescribed by physicians. And, during the course of its 12 turbulent years, it came up with seven findings of distinct philosophical, if not always statistical, import.

Result One

The Soteria project created, staffed, and operated (until the money ran out) two facilities, on whose model several current European treatment centers are now operating, that worked from a totally different perspective than its hospital ward comparison settings. The medical model of treating mentally disturbed individuals, with drugs, in hospitals, and by mental health professionals, was muted, if not denied, in the experimental settings. And, in short, the Soteria nonmedical model worked.

Result Two

Until recently, research on psychosocial interventions has been plagued by a major practical problem. Unlike many drug studies, they were unable to define precisely and consistently the nature of the interventions/processes taking place and being studied. Psychosocial approaches, by definition subjective, produce results difficult if not impossible to quantify.

Nonetheless, the Soteria project successfully established and defined replicable social environments whose characteristics were stable over time. Hence, it defined a process with known ingredients and knowable effects. Despite their highly individualized relationships with residents, staff perceived Soteria interventions to be similar across the two settings and very different from those occurring in the social environments of the control facilities. Basically, staff perceptions in the two experimental programs differed significantly from those of the control facilities on 8 of the Moos's 10 variables (see note, page 254). Their ideas about the degree of autonomy allowed and order and organization were similar. But staff at Soteria and Emanon viewed their milieus as offering higher program levels of involvement, support, spontaneity, personal-problem orientation, tolerance of anger and aggression, and lower levels of staff control and program clarity than did hospital personnel. These different patterns remained stable over the project's life. (See Wendt et al., 1983; Mosher et al., 1995.)

Result Three

Many wards that deal with acute psychosis rely upon forced injectable medication, seclusion (isolation in a padded cells), restraints (binding to a bed or chair), and electroshock therapy to control unmanageable psychotic behavior.

The two Soteria project facilities used none of these restraining measures as part of their treatment repertoires. They successfully dealt with acutely psychotic and usually unmedicated clients for more than a decade without them. Rarely were clients hospitalized directly from the houses. Rarely did clients get into enough trouble in the community to be hospitalized. Basically, clients admitted were successfully cared for in the houses without the use of the usual chemical/physical restraints. (See Mosher, 1991.)

Conclusion: Acute psychosis, in a properly designed environment, can be dealt with interpersonally, without the mechanical and chemical controls used routinely in most hospital settings.

Result Four

Most treatment of illness is pragmatic; practitioners look and listen, make a diagnosis, and do what they think will fix the problem. When a valid and reliable diagnosis is followed by causally based treatment, theory becomes unimportant compared to observation and the factual results of laboratory and other tests. Psychiatry, broadly defined, is at a serious disadvantage with regard to physical medicine in this regard: Diagnosis, because it results basically from personal judgment, can be unreliable and unstable over time. Unlike medical diagnoses, psychiatric ones cannot be validated by laboratory tests, X-rays, and the like. Treatment based on correcting the cause of the problem is only hypothetically possible.

Concurs Kate Millett,

> The entire construct of the "medical model" of "mental illness"—what is it but an analogy? Between physical medicine and psychiatry: The mind is said to be subject to disease in the same manner as the body. But whereas in physical medicine there are verifiable physiological proofs—in damaged or affected tissue, bacteria, inflammation, cellular irregularity—in mental illness, alleged socially unacceptable behavior is taken as a symptom, even as proof, of pathology. (There are exceptions to this: brain tumors, paresis [tertiary syphilis], Huntington's chorea, and Alzheimer's disease—in each of these there is indeed physical evidence of cellular damage. However, these conditions are not what we mean by mental illness. What we generally mean—schizophrenia, manic depression, paranoia, borderline personality disorders, and so forth—are all illnesses which are established upon behavioral and not physical grounds). Diagnosis is based upon impressionistic evidence: conduct, deportment, and social behavior. Furthermore, it may not even be experienced by the afflicted part, but instead may be observed by others who declare such a one afflicted. (1990, p. 311)

So, *theory* tends to rule treatment. Faulty genes, chemical imbalances, instinctual conflicts, learned deviant behaviors are examples of theories that guide psychiatric interventions. The Soteria project was able to eschew such approaches. Rather, it successfully put into operation and researched a nontheoretical theory of interpersonal phenomenology. Simply put, the Soteria credo, transmitted via staff-resident interactions, was "what you see, hear, and feel is what you've got—deal with it as best you can." *No* prescriptive rules governed Soteria staff's therapeutic approach. From this stance evolved, bottom-up, a number of techniques (see pages 125–164), which were neither imposed nor theoretically predetermined. Such techniques grew out of the repetitive interactions that took place between and among residents and staff at Soteria and Emanon.

Loren also identified a set of umbrella milieu characteristics, derived from the project's clinical work and summarized in Loren's and Lorenzo Burti's book, *Community Mental Health* (1994):

The important [milieu characteristics of residential alternatives to hospitalization] are commonsensical to clinicians who have dealt extensively with psychosis. The environment should be quiet, stable, predictable, consistent, clear, and accepting. The milieu functions that should be emphasized early in the course of a person's stay in this type of environment are: (1) *control of stimulation* so as to prevent the person from being overwhelmed by incoming stimuli; (2) *provision of respite or asylum*—that is, a place to be away from where the psychosis evolved; (3) *protection or containment* of poorly controlled behaviors engendered by the psychosis; (4) *contact with people* in touch with, and supportive of, the person's immediate experience; (5) early on, *validation* of the person's experience as real, even though it cannot be *consensually* validated. Hallucinations are all too real to the psychotic person. They should be acknowledged and respected as part of his/her experience, and an attempt should be made to understand them and how they are reflected in feelings and behavior. In no instance should they be labeled as "not real" or "only part of the illness." To do so would impede the development of a relationship, since it would affirm yet another disjunction between how the client experiences the world and how it is experienced by representatives of "reality." Bringing the subjective and objective reality together takes time and can best be done in the context of a positive relationship. This relationship is best facilitated by planting oneself solidly in the client's shoes. This may call for a temporary suspension of one's own objective reality—an often frightening experience. We encourage this stance because we've so often found it to be helpful. Try it, you might actually come to like it!

The five important functions of [residential alternatives to hospitalization] as psychosis is subsiding, are more . . . complex and require increased participation on the part of the client. By structure we mean close ongoing relationships with lots of feedback—not a highly organized program of daily activities. While sometimes useful, such prescriptive activities are not usually individualized, flexible, and responsive enough to suit the clientele's needs.

Involvement means setting the expectation that the client will begin to resume participation in her/his life, beginning with personal activities (doing laundry, setting appointments, etc.) and chores necessary for house maintenance (e.g., cooking, cleaning). *Socialization* includes gradually expanding the circle of people with whom the person relates, first within the setting, then outside. *Collaboration* and negotiation denote an interactive process that will begin to identify goals and strategies for achieving them. The result of this process will be a map for the future— a discharge *plan,* if you will.

Obviously many of these functions go on at the same time, and different ones will be more in evidence on different days. They should not be viewed as occurring in a stepwise progression. (pp. 121–122)

Since the mid-1950s, it has become usual and customary for doctors to use antipsychotic drugs to control the outward symptoms of acute psychosis. In addition to their therapeutic properties, these powerful drugs can have a number of short and long-term side effects and toxicities. Many patients experience these drugs as unpleasant in general; some have terrifying, uncontrollable neck and face muscle spasms (dystonia) soon after their administration. Others develop involuntary finger movements (tremor) and facial and other muscular stiffness like that found in Parkinson's disease. The result can be an expressionless, zombie-like individual, who moves slowly and stiffly. Others suffer a motor restlessness syndrome (akathisia) or become immobile (akinesia). Later, about 5 percent per year (that is, 20 percent in four years) of persons treated continuously with these drugs develop uncontrollable twitching of the tongue, facial, and neck muscles (tardive dyskinesia—late occurring abnormal muscle movements). This iatrogenic condition is untreatable, usually irreversible, and always disfiguring.[19]

At two years, the 43 percent of Soteria's residents who had not been exposed to the dangers of antipsychotic drugs had even better outcomes than those of the Soteria group as a whole. While difficult to quantify, the saving in reduction of human suffering from medication effects warrants serious consideration.

Result Five

The fashionable disease model of "schizophrenia" posits that, while environmental factors may trigger or ameliorate the course of this illness, its basic outcome is determined by genetically determined, biochemically mediated chemical transmitters in the central nervous system. Based on this theory, biochemical intervention with the antipsychotic drugs that change the levels of a number of these transmitters should be the mainstay of treatment.

---

[19] Breggin (2000) notes the inadequacy of the length of most drug trials given the duration of time the drugs are typically prescribed: ". . .Psychiatrists commonly tell their patients, 'It can take eight weeks or more for the drug to take full effect.' Yet there is little evidence in support of this assertion, given that clinical trials seldom last beyond four to six weeks" (p. 38).

The Soteria project revealed the power of psychosocial processes to effect the short—(six-week) and long-term (two-year) course of what psychiatry labels "schizophrenia." Contrary to many expectations, the social environments at Soteria and Emanon were as effective in significantly reducing overall levels of acute psychotic symptoms (for example, inability to communicate logically, agitation, unfounded beliefs, hearing voices, and so forth) within six weeks as hospital treatment with antipsychotic medication. Most (75 percent) of the residents at Soteria and Emanon either never received or received only briefly these medications during their acute psychotic states. (See Mosher & Menn, 1978b; Mosher et al., 1995; Mosher & Bola, 2004).

Since residents spent most of the follow-up period in the community, accounting for their general continued well-being is important. Most responsible seem to be the informal friendship networks made up of exresidents, volunteers, students, and staff that grew up around the experimental facilities (see pages 65–77 for a detailed explanation of this process). These networks, sometimes through active recruitment, were almost always able to absorb graduates of the houses. The facilities themselves served as contact and support liaison points. Informal peer groups organized employment, housing, socialization, and recreation. These networks appear to have eased the transition from residence to independence.

Loren and John Bola recently analyzed the combined two-year outcome data from both cohorts using newly refined statistical methods that allow adjustment for missing observations, differential attrition between groups, subject loss, proportion with *DSM IV* schizophrenia, and length of postgraduation follow-up period. The basic results: All Soteria residents did significantly better two years after entry to the program on an eight-variable global outcome measure (that tracked rehospitalization and psychopathology as well as independent living, working, and social functioning) than did controls. Soteria residents diagnosed with *DSM IV* schizophrenia also did significantly better than controls at two years. (See Bola & Mosher, 2002, 2003.)

Result Six

Madness, psychosis, lunacy, insanity, "schizophrenia," disturbed and disturbing behavior, manic depression, and so forth are generally the purview of mental health practitioners. Dealing with "illness" is usually seen as needing special education and experience. Certainly as "diseases" they need medical doctoring. So goes the medicalization of madness.

In the Soteria project, the medicalization of newly diagnosed psychosis was muted and proletarianized. A sympathetic staff without formal medical training could relate to insanity, which was for them understandable and rarely threatening. While such personnel may serve in other mental health settings, at Soteria and Emanon they had primary therapeutic responsibility and power; they did not function as extensions of medically trained staff. Yes, they received training and supervision, but they made and took responsibility for quick, important decisions.

There was no protocol, manual, or hierarchy. They were on their own. This is the heart of empowerment, and, at Soteria and Emanon, it usually seemed to work for both residents and staff.

Result Seven

How much treatment at Soteria cost compared to the cost for usual treatment—psychiatric hospitalization and medication—is, unfortunately, difficult to answer definitively, primarily because the project's design in 1970 did not call for collecting data that would yield sophisticated cost-benefit analysis.

In terms of today's dollars, the daily cost of treating an acutely psychotic individual in various types of facilities is about

- $680 on a psychiatric ward of a general hospital
- $365 at a state hospital (these facilities do not usually treat "acute" patients)
- $150 in a residential alternative to hospitalization like Soteria

Because of large average differences in length of stay in the three facilities, however, one can be misled by comparing these numbers directly. This admitted, some aspects of comparative cost/benefits to individuals treated at residences like Soteria and in psychiatric hospitals bear noting. Individuals treated at Soteria and Emanon

✎ had outcomes at six weeks comparable to those of hospitalized patients

✎ had significantly better overall two-year outcomes than those of hospitalized patients (see Result Five)

So, experimental subjects benefitted more than did controls. Unfortunately, the dollar savings that might have accrued from these better outcomes cannot be reliably quantified. The project was able to determine direct treatment costs for the initial six months of care for subjects (N=79) in the first cohort (1971–1976). Both experimental and control subjects received about $4,000 in 1976 dollars ($12,800 in today's dollars) worth of treatment in their initial six months (Mosher & Menn, 1978). Most of this cost for the Soteria/Emanon persons was the result of five-month initial stays (on average) in one experimental facility or the other. Costs for subjects treated in hospitals included only an average of 30 days of inpatient care. The balance of their costs came from extensive day care, individual and group therapy, and medication visits.

Thus, in practice, the Soteria/Emanon model cannot be said to have been cheaper—at least for the initial six months. While Soteria graduates used fewer mental health resources in the community than ex-patients, Soteria study data are not sufficiently detailed to yield a cost-saving comparison between the groups.

In the 1990s, however, a residential alternative to psychiatric hospitalization called McAuliffe House (Maryland), which was in many ways like Soteria House, was compared with treatment on the ward of a general hospital in a random assignment study. Costs for the two facilities were compared in a six-month all-inclusive study that considered costs of residential, outpatient, medical, crisis, and day care; psychosocial rehabilitation; supported living arrangements;

federal assistance programs like Supplemental Security Income and Social Security Disability Income; jail time and police 911 calls, and the like. The six-months' cost was about $19,000 for residents in the alternative facility and $26,000 for patients in hospitals. (See J. M. Fenton, L. R. Mosher, J. M. Herrell & C. R. Blyler, 1998 and W. S. Fenton, J. S. Hoch, J. M. Herrell, L. R. Mosher, & L. Dixon, 2002.)

While the basic philosophy, social structure, type of staff, relationships formed, and basic attitudes were similar in McAuliffe House to those of the original Soteria/Emanon facilities, there were important differences:

- The project admitted any voluntary client *deemed in need of hospitalization* regardless of age, diagnosis, marital status, length of illness, suicidality, homicidality, or type and number of symptoms. Among other things, this open-admissions policy meant that the subjects in this study were much older (on average, 37 years) than the 20-year-olds typical at Soteria. In addition, McAuliffe residents had had an average of 12 previous hospitalizations (compared to the 0.5 of Soteria's population) and suffered from all the major *DSM IV* "severe" diagnostic symptoms (schizophrenia, schizoaffective disorder, bipolar disorder, major depression, and so on). Ninety-five percent of people admitted to McAuliffe came with diagnoses of psychosis. They were representative of long-term chronic clients of the public mental health system and were frequently readmitted to acute intensive care.

- Conventional (that is, nearly universal) use of psychotropic drugs was usual in both McAuliffe House and the hospital. Thus, nearly all the subjects were taking one or more psychiatric drugs.

- Initial lengths of stay were much shorter at McAuliffe House than at Soteria both for the alternatively treated groups (19 days) and for those hospitalized (12 days). Brief stays meant that individuals suffering from acute episodes of mental distress could be treated less expensively at McAuliffe than in the hospital ($3,000 vs. $5,000). The alternative setting was about 44 percent cheaper than the hospital, despite the fact that residents spent more time in McAuliffe than in the hospital.

✎ Clinical outcomes were comparable for ex-patients and ex-residents (Fenton et al., 1998).

McAuliffe House moved the Soteria model of care for acutely psychotic persons more into mainstream psychiatric thinking, largely because it accepted the use of antipsychotics and other psychotropic drugs as a fact of clinical life. The result was that about 90 percent of persons who would have otherwise been hospitalized were treated in a nonhospital residential alternative at substantial savings to taxpayers. In fact, if one extrapolates, this study's six-month cost savings to one year, the subjects treated alternatively would have saved the system about $14,000 per client per year!

As a result of this study, Maryland asked the federal government for a waiver in its Medicaid program to allow the state to pay for "crisis residential care." Thereafter, a number of new programs based on the McAuliffe House (modified Soteria) model were developed statewide.

For the original Soteria model to be dramatically cost-saving, shorter initial lengths of stay would have been necessary. Thus, Luc Ciompi's Swiss Soteria-Bern, one of only two fairly exact Soteria replications, was slightly more expensive than psychiatric hospitalization until initial lengths of stay were reduced to three months or less (personal communication, 1992).

Why Soteria Worked

In light of the results just described, it is clear that the Soteria program was significantly more helpful for persons newly diagnosed as having "schizophrenia" than was traditional hospital and neuroleptic treatment. This book describes specific aspects of the interventions at Soteria. Three decades after the doors closed at Soteria (and Emanon), Loren and Voyce tried to trace the dots described in this volume—What, *overall,* was different in these milieus from those offered by usual approaches?

Soteria worked, they believe, because of the interaction of a number of factors, the most important of them the intangible and immeasurable qualities of the dedicated people who chose to work there. *Soteria and Emanon staff saw the residents they were there to help as valuable, if flawed and unhappy, individuals whom they expected to improve.* Probably the single most important part of why residents at Soteria became less damaged was the direct result of the relationships established among the participants—staff, clients, volunteers, students, anyone who spent a significant amount of time there. It is, of course, fair to ask, How can one establish a confiding, significant relationship with someone who is disorganized and psychotic? At Soteria, the staff's sympathetic attitudes and positive expectations, along with other, less subjective, factors, made such essential social interactions possible.

Soteria's staff were psychologically strong, independent, mature, warm, and empathic, traits they shared with most of the staff of the control facilities. Soteria staff were, however, more intuitive, introverted, flexible, and tolerant of altered states of consciousness than workers on general hospital psychiatric wards (Hirschfeld et al.,1977). These cognitive and attitudinal variables were highly relevant to Soteria staff's work. Soteria data do not reveal whether these differences were state-related characteristics growing out of staff's experience at Soteria or were preexisting personality traits they brought to the job. But wherever and however these qualities developed, Soteria staff's ability to relate to the residents and to each other was vital to the program's success. (See *Some Problems and Some Solutions,* pages 125–164.) Because they worked 24- or 48-hour shifts, Soteria staff could *be with* residents (see pages 169–201) for periods of time that staff of ordinary psychiatric facilities could not. Thus, staff were able to experience, firsthand, complete "disordered" psychological and biological cycles. (Ordinarily, only family members or significant others have access to such experiences over an extended period of time.)

Soteria House was a homelike, nonmedical and unmedicated, normalizing place with a quiet, safe, supportive, protective, and predictable social environment. Similar milieus can be established in a variety of places: They should

- be small—housing no more than 10 persons, including staff
- be the psychotic person's place of residence for as long as necessary
- encourage involvement from significant others
- have a ratio of helpers to residents between one to one and two to one

Soteria's proposed staffing-to-residents ratio was one to three. Its actual optimal ratio—one to one—was usually made possible by the generosity of volunteers and the help of residents (who usually stayed about five months) well enough into recovery from their own psychosis to enter into close, supportive relationships with other residents in more difficult straits.

For many reasons, such environments cannot usually flourish within psychiatric hospitals or on their grounds. Perhaps the paramount impediment is their staff's widespread belief in schizophrenic chronicity and biomedical philosophy.

From ethnographic and anthropological perspectives, the social processes differed greatly between the houses and the control facilities (general psychiatric wards). Five characteristics at Soteria and Emanon set them apart from the hospitals: The houses

- avoided codified rules, regulations, and policies
- kept basic administrative time to a minimum to allow a great deal of undifferentiated time
- limited intrusion by outsiders
- worked out social order on an emergent face-to-face basis
- followed a nonmedical model that did not require symptom suppression.

Wilson's (1974, 1983) description of the hospital procedures based on labeling and aimed at discharge shows the essential differences in approach between the control and experimental facilities (See pages 27–30).

Soteria succeeded in part because its staff unconsciously embraced the principles Jerome Frank found to be essential for positive psychotherapeutic outcomes in 1972.[20] They are the

- ✎ presence of what is perceived as a *healing context*
- ✎ development of a confiding relationship with a helper
- ✎ evolution of a *plausible causal* explanation for the reason the problem at hand developed
- ✎ generation of positive *expectations* by the therapist's personal qualities
- ✎ provision of *opportunities for success* through therapeutic processes

Certainly the two California facilities came to be seen as healing contexts, though whether they were perceived to be more helpful than the hospitals remains unknown. A major defect in the Soteria Project was the lack of a measure of client satisfaction. Actually, because of Soteria and Emanon's uniqueness, they might well have been seen as healing contexts only after some period of time, while hospitals immediately enjoy this expectation by shared cultural definition.

Because social interactions were highly valued at Soteria, "confiding relationships" were difficult to avoid. In addition, the milieus' contexts were structured to remove usual institutional barriers to the growth of such relationships.

Loren has already emphasized how important finding meaning in psychosis is to recovery, an approach synonymous to Frank's "plausible causal explanation." Both staff and residents expected recovery from psychosis, and each new generation of both groups came to Soteria embracing the same optimistic culture. The ambiance among both the afflicted and their helpers was typical of the "positive expectations" at Soteria. What could be more optimistic than to expect

---

[20] Frank's massive review of studies of therapy found, to his amazement, that variables ordinarily thought to be predictive of outcome, such as therapist experience, duration of treatment, type of problem, patient characteristics, theory of the intervention, etc., generally bore no relationship to client outcome.

recovery of persons experiencing the most severe, and putatively least curable, of crises, "schizophrenia"? See particularly *Some Problems and Some Solutions* (pages 125–164) for examples of how problematic behaviors and situations were consistently framed in positive terms. Staff encouraged residents to deal with their often very serious conditions in ways that helped clients not only to retain or even to create self-esteem but also, often, to learn something helpful about how to cope better.

The community set modest, achievable goals and noted progress towards them with encouragement. In fact, very disorganized persons can find "opportunities for success" relatively easily. A bath after weeks of not bathing is a major accomplishment!

While Frank's atheoretical formulation by no means accounts completely for why Soteria worked, it does provide a useful set of generic explanatory principles to apply in evaluating therapeutic programs.

Soteria's successful black box remains open to further interpretation.

From the Microcosm to the Macrocosm

The Soteria project suggests that newly diagnosed schizophrenic patients can be treated as well or better and at no greater cost in a community setting as in hospital. These results are consistent with those of others who have studied nonhospital alternative treatments.

Roger B. Straw (1982) found that in 19 of 20 studies he considered, outcomes were as good or better in the alternative groups than those in hospitals. In addition, as Loren has noted, residential care is considerably more cost-effective than hospitalization. Have these presentations of scientific evidence resulted in a shift away from the use of hospitals to use of alternative methods of care in the United States? Basically, the answer is no.

The evidence has not persuaded private practice-oriented psychiatry in this nation that nonhospital alternatives are a useful ingredient in the therapeutic smorgasbord. This is no longer true in

American *public* mental health, where the notion of crisis residences has caught on (B. A. Stroul, 1987).

The Soteria experiment changed the lives of many people. Voyce, Loren, and the members of the staff who have tried to collect and write down the experience of this unique place in mental health history are humble about how little they've succeeded in transmitting, despite their best efforts. When the findings reported here become known, more attempts to replicate its setting, methods, and results will be welcome.

A study that implicitly calls into question the medical model, the need for psychiatric hospitals, the efficacy of antipsychotic drugs, sometimes even the mental health professions themselves, is unlikely to be popular. At this point, only a few have attempted to replicate the Soteria model. The most venerable, the Swiss Soteria-Bern project, running for 20 years since its establishment by Luc Ciompi, is coming up with results similar to those reported here. Soteria also has some offspring on the U.S. East Coast, and several grandchildren in Europe. (See pages 2–3.)

Resisting Soteria's Teachings

Why, in the era of "scientific" psychiatry, have these types of facilities and clinical care paradigms not been widely implemented? The answers are both complex and elusive. One, at times, is that studies like those reported here were seen as either insufficiently rigorous, or as not providing convincing evidence, or as based on one-time, unreplicable products of the investigators' enthusiasm and dedication.

If the evidence presented is in itself acceptable, however, why is the next step—its application to clinical care settings—not? Loren thinks that the implementation of such alternatives might be considered unacceptable because they represent a threat to inhospital psychiatry's turf. The major element of the Soteria program—typical to a greater or lesser extent for most alternatives, was, put positively—

its rehumanizing of madness. Put negatively, as from the standpoint of traditional hospital psychiatry, it was the demedicalizing of psychosis. To defend itself against the incursion of Soteria-like facilities, hospital-based psychiatry has manned four big guns.

1. In spite of the stunning cost-effectiveness of facilities like Soteria/Emanon, no third-party payers in the United States are willing to underwrite mental care in such residences. Traditional psychiatry has not actively moved to *prevent* third-party payment for alternatives; however, it has not *sought* it.

   The ultimate viability of alternatives in the therapeutic marketplace resides with funding sources (which is why Soteria-like facilities are becoming available in public systems but not in private ones). The degree of interest these fiscal intermediaries have in paying for innovations in care is strongly influenced by the prevailing *Zeitgeist*. In the last several decades, there has been a substantial shift in the spirit of American psychiatry—away from a socioenvironmental emphasis to a more medical-biological point of view. Biomedically-oriented mainstream psychiatry puts little pressure on insurance companies to pay for what it views as nonmedical treatment. Another relevant manifestation of the biomedical *Zeitgeist* is that psychiatry is doing what it believes it must to continue to qualify for third-party payment, that is, it is continuing to advocate and use hospital-based wards.

2. Community psychiatry has been medicalized. It is ironic that the now nearly 40-year-old community psychiatry movement (a *social* psychiatric reform) in the United States has moved the mental health system into closer juxtaposition with the somatic health system. That is, the relative isolation of mental health before the 1960s—as manifested in state hospitals usually distant from patients' friends and families—was broken down with the advent of community mental health, with its emphasis on inpatient care on wards in local general medical hospitals. The growth of such wards was spurred by

psychiatric coverage in health insurance programs and by government-sponsored Medicare and Medicaid. Payment for inpatient care in general hospitals has often been America's only consistently available mental health benefit. These two factors account in large part for growth of these wards and their becoming the principal sites of inpatient care.

The process of bringing "mental illness" back into the mainstream of medicine was given further impetus by a flurry of developments in medical technology. A whole array of new and sophisticated techniques became available for use in the search for the "schizococcus," an ironic turn of phrase that nonetheless conveys the desperation in medicine's search for a specific one-factor etiology causing "schizophrenia." Other cocci are being sought for other specific forms of mental illness. Application of these techniques to "mental illness" has provided a deluge of new information but has as yet failed to discover specific etiologic factors in psychosis. In addition, in a characteristically American fashion, a new generation of technology-oriented biological psychiatrists has risen to positions of influence and power in many medical school departments of psychiatry.

3.   Neuroleptics have been seen as salvation: The answer at last? Or wishes transformed to myths? Another important factor in the progressive medicalization of madness has been the introduction and widespread use of neuroleptic drugs, which are widely believed to be efficacious treatments for psychosis. Drugs can only be prescribed by MDs; thus, so long as drugs are viewed as *the* answer to mental illness, physicians' power and control over the treatment system are inevitable and will increase.

Because pills are given to individuals, they maintain medicine's traditional focus on a person as diseased. This can prevent the doctor and the system over which s/he presides from looking at the family and wider social contextual factors that might have exerted important influences on the development of psychosis—and might also therefore be amenable to intervention. Thus, medications narrow conceptual sights and limit treatment possibilities.

4. The virtual death of psychoanalytic interest in seriously disturbed and disturbing behavior is a last factor. The 1950s and early 1960s seemed the heyday of psychoanalytic influence on traditional psychiatry. Psychoanalysts and analytic theories were widely used for both descriptive and etiologic purposes. For a number of years, it was almost *de rigueur* for residents in the best—known training programs to enter analytic training.

In the late 1960s and through the 1970s, psychoanalytic influence has been overwhelmed by waves of findings from the new technologists and technology. The early appeal of analytic constructs has been replaced by more reliably identifiable and quantifiable neurotransmitters, endorphins, and so on. Whether these high-tech findings have made a substantial contribution to clinical practice remains unknown.

This evolution is complex in its derivation, but nevertheless psychoanalysis as a discipline does not seem to be as interested in psychosis as it was during its halcyon days at midcentury. The neuroleptics, development of rapid turnover wards in general hospitals, and community psychiatry each contributed to the apparent withdrawal of psychoanalysis's cathexis of psychosis.

Politics: Internal

For all these and other reasons, the impact of the Soteria/Emanon data has been modest. But even during the life of the project, the tugs between the demands of the conventional medical establishment and the ongoing experiment were intense. Soteria's real issues, actually more political than scientific, stemmed from the clash between two paradigms: To obtain grant support, psychiatric research must conform to a set of logical positivist guidelines sacred to those who decide who will receive the National Institute of Mental Health's—

that is, the taxpayers'—money. Soteria's application did what was required to compete, and a proposal meeting these criteria was designed and submitted. Yet, the actual plan rejected the funding institution's paradigm in favor of an interpersonal-phenomenologic one. (Phenomenology itself developed to reject 19th-century rationalism's confining methodology as framed in logical positivism.)

So, from the get-go, the Soteria project contained an irreconcilable paradox. This *internal* problem could be largely dealt with by acknowledging it and separating the research from clinical functions. There was, however, always a tension between the two. In retrospect, the most adverse consequence of this constant tension was a lack of firsthand, moment-to-moment documentation of the internal workings of Soteria and Emanon. Neither staff nor clients regularly and spontaneously wrote about or recorded their experiences because, they reasoned, to do so would amount to buying into the research, and the antiresearch culture of Soteria was nearly as strong as its antiestablishment and antipsychiatric drug stances. Science, traditional values, and neuroleptics were all seen as sources of denigration and invalidation.

What appears in this book, therefore, is but a small sample, much of it gathered from the authors' personal experiences, of the extraordinarily rich and complex set of interactions that took place at Soteria (and, sometimes, Emanon). Much, even most, however, is lost.

External Politics: Demedicalizing Madness

But it was political pressures from outside, compounded by management failures, that were ultimately the project's undoing. Looking back, now almost 35 years after the idea for Soteria began to take shape, Loren thought that its end should have been visible in its beginning. Only those with vision clouded with youthful enthusiasm, idealism, and naïveté would have embarked on such a high-risk venture.

The Soteria project had the capacity to tread on more sets of sensitive and powerful professional toes than any mental health experiment in recent memory. The fundamental nature of the threat, in all cases, was its demedicalization of madness.

First, Soteria explicitly disavowed that "schizophrenia" was a medical disease. Although many psychiatrists would just as soon not deal with the poor souls so labeled, the profession as a guild needs schizophrenia as illness to justify its existence. The endless and, thus far, fruitless search for the biological cause(s) of "schizophrenia" helps provide a reason for psychiatry's status as a *medical* subspecialty: To demedicalize madness would call the entire profession's existence into question, an especially painful result in light of psychiatry's current campaign to establish itself as a new entity, *scientific psychiatry.*

Second, a successful experiment at Soteria could dehospitalize (or deinstitutionalize) the treatment of schizophrenia. At present, there are about 130,000 psychiatric beds in U.S. hospitals used and reused at a great rate by persons labeled "schizophrenic." Some occupy such beds for their entire lives. Consider the consequences of emptying, say, half of these beds. Large numbers of professional caretakers would have to redefine how and where they work. Many would become unemployed. Such a change would constitute a serious crisis for the mental hospital industry. Large institutions do not take kindly to being replaced by small noninstitutions.

Third, the Soteria project was designed to provide an interpersonal treatment alternative to the use of the antipsychotic drugs. These agents, called, rather interchangeably, tranquilizers, neuroleptics, or antipsychotic drugs were developed and first used in the early 1950s. Chlorpromazine (Thorazine) was the prototype.

By the late 1950s these drugs were in wide use. Their rapid spread is a remarkable social phenomenon in itself. Smith, Kline, and French, Thorazine's manufacturers, trained and sent out "assault troops" (Braden-Johnson, 1990) to alert every psychiatrist and psychiatric ward to this new wonder drug and strongly encourage its use. By the time the Soteria project started, prescriptions of these substances for persons called schizophrenic were almost mandatory.

Their use is still so ubiquitous that they are usually administered to psychotic persons immediately on their arrival at emergency wards or mental hospitals. It is clear that they do, in fact, work—roughly 70 percent of persons labeled "schizophrenic" experience a substantial reduction in symptoms when treated with them. The problems: Not everyone responds, and the drugs all have serious short- and long-term side effects and toxicities, many of them irreversible and untreatable.

Most serious, reducing symptoms of disturbed and disturbing behavior does not effect reintegration. It merely mutes inconvenience.

Imagine the boardrooms of the pharmaceutical companies that manufacture these drugs if a viable nondrug alternative treatment were established safe and effective. Some actions would be taken to insure the continued profitability of these agents.

Data supporting a nonneuroleptic approach are unlikely seriously to affect their use, because drugs

- are easy to administer
- are widely acknowledged as the "mainstay" of the treatment of schizophrenia
- provide many psychiatrists with large incomes
- result in handsome support for the guild's organization (the American Psychiatric Association)

And drugs are under the control of MDs. (See pages 18–22 for more on Soteria's approach to medications.)

A fourth and final political problem area for Soteria was its use of nonprofessionals as the primary treatment personnel. Although trained on the job and supervised by professionals, the front-line staff were not required to have formal training or degrees in mental health. A number of staff members had a good deal of relevant training and experience, however, and some were in the process of study in mental health-related professions. In fact, on many psychiatric wards, employees without degrees (usually called "psych techs") are the backbone of the staff. Nevertheless, to elevate such persons to therapists, with implied curative powers would not make mental health professionals happy.

Deprofessionalization has no more adherents than demedicalization.

Scientific Review

That the Soteria research might be a lightning rod attracting ambivalence at best, or hostility at worst, from mental health professionals is not surprising. What is interesting in retrospect is that the project was supported for as long as it was. The simplest explanation is that the design and conduct of the research was too good to be rejected by the scientists sitting in judgment on it.

Yet, the review process itself was Soteria's eventual undoing. Because of frequent examinations calling for a great deal of time and energy compiling progress reports, writing new applications, and preparing for site visits—rituals that extracted tolls—both actual research and clinical work became difficult. At each site visit, a new set of consultants attempted to redesign the study, and over time it became so complex that collecting all the data became virtually impossible. The project's ultimate demise was guaranteed when Loren, who had conceptualized the treatment and designed the research, was forced into a peripheral role by the actions of a group of hostile reviewers. His exclusion occurred five years into the project, when the successful establishment of Emanon (a replication facility) made the enterprise begin to look viable.

Marginalizing a project's conceptualizer is a nearly unheard-of function of scientific review. Evaluators rationalized that Loren was too biased to report the data honestly—an ugly, ungrounded assumption belied by the fact that Loren, aware of the problems of experimenter bias, had used independent evaluators to avoid it. Removing Loren from Soteria, which he had fathered and nurtured, was analogous to taking a well-treated child, about whose potential abuse someone worried, from its biological parents and placing it for adoption.

Fortunately, control of the data from the 1971–1776 cohort of subjects remained with Loren, who has analyzed them extensively and published his results. The data from the second cohort of subjects (1976–1982) were not completely discussed until 1992, because those data were caught up in a lawsuit growing out of disputes among the project's several sets of adoptive parents attempting to succeed Loren.

Ironically, those data are now available in large measure because of his continued commitment to answering the original simple, but politically dangerous question.

Can the disturbed and disturbing among us be helped in a setting that is demedicalized, dehospitalized, dedrugged, and deprofessionalized? (Part of the answer rests in still another question, which begs for study: What would the six-week outcomes of experimental patients in a Soteria-type atmosphere have been had they been given neuroleptics?)

But the Soteria project was trying to find an answer to the first question and had begun to do so. And, after a third of a century of looking, Loren is not yet prepared to quit.

This book provides data about settings, personnel, and practices that differ dramatically from those found on psychiatric wards. Yet every resident admitted to Soteria (or Emanon) would otherwise have been a patient in a psychiatric hospital. It is remarkable that these two communities, with the techniques described here, dealt as effectively with acute psychotic behavior—mostly without the aid of neuroleptic drugs—as psychiatric hospitals and their medications dealt with patients.

At Soteria, people designated as "schizophrenic" were valued, validated, attended, and empowered. They engaged in real relationships with caring individuals in a nonjudgmental, reciprocal, social subsystem under the guidance of an extended, peer-based, natural social network. Such treatment for "schizophrenics"— whatever they are—is almost unheard of today.

This book and the associated research results indict current overmedicalized approaches based on theories of brain disease and dominated by psychopharmacology. There are alternative ways of dealing with madness. The Soteria project has established the scientific credibility of one of them.

The Voices of Soteria

Loren R. Mosher, MD

ALMOST FOUR DECADES from Soteria's conceptualization until today. Thirty-three years since its opening. Twenty, since its closing. Soteria—in all its internal and external manifestations: Soteria—

- a time, a place, a space, a window of opportunity, a happening, a scene, an event, a sentinel, a curriculum-free university, a network, an asylum, a safety net, a hurricane hole, a springboard, a circus, a spiritual center, a crash pad, a soup kitchen, a lovers' nest
- person *to* person, person *with* person, persons *around* persons
- involvement, attentiveness, emotions, communication— abortive, indecipherable, fruitful
- feeding, watering, cleaning, creating, revolting, searching, learning, finding, knowing, despairing, hoping, regressing, growing, defending, rejecting, healing, failing, dying, being, starting, ending, reaching, knowing, disavowing, seeking
- meeting and addressing God, devils, and the cosmos
- solitude, parties, sadness, joy, pain, glory, bedlam, serenity, salvation, retreat, acceptance, rebellion
- invalidation, marginalization, confrontation, rejection, avoidance, degradation, denigration, ambivalence

✎ groupies, heretics, heroes, angels
✎ mainstream, parallel course, empty creek bed
✎ to grow and reproduce, or to wither and die?
✎ a family without common genes

This retrospective doesn't provide 20/20 vision, nor should it. I offer but one Pirandelloscopic view. How did Soteria happen? Why?

Soteria's is a personal story. It could not be otherwise. To write it impersonally would be hypocritical. Without intimacy, Soteria could not have been. Because of intimacy, it was scrutinized to death.

How did a "schizophrenia" project that, naively in the beginning, confronted four of the sacred cows of mental health come to be? What led me to question

1. the medical model of madness,
2. the necessity that hospitals "treat" this "disease,"
3. the usefulness of neuroleptic drugs in the treatment of disturbed and disturbing behavior, and
4. the essential intervention of professional mental health workers in restoring sanity?

Soteria left little that was sacrosanct in the mental health arena unquestioned.

Starting Out (California)

My journey towards the philosophy that Soteria briefly embodied began during World War I when an atheist sailor from California met and married a staunch Irish Catholic from the Bronx. They returned to his native state, where he taught school in Monterey, and she bore four sons. I was last, a replacement for my older brother, who died of pneumonia. Although I was not the girl they had hoped for, my mother adored me. Sickness continued to strike the Moshers; my mother had a mastectomy a year after I was born, a sickly boy with allergies and asthma who was twice given up for lost. During the Second World War, when I was nine and enrolled in a Catholic military boarding school, my mother died slowly of cancer.

The result of her death was a family diaspora. One son away in the military; another, sent to a cousin's to attend high school; the last, a migrant guest. I lived with a grandmother and two uncles (one of whom, Uncle Ross, became a surrogate father to whom I stayed close until his death in 1987). Then, I moved in with my father, to be joined by his new wife and, again, to shift locations. Finally, we moved to what—after six years on the road (1942–1948)—became "home." I went to eight different schools before my freshman year in high school; in eighth grade, I was readied for the "manual arts" track, a fate from which I was saved by intervention from my father, who as a former teacher knew what that meant. He also suspected that I was not too stupid for college.

Here, in California's Marin County, we settled into a certain residential and educational stability at last. Two years later, however, my stepmother died of complications of alcoholism, giving her family relief from the psychological afflictions of her disease.

In high school, I was recognized—for the first time—as bright and witty. Having basically raised myself from ages 8 to 14, I saw no reason to stop, and I enjoyed extraordinary adolescent freedom. Because of the demands of farm life, California allowed 14-year-olds drivers licenses until the early 1950s, and, at 14, I had both a license and a car. I worked odd jobs during school as well as all summer, usually at the Sierra Nevada resort area where my Uncle Ross lived. He provided me with an elderly Arabian stallion on which I explored the surrounding wilderness. Life was great: Friends, sports, social activities, beer, speeding, and chasing girls.

Unchallenged by but challenging in school, I spent many hours sitting in the principal's office and "at the dentist." That particular caper ended when my forged excuses were detected, and I no longer had Friday afternoons off.

Because my grandfather, a carpenter and contractor, had helped build Stanford University, because my eldest uncle (a child prodigy on the piano) had been partially raised on campus by Mrs. Stanford's sister, and because my next older brother was enrolled, Stanford was obviously the university for me as well. Arrogantly, I filled out only one college application. I was lucky.

Realizing my need for substantial cash for the upcoming fall at Stanford, I spent my prefreshman summer working in the oil fields of

Wyoming and Montana among the "roughnecks"—the men on derricks whose main job is to wrestle used drilling pipe out of the well so blunt bits can be replaced by sharp ones. (I doubt if any other Stanford matriculants spent their summer working 80 of its 84 days— we had every third Sunday off.) Except for the driller, who was married and lived in a trailer with his wife and child, my fellow itinerant crew members were single, promiscuous, alcoholic, brawling, high school dropouts, mostly from Texas. For liability insurance purposes, roughnecks had to be 21 years old. (Fortunately, I already had a fake ID, obtained for the usual reason, to so prove.) My story was that I was working *after* college to get money to go to medical school. Presto chango, I was "Doc." My practice was luckily limited to simple first aid, common ailments like colds, and sexual complaints like the "crabs" and gonorrhea. I referred all penile sores and exudates to specialists at the nearest hospital about a hundred miles away. Because of the isolation of the drilling sites, however, I provided psychological reassurance to this community while, if doing no real physical good, at least doing no harm.

This was a sentinel summer for the wild child. I was given high status because I seemed smart and was "going to be a doctor." I was astonished (and delighted) at how important I suddenly became, not only among the rig's crew but also among members of the tiny community that the 15 of us had invaded. Everyone went out their way to be sure I was safe, protected, and well cared for.

The ex-gambler who owned one of the bars, the restaurant, the store, and the filling station, in this gold mine ghost town rented me a room (albeit without running water or electricity) in his house. He taught me how to cheat at dice to augment my income. (The trick was in learning to hear the particular pitch of the higher numbered dice rattle as they slid down the smooth felt of the walled cup's interior. More noise advised a reshake until the cheater heard a subdued rattle indicating that most of the dice slipping along the cylinder were among the five lower numbers. Without turning the dice over, I then rolled out the higher-numbers facing away from the cup's wall.) Needless to say, this technique, which was not known to me alone, improved my chances. Smooth-walled dice cups are now illegal in most states.

On Saturday nights, the town's weekday population of about 100 swelled fivefold, as cowboys and Indians from the surrounding mountains converged to drink to stupefaction in the two available bars. The roughneck outsiders noticeably stirred up the local social system previously accustomed only to three groups: The townspeople; the cowboys from nearby ranches; and the Indians from the reservation. On one occasion, my drilling crew rescued me from an angry knife wielding warrior not pleased to discover me in bed with his wife. This caring community was quite a launching pad for a college freshman-to-be.

Higher Education (Stanford and Harvard)

Stanford in 1952—nicknamed "the Farm" because of its sprawling underpopulated campus—was known as a WASP party school. Although a WAS but not a P, I was both a fallen-away WASRC (an unworkable acronym) and much poorer than almost all of my classmates. I liked the party idea, but the fact that I had to earn almost all my nontuition funds crimped my hedonism somewhat. I also had to retain a *B* average to keep my scholarship. My dormitory jobs got me free room and board, and my fraternity's connections earned me access to the easy work at high pay as a sports "monitor" (a euphemism for quasipolicing) usually reserved for off-season athletes.

Come September, 1952, I arrived at Stanford from Marin County with two friends in one large car. We have remained friends: The two were on basketball scholarships; I was the resident intellectual—a role I've played ambivalently for most of my life. After my peripatetic childhood and high school summers, college seemed tame—or at least predictable. I did the expected fraternity gig; becoming a nonjock in a jock house because of my older brother's affiliation. Actually, with another medical-school-bound hellion, I kept the house from being shut down because of its overall poor grades.

Nonjocks did have a role.

I had decided in the eleventh grade I wanted to go to medical school. Always ambitious (but denying it all the way) I thought I ought to go to the very best medical school; in those days Stanford was not it. So I applied to Harvard, Hopkins, McGill, and Stanford. I was accepted at the latter two but—insulted that I'd been turned down by the Stanford of the East (Harvard)—I decided after two years at Stanford Medical School to take a year off to make some money and to see if I could get into Harvard. I could, and I did. In 1959, accompanied by my then true love (a nurse), I went off to Boston to finish medical school. While at Harvard, I met the woman who would become my first wife and the mother of my three children.

My reasons for choosing a career in medicine are not entirely clear, but they seem, in part at least, related to my family's emphasis on both practicality and individual freedom. Also, my childhood was replete with serious illnesses, and my decision to enter medicine could reflect my gratitude to and identification with the warm, competent, interested woman who was my doctor throughout my sickly childhood. My reasons for deciding to specialize in psychiatry are also somewhat murky, though several experiences in medical school were clearly important.

In my second year at Stanford Medical School, I came down with a case of "medical student hypochondriasis" severe enough to lead me to seek psychological treatment. In psychotherapy for more than a year, I experienced firsthand the healing possibilities of a caring, human relationship. The following summer, a special psychiatric fellowship introduced me to the broad range of interests that could be pursued in this field. In addition, psychiatry's humanistic possibilities stood out in strong contrast to the technological, mechanized aspects of many other medical specialties. These experiences were followed, during my third and fourth years in medical school, by excellent clinical psychiatric clerkships (at Harvard, where I later did my residency). These experiences, along with the fact that many of my best friends were going into psychiatry, crystallized my choice.

My internship year was also crucial to my orientation to the field. During that year, I was, for the first time, really responsible for the care of other persons. Confronted daily with sickness, unkindness, and death, situations over which I had little influence or control, I sought a means to cope without embracing the dehumanizing, objectifying position in which I so frequently found myself. Fortunately, I found both solace and a humanistic model in existential/ phenomenological thought.

Reading Rollo May's *Existence: A New Dimension in Psychiatry and Psychology* (1958), which had been recommended to me during medical school, I explored the writings of men like Boss, Jaspers, Kierkegaard, Bergson, Merleau-Ponty, and Sartre. Their stress on the uniqueness of individual experience, on not pigeon holing in the guise of "science," on the importance of subjectivity, and on nondoctrinaire theorizing stood in sharp contrast to the authoritarian and paternalistic attitudes that had often characterized my other medical training. The openness and specificity of the phenomenological philosophy such thinkers often expressed had profound relevance to diseases at medicine's borderlines—ones for which no pathological lesion, no specific etiology, and no effective treatment had been identified. "Schizophrenia" is the 21st century's best example of such an "illness."

Starting Out at the "Psycho" in Boston

Armed with this conviction and my phenomenological philosophy, I arrived for my psychiatric residency at the Massachusetts Mental Health Center (its doors closed forever in 2003). At this institution, long known as the "Psycho" because of its previous name (the Boston Psychopathic Hospital), I was greeted by a white-haired, rotund Santa Claus, who quickly divested me of any remaining pretensions about "curing" patients. The late Dr. Elvin V. Semrad instructed me to go and sit with patients, not expecting to "treat" or to "cure," but to investigate their lives with them. Thus, my mentor immediately banished the *doing to* stance of the usual medical therapeutic model and replaced it with a *being with* investigative attitude quite in keeping with my phenomenological bias.

In addition, he specifically *proscribed* intellectualization as a means of dealing with human miseries we couldn't comprehend. Going to the library, Elvin said, in search of the "answer" to the "problems" with which we were trying to deal would only contribute to our misunderstanding and confusion. Even at this early stage of our careers, he encouraged us to learn from our experiences rather than from secondary sources. He knew, of course, that his advice would only be partially taken—wisdom in any field depends on both formal and experiential knowledge. Elvin's approach was a matter of focus and emphasis on how one deals with the anxiety associated with the uncertainty, unpredictability, and incomprehensibility of psychiatric problems.

The model Elvin explicated of *being with*—understanding, accepting, and seeing human relationships as potentially helpful—has dominated my thinking ever since and throws light on much of what the Soteria Project attempted. His encouragement to relate to "schizophrenics" as people with very serious life difficulties, to treat them with dignity and respect, and to attempt to see things as they saw them, was a critical piece of my subsequent development.

Many institutional factors, however, interfered with Elvin's chosen processes. Patients were often dealt with as if they were things; decisions that made the staff, not the patients, more comfortable were rationalized; and physical treatments such as electroshocks were applied to relational problems. What became obvious was the fragmentation of the patient among various people who played specific institutional roles—for example, the doctor was in charge of the person's head; the social worker, her family; the nurse, her social behavior; the occupational therapist, her psychomotor coordination, and so on. As I watched the obvious primacy of institutional staff and training needs over those of the patient, I began to wonder what real therapeutic impact such hospitals could have.

A microcosm of this sacrifice of patient to staff was the problem patient case conference, a peculiar psychiatric ritual that went as follows at the Massachusetts Mental Health Center between 1962 and 1964. The chief resident selected a case to be presented to a consultant, usually a senior staff member. I soon learned that there was more on the agenda than conferring, teaching, and learning. One of the chief resident's frequent hidden agenda items was, How do we get rid of this pain in the ass? Chief residents took flak from their superiors about keeping patients for a long time, particularly if the latter did not seem to be "benefiting from the treatment being given." (This failure to thrive usually meant the patient was causing trouble by noisily behaving oddly—quiet madness was better tolerated.)

Most of the conference was occupied by a long presentation by the first-year resident in charge (me, on many occasions), which left little time for input from the nurses and occupational therapists who spent the most time with the patient. Finally, the consultant interviewed the patient. Although alerted that the interview was to be expected, patients were almost never told why they had been selected or what to expect as its possible consequences.

Their bewilderment was not terribly surprising. It took me almost six months into my first year of residency to figure the *really* important agenda in these conferences, and until then I could not forewarn my patients. Frequently, the case conference concluded with the consultant's recommendation of a course of action the chief resident knew the first-year resident opposed. When I occupied the latter position, I sometimes saw my patients prescribed either electroshock treatments or transfer to Boston State Hospital (a place I'd not send my worst enemy). In either case, the action was rationalized as "best" for the patient, what s/he "really needed at this point in the course of his/her illness." This last phrase effectively shifted the responsibility for the decision from the institution and its medical staff to the patient. The fact that the choice was motivated by institutional priorities and that the patient was absolutely excluded from the decision-making process was never acknowledged.

My quarrel is not, necessarily, with the decision itself but with the false attribution of responsibility to the patient by powerful, respected persons in a ritualized context. The person least able to sustain his/her self-esteem was made to shoulder responsibility for our inability to help. If anything defines the psychiatric patient, it is a sense of failure and consequent loss of self-esteem. *We are not being useful therapeutically when we add yet another apparent failure to the load, especially when that failure is really ours.*

Because I accepted the myth that the hospital's primary role was trying to respond to the needs of its clients, the clear perversion of this goal led me to question the validity of institutions like the Massachusetts Mental Health Center. At the same time I recognized that society needs some way of dealing with what it calls madness. Hence, to seek the abolition of psychiatric hospitals without a viable alternative seemed impractical.

I emerged from my residency training with two conflicting sets of attitudes:

✏ First, human relationships could be therapeutic for even those whose distancing maneuvers were most masterful ("schizophrenics")

✏ Second, a variety of institutional factors seemed directly in opposition to the establishment of such relationships.

This latter, in hindsight, seems a symptom of early infection with devianococcus, a condition that proved incurable.

The National Institute of Mental Health: The Yellow Berets[21] (Maryland)

To complete my residency, I went to work at the National Institute of Mental Health's intramural research program.

There, my involvement in a family study of identical twins, discordant for "schizophrenia," and my contact with Lyman C. Wynne's research group raised my consciousness with regard to the importance of the family—positive and negative—in human psychological development. In the current context of highly developed family-systems theories, this statement may seem remarkably naive. Yet, it must be remembered that this period preceded the appearance of Wynne and Margaret Thaler Singer's remarkable publications of 1963 and 1965. Although I was taught family therapy during my residency,

---

[21] The term applied to MDs who chose to work for the Public Health Service to avoid possible assignment to Vietnam.

it was regarded as "experimental" and accorded little status within an institution dominated by psychoanalytic theory and practice.

During the mid-1960s, I was not only treating and studying families but also beginning my own. In 1964, my son Hal was born; Tim arrived in 1965; Missy, in 1968.

My two-year stint at the National Institute of Mental Health was overall a positive experience—especially in terms of learning research methodology—but it also brought up some troubling questions. I became concerned about certain ethical considerations in research. How, for example, does one justify unearthing and eventually publishing a family's secrets? Or doing "research" that has little direct value for the human guinea pigs involved? Or keeping patients in a hospital for purely research purposes? These questions showed that the gestational devianococcus I had acquired in residency was still viable. Considering my indecisive state at this point, it is fortunate for many reasons that the National Institute of Mental Health sent me to England for a year's study.

As a student of phenomenological/existential psychiatry and psychology, I had come across Ronald D. Laing's books. I thought *The Divided Self* (1959) an excellent account of a clinical situation; it resonated so closely with my experience that I wondered why it was causing a stir. While attempting to write a scientific proposal that would support a year of study abroad, I realized that spending a part of my time in London with Dr. Laing could better ground my understanding of the family's role in psychosis. I had heard him speak at the National Institute of Mental Health of his family studies in 1964, so I wisked off a letter inviting myself to study with him during the year.

Kingsley Hall (London)

Dr. Laing in response wrote of the formation of the Philadelphia Association and its plans:

> A number of us who have formed ourselves into a company
> called the Philadelphia Association have just recently been
> given a building in London called Kingsley Hall at which we

hope to set up a small therapeutic community particularly for schizophrenics.

The initial stages in this are bound to be more empirical and improvised than systematic plans in advance. However, I think you might well find that this was a context in which very useful research could be conducted. Particularly, I think [study is possible] at the interphase between the internal life of the community and the formal and social networks of patients. We are not registering this community as a nursing home and people will not be labeled "patients," although they will be people who would otherwise be committed to hospital as diagnosed schizophrenics. We will have to improvise alternative role relationships between those of us who are relatively able to cope with external realities and those of us who are relatively unable to do this but are involved in other issues.

Dr. Laing's plans for Kingsley Hall further quickened my interest in his work.

Upon my arrival in London in early June, 1966, I called him, arranged an appointment, and arrived, prepared with 50 minutes of suggestions about the kind of program I would like to have him run for me. I emerged some two and a half hours later with a notebook with names of other people involved in the "network," and no program whatsoever for myself. Our talk ranged over many topics, mostly developments at Kingsley Hall, and I remember asking, "Would you try to prevent residents from killing themselves in Kingsley Hall?" As I reconstruct that discussion now, the answer was, "In theory, no." In fact, however, mutual human concern would make inaction impossible if residents thought someone was in serious trouble.

Dr. Laing then told a story from several nights before when an angry interchange between two of the people living at Kingsley Hall had resulted in one man's flight into the night in a rage. The remaining residents decided as a group to go to an apartment they knew he frequented, see how he was, and invite him back. In broad Scottish accent, he recounted a Laurel and Hardy scene of six people running across the streets of East London to an apartment building, scrambling up the stairs, and knocking breathlessly and furiously on a door. Much to their (and my) relief, in no danger or difficulty, their fellow resident was quietly cleaning up.

Armed with Laing's list of names, I contacted the appropriate people and arranged a visit to Kingsley Hall, which at this time had been open for about nine months. On the tube, Kingsley Hall is about one hour from the West End of London. I got off the train and asked the ticket seller for directions: "Turn right, over the bridge; take the second turning on the left; then, the first, on the right." Kingsley Hall loomed large in its predominantly working-class neighborhood of single-family brick row houses. It sat beside a park and appeared to stand alone. The bell didn't seem to work, so I knocked loudly several times. One of the "more-together" (Laing's phrase) residents eventually answered the door, and I was ushered through a cluttered vestibule into the meeting place.

In the still-daylit evening, the conference took place in the hall that occupied a major portion of the downstairs, There, around several rickety tables, sat 11 men and a woman—mostly mental health professionals—on folding chairs under the benign gaze of Mahatma Gandhi. (His portrait, enshrined over a small altar in the middle of the room. commemorates his early 1930s stay at Kingsley Hall while he was conducting negotiations with the British Government.)

Of the topics discussed at that first meeting, I recall most vividly the detailing of problems associated with Mary Barnes, a resident who refused to eat. (Eventually, her psychiatrist, Joseph H. Berke, collaborated with her on a book [1971/1994].) The discussion of what should (or could) be done about her fast was disconcertingly close to a clinical psychiatric case conference. Joe presented the problem, and the rest of us attempted to give him advice:

- Largactil (a neuroleptic drug)?
- tube feeding?
- hospitalization?
- wait and do nothing?
- take food to her room (but how to avoid that as a unique privilege)?

For the moment it was decided to try and get a better idea of what she *actually* was eating and drinking and do nothing. (Later, Joe did feed her in her room.)

Following our discussion, we adjourned upstairs for dinner; there, I met, for the first time, several wives and other friends of the members of the discussion group. In addition, I met the "less-together" (also Laing's phrase) residents of Kingsley Hall. The latter, a mix of expatients from British mental hospitals and foreigners in various stages of disorganization, were attempting to pull themselves together in the new communal "treatment" setting.

Upstairs, I felt for the first time the discomfort that would accompany in some degree all of my many visits to Kingsley Hall. Why? To begin with, I felt a stranger in this group, some of whom had lived together for as long as a year. As time passed, I came to know most of the people fairly well, yet I never relaxed at Kingsley Hall. The major barrier to inclusive relationships, I now believe, was an unspoken community rule against the ordinary social amenities. Introductions, handshaking, and get-acquainted small talk were virtually forbidden. Thus, I always felt like an outsider who had come to dinner in someone's home where he was uncertain of genuine welcome.

By fall, the site, the topics of discussion, and the composition of the group had shifted considerably. Tables and chairs had been replaced by mats and cushions on the floor. A number of the original group's professionals had dropped out or attended irregularly, and it had been proletarianized to include spouses, friends, one-time visitors, and the less-together residents who chose to attend. No longer were "cases" discussed and advice sought. There was usually no formal agenda; meetings were called because a problem had arisen in the community or to greet a visiting dignitary. The meetings changed from problem-solving discussions among experts to a forum where Dr. Laing (now Ronnie) could present his views.

The experience crystallized for me with varying degrees of certainty a number of ideas. I decided, for example, that madness need not be—and is probably better not—treated in hospitals. Openness, lack of rigid role definitions, and a social context relying on minimal status and power hierarchy can happen by, with, for, and around mad persons. Medical and psychiatric trappings are at best irrelevant and at worst harmful for the mad.

Kingsley Hall also showed me a number of pitfalls to skirt:

1. Persons on inner voyages should not be treated as museum pieces. They suffer discomfort and mistrust in the inexplicably changing environment bound to be engendered by a steady stream of strangers.

2. While cleanliness and organization have no direct relationship to mental health, most members of Western civilization have learned to expect a certain degree of both, and, it seems to me, learning to function in the "normal" world includes some minimal conformity. I felt critical of the run-down, dirty state of the house, the chaotic disorganization of its money matters, and the at best haphazard gathering and preparation of food there. (My middle-class upbringing must, of course be taken into account here.)

3. Although we may disagree with much of what goes on in the adjacent community, it is nevertheless indubitably *there*. It seems pointless and contrary to the primary functions of such a setting—allowing individuals sufficient time and space to go on their own trips—to act either as though surrounding society does not exist or is there only to be attacked. In a sense, such a stance contradicts a cardinal tabu of Kingsley Hall—the attribution to or the imposition of one's views on others. Thus, the isolationist, anti-everything-out-there position I perceived at Kingsley Hall was, for me, unrealistic. I believed then and now that the world "out there" can kill you, if you are unwilling to deal with it realistically.

4. Internally, the covert rule against social amenities was another way in which the adolescent, rebellious attitude of Kingsley Hall may have interfered with its function as a refuge. Perhaps, however, Kingsley Hall's style was a necessary precursor to the more mature communities such as Soteria and those now run by the Arbours and Philadelphia associations.

Soteria

5. Finally, at Kingsley Hall I saw too many profoundly miserable people left to themselves because they were "into their trips." Kingsley Hall relied solely on altruism and friendship to generate interpersonal involvement: While the aim sounds noble, the result was that unattractive residents spent large amounts of their time alone on their "trips." Although this solution could be fraught with its own problems, I concluded that some salaried staff, whose job it was to be nonaggressively involved with spaced-out residents, would achieve better results than leaving the mad to their loneliness and misery.

The design of the Soteria project addresses both my positive and negative impressions of life at Kingsley Hall. Either way, Laing's project was seminal for the later California experiments.

Full-Blown Devianococcus (Yale Medical School and the Connecticut Mental Health Center)

Before leaving for my year's fellowship in London, I had been part of the booming assistant professor recruitment circuit. The decade of the 1960s was halcyon days for academic departments of psychiatry—principally because of large infusions of federal dollars (primarily through the National Institute of Mental Health). On paper, I glittered: Stanford AB, Harvard MD (with honors), Harvard residency training, research credentials from the National Institute of Mental Health intramural program, and a year's fellowship at the Tavistock Clinic in London.[22] No sign of deviance yet. My career track seemed clear:

- assistant professor, with several research papers on families of schizophrenics
- associate professor

[22] The "Tavie," as the British National Health Service's only solely psychotherapeutic and psychosocial research institution is known, provided government-supported psychoanalysis (mostly from the standpoint of object-relations theory). Its best-known physician was John Bowlby.

- chair of psychiatry at a somewhat obscure medical school
- chair of an important psychiatry department at a major university

Such a path was normative for someone with my background and experience, and many of my fellow residents in Boston and clinical associates at the National Institute of Mental Health traveled it happily. My journey was to start at Yale under the tutelage of Theodore Lidz, one of the family study pioneers of the 1950s. I was the bright young man recruited to bring the new, "hard," family-study methods to Yale while continuing to respect the revered tradition of Lidz, Stephen Fleck, and Alice R. Cornelison.

Returning to New Haven from a year in London guaranteed culture shock. London (1966–1967)—the heyday of the Beatles, the miniskirt, LSD, and a large counterculture. New Haven (1967–1968)— at least, the Yale department of psychiatry—conservative, psychoanalytic, and dominated by powerful, established full professors who had achieved the rank that allowed them to choose what they wanted to do. Most were sequestered, writing their latest books. Assistant professors like me did most of the day-to-day teaching and patient care.

Another assistant professor had just been fed to Vietnam, and I was asked to take over the 20-bed ward he had headed up in Yale's new mental health center. Gerald L. Klerman, the Center's chief and my mentor during my residency, had climbed to the heights of psychiatric power and influence. Given his support, I thought the ward would be an excellent place to try out some of my notions about focusing primary attention on the expressed needs of the patients who came for care. In my naïveté, the circumstances seemed ideal. The institution itself was new, its chief was also a "Semradian," and the department was filled with bright, psychodynamically-oriented staff.

Then as now, the guiding principle of my clinical work was straightforward: Ask your clients what they want, and do your best to help them get it. If what they want is beyond your ability to help them get it, say so. If what they want can be better achieved elsewhere, tell them where they might go, and help them get there.

To teach these principles to the various trainees on the ward, I welcomed their observation of my intake interviews with each new patient. I asked each patient a simple series of questions:

✎ Why are you here?

✎ What happened in your life that resulted in your coming (or being brought) to a psychiatric ward?

✎ What needs to be done to "fix" the situation, and how can we help you with the "fixing" process?

Unless there was persuasive evidence they were imminently dangerous to themselves or others, patients who had been forced to enter the ward could leave, if they could find no reason to stay and if there was nothing we could do to help them. Based on this "consumer model," all ward activities (such as community meetings and group, individual, and occupational therapy) became optional. A number of previously "required" activities disappeared. Acting as enforcer, I believe, makes it nearly impossible to serve as helper. Ergo, I instructed staff to inform, invite, and encourage patients to attend activities but not to try to force them to participate either by physical or psychological coercion. In an attempt to demystify and proletarianize the staff's functions, we phased out post-community and post-group therapy staff-only meetings. Unless there were very unusual circumstances, the doors were always open. Patients made their own choices as to their activities. The program was destructured so that it incorporated only elements in which the patients were interested, and I strongly encouraged staff to spend their time with the clients rather than playing grab-ass in the nurses' station

It was not long, however, before this psychiatric Walden came under fire. How could we (especially me) allow *patients* to decide what they needed? Obviously, such a position abrogated our responsibility as the treating physicians and indicated over-identification with the patients. Did we not know that patients *really* needed and wanted structure and limits set? Why did we allow such "acting out"? *Acting out?* A typical example of such behavior occurred when two patients returned from a movie (their whereabouts known by staff) in town after 11:00 PM. They found the front door of the mental health center locked and had to call the guard let them in. The following morning this "incident" (which required a special report) was sternly brought to my attention as an example of the patients' destructive acting out.

This ward did not conform to the dominant, analytic philosophy. Those who knew its reality least were most critical, often basing their negative conclusions on faulty evidence. But did my ward have more "incidents"—more suicide attempts, more violent episodes, more patients sent to the state hospital, more patients signed out against medical advice—than did the other wards at Yale? At the time, I assumed that it did, and I took the criticism seriously: It came from powerful, respected doctors.

After leaving, however, I studied all the available data to compare my ward to two similar facilities located on the floors above and below. In no instance could I substantiate that my free-form ward had more "incidents" than the other two. Hence, I could only conclude that the conclusions were unwarranted attributions, no matter how famous, respectable, and powerful their originators. My study taught me an important and painful lesson in the power of the social context to invalidate so thoroughly that the victim comes to embrace the position of his persecutors as "reality"—a paradigm utterly applicable to the development of madness.

I left, having learned firsthand the process of labeling, stigmatization, and distancing that hospitalized mental patients experienced routinely.

The Antibureaucratic Bureaucrat (Maryland and Washington, D.C.)

Administrators at the National Institute of Mental Health, although they didn't know it, were offering me as much a refuge as a positive choice. Luckily, they could only read my printed CV, not the scribbling between the lines. Without realizing it, they had hired a questing, antiestablishment rebel, but it was several years before my deviance drew serious notice and criticism.

My dislike of many neuroleptic drugs (and certainly my reluctance to overdepend on them) is reflected in the approach taken at Soteria. The reasons for my stance are neither obscure nor simple. I prescribed neuroleptics during residency training with Dr. Klerman; my first psychiatric paper was a drug study; none of my mentors was militantly antidrugs. Even the Kingsley Hall experience did not contribute significantly to my view, because a number of the persons living there took neuroleptics as prescribed by MDs not associated with the Philadelphia Association. I began to be sanguine about the overuse of antipsychotics at Yale, where my resident and medical student trainees frequently said that such drugs were the only really useful treatment in psychiatry. My experience has taught me otherwise, and I wanted to be sure that my students did not retain exaggerated expectations about the usefulness of the neuroleptic drugs.

My first two years as Schizophrenia Center Chief at the National Institute of Mental Health led me inexorably to an antidrug position, which is fundamental but not absolute. It seemed clear to me that the National Institute of Mental Health was devoting an inordinate proportion of its resources to psychopharmacologic studies—especially in view of the fact that the studies would have, in all likelihood, been conducted and paid for by the drug companies, whether the government contributed or not. I have no quarrel with public money being used to conduct studies that the pharmaceutical houses would not do, or with taxpayers' dollars being used to assure that company-conducted studies be methodologically sound, rigorously conducted, and properly interpreted. By 1968, however, it seemed to me that psychopharmacologic research had become sophisticated but repetitive, especially in view of the fact that the neuroleptics developed early on were as good (or as bad) as those being endlessly and expensively tested with federal money. In addition, the relationship between the drug industry and the National Institute of Mental Health was too clubby. For example, even I attended meetings of, and was eventually admitted into, the American College of Neuropsychopharmacology, an organization dedicated to drug therapy.

Even by 1968, I wasn't convinced schizophrenia was an organic illness, though my mind was not then made up on the subject. There are vast differences among people so labeled. Then as now, "schizophrenia" is considered to encompass a long list of symptoms (see page 64). And you can get that label without sharing a single characteristic with some other person also diagnosed schizophrenic. No blood test or brain scan or other external validating criterion for "schizophrenia" has ever been established. Instead, diagnosis boils down to the subjective impression of the interviewer.

I am convinced now that "schizophrenic" behavior results from psychosocial experiences and is not biological in origin. As Chief of the schizophrenia center, however, I had no objection to people approaching the condition from a disease standpoint. Still, I did (and do) think that both disease and social models deserved equal time and equal money. My attitude towards both biologically and socially oriented research proposals was positive, if they obeyed scientific canons of science and produced sound answers.

While I was chief, three or four "causes" of "schizophrenia" and four or five "cures" for it were discovered. My all-time favorite cure was kidney dialysis. The man heading this study was a psychiatrist with considerable charisma, perhaps gained during his prepsychiatric days as a preacher.

He and his staff housed persons having "schizophrenia" in pleasant, comfortable places, treated them kindly, and showered them with attention. He really cared for his patients and approached them humanely and sensitively. To meet his experimental protocol, however, he also made them undergo twice-weekly dialysis, even though their kidneys were normal.

Guess what? The patients improved.

His conclusion: Dialysis cures schizophrenia.

No harm was done; in fact, his patients had a nice time. But the National Institute of Mental Health is a political animal. We were forced to spend several million dollars studying dialysis done on "schizophrenics" by other people in other places to test his hypothesis that kidney dialysis could rescue people from madness.

Guess what? It didn't work. I had told them that it wouldn't. His positive results were a product of kind attention and positive expectations.

The dialysis cure was absurd, but it was symptomatic of a darker reality. Even in the late 1960s, the notion that schizophrenic symptoms could be controlled by pills (or injections) was widespread.

Because there were no large companies marketing psychosocial therapies, I believed public money should be devoted to the evaluation of their effectiveness. When I became better acquainted with the peer review process and witnessed the difficulties necessarily impressionistic and subjective psychosocial treatment studies had getting approved (in contrast to the methodologically high-tech but *simpler* drug studies), my antiauthoritarianism began to emerge. The Soteria study was in part an attempt to change the federal and medical reward system.

A second major reason for my deviant position vis-à-vis drugs was the appearance in 1968 of Philip R. A. May's extraordinarily influential book on treatment of "schizophrenia." Although, to his credit, May presented his findings in a straightforward way, others exaggerated them, and he was widely quoted as having shown that "milieu" and individual therapy were "ineffective." The study's limitations were buried in a crescendo of praise. Smith, Kline, and French, who supplied the drugs used in the study free of charge, distributed a copy of the book to every psychiatric resident in the United States. They gave it away at psychiatric meetings and quoted from it in their ads. The pro-drug pendulum was gathering force—the years 1968–1973 were particularly good ones for the phenothiazinologists.

The Soteria Project, designed in 1969–1970, eschewed extensive dependence on neuroleptic drugs on good experiential and scientific grounds: "Schizophrenics" major obstacle to surviving in the community was usually their imperfect psychosocial skills, a defect everyone agreed could be little affected by neuroleptics. In addition, it soon became clear that the type of staff we wanted to hire would not accept their use. While in 1969–1970 I was as ignorant or as oblivious as my colleagues about tardive dyskinesia as a frequent long-term toxicity from neuroleptics, I was quick to seize upon George E. Crane's courageous 1973 review of the literature showing the causal relationship between them. By then, however, the neuroleptic drug issue had already polarized opinion about the Soteria project

Things were almost as turbulent at home as at the office. To our family's joy, our daughter was born in 1968. To our family's sadness, the marriage crumpled.

My position about neuroleptics probably brought more attention to my deviance than everything else. This issue, couched in scientific terms, How can you question the value of agents of proven safety and efficacy? was usually entwined with an ethical parallel—How can you justify withholding a treatment of known value? Although the questions seem simple ones grounded in solid data, they are not. Neuroleptics are *not* universally "agents of proven safety and efficacy," and they are *not* always "treatments of known value." I neither prescribed nor avoided neuroleptics across the board. When they looked helpful, I suggested them. If they seemed to be working, I continued them under careful scrutiny. And when the benefits—as often—did not seem to outweigh the risks, I avoided them. Although in papers and talks I always made clear that I both believed neuroleptics to be efficacious on many occasions and used them when appropriate in my practice, my position was often simplified into a doctrinaire antineuroleptic (and hence antiscientific) stance.

Today, my position is that, since no real alternatives to antipsychotic drugs are currently available, to be totally against them is untenable. Thus, for seriously disturbed people, I occasionally recommend them—as part of collaborative planning with my client—but in the lowest dosage and for the shortest length of time possible. Instead of antipsychotics, however, I prefer to calm acute psychosis and restore sleep/wake cycles with an initial course of minor tranquilizers accompanied by in-home crisis intervention.

Adding what *seemed* injury to insult was my position as head of the National Institute of Mental Health's Schizophrenia Center. Disgruntled would-be principal investigators attributed to me power and control, which I simply did not have, over decisions about grants' approval and funding. Despite repeated clarifications, many of them were unable to understand that I neither reviewed nor decided which grants would be funded. Despite the fact that my most severe critics had almost all sat on the peer review committees that make these decisions, several remained convinced, their own experience and knowledge to the contrary, that I must be subtly controlling the process—and thereby depriving *them* of grant support (paranoia is not confined to those diagnosed as mentally ill).

The data do not support their beliefs: In the years between 1968 and 1975, during an era of essentially level research budgets, the National Institute of Mental Health's support of biological studies of "schizophrenia" grew by nearly 300 percent. Were I attempting to undercut this kind of study, I failed miserably.

This review of my psychopharmacologic history is germane to the context of the Soteria Project, both in its protocol and in the incredible obstacles it faced. The first Soteria Project grant, submitted to the National Institute of Mental Health in the spring of 1970, was given a disappointing evaluation that presaged well the project's future with peer reviews. Our application for five years of support in three settings (two community residences and one general hospital ward) received funding, but there was money only for a year-and-a-half study of the "feasibility" of establishing Soteria House. The project never succeeded in banishing this kind of ambivalence and mistrust. Its eight reviews and five site visits in ten years set records for scrutiny over the spending of taxpayer dollars. Time spent preparing grant requests was time lost from the therapeutic and scientific work of the project.

In spite of bureaucratic federal resistance, however, by 1974, we had two houses going. That same year, I began presenting the first papers reporting Soteria's outcome data. We would collect the data and send them to the National Institute of Mental Health, where my staff would analyze them as fast as they arrived. We produced papers by the carload.

That was a mistake. We wrote too much too soon, allowing the enemy—mainstream biologic psychiatry—to identify us as early as 1975.

Our results were very positive, but, rather than heralding the findings as a breakthrough, the Soteria review committee sniped that the "credibility of the pilot study [was] low." Our grant was reviewed more times by more committees than any grant in the history of the National Institute of Mental Health. Why? The Soteria approach questioned many of the psychiatric beliefs that the profession holds dearest. For example, it showed that persons diagnosed schizophrenic could improve without hospitals, trained staff, and neuroleptics. It also rejected the medical model of "schizophrenia."

Although, with the wisdom and support of Voyce and others, Soteria House limped along until 1983, my termination as research director presaged the eventual demise of the scientific portion of the project. Until 1976, project data were quickly analyzed, presented, and published. Until very recently, however, the post-1976 data were not readily available in the scientific literature. But in the past couple of years—more than three decades since Soteria's doors opened; two, since they closed—John R. Bola, PhD, a professor of social work at the University of Southern California, and I have published several papers on the project. See Mosher (1999, 2001a & 2001b); Mosher and Bola (2000); Bola and Mosher (2002 & 2003).

My successors published nothing. I was outraged but helpless to stop their inaction. I thought Soteria was too important to kill, so I played the good mother in Solomon's court: Rather than cut the child in half, I made the ultimate sacrifice and sent it to a stranger's care. No federal Solomon, however, rewarded the good parent, and thus ended a rare experiment of madness dealt with in a demedicalized, dehospitalized, deneurolepticized, and deprofessionalized context.

My recovery from these personal and professional setbacks took a good four years, becoming complete only when I became a gentleman of Verona, spending a productive 1980 in Italy, studying the new community psychiatric system it was designing without large state hospitals. Meanwhile, the Soteria Project was somewhat redesigned by the new research director I was forced to recruit and took on subjects until early 1979. It successfully competed for continuing federal support except for an 18-month period in the early 1980s. A third research director, who had to be hired when number two saw the handwriting on the wall, also quit abruptly. Soteria's final two years of support for data analysis became the subject of a lawsuit that prevented funding, becoming only fully available in 1991. As the good parent, I stepped back in to direct the final data analyses (none had appeared between 1979 and

1989). Between 1984 and 1988, Bob Vallone[23] and I continued to work on the available data, hoping, eventually, for a favorable settlement.

We were able to pull together a small but basic portion of the data collected between 1976 and 1982. Its protocols had been progressively reinvented by each new review group, research director, and statistician, however, and much of its rich, complex contributions disappeared among disruptions, new settings, different data analysts, and incompatible computers.

The Italian psychiatric revolution that I found so astonishing and so promising was awarded a reception in the United States that was at best lukewarm. Because I did not share my colleagues' enthusiasm for the wonders of reductionistic biologism, I had been replaced as the National Institute of Mental Health Schizophrenia Center Chief during my stay in Italy.

Soteria and its offspring Emanon died—mainly because of lack of funding and leadership—not long after my return from Italy. At the same time, it quickly became clear that the data analysis would not go forward.

The Sun Also Rises

What I had learned from Soteria and from my wise and imaginative Italian colleagues could not, however, be taken away. In the late 1980s, I became a professor of psychiatry at the Uniformed Services University (Bethesda, Maryland), continued to consult with many community-based programs, and participated in an extraordinary five-year series on "Alternatives to Traditional Psychiatry" held at the Esalen Institute in California. In 1988, I married Judy Schreiber. In 1989, Norton published Lorenzo Burti's and my book on community mental health, containing the latest Soteria data analyses. The new, shorter edition (1994) volume publishes some of the 1976–1982 Soteria data and provides a research-based characterization of Soteria's milieu.

---

[23] See page 117.

In 1988 I became the Clinical Director of the Montgomery County (Maryland)'s public mental health system. While I was there, we established an alternative to psychiatric hospitalization (McAuliffe House) based on the Soteria model. Earlier, in 1977, I had helped establish a similar refuge (Crossing Place) in Washington, D.C. Both houses loosely followed Soteria's treatment principles, social structure, and staffing patterns. In contrast to Soteria, however, they were (and are today) very much a part of the local treatment systems. As such, they accepted all types of applicants (mostly the long-term mentally ill), provided more or less defined lengths of stay, and offered most residents some form of psychotropic medication. Our random-assignment study of McAuliffe House in comparison to the "usual" treatment given in the psychiatric ward of a Montgomery County general hospital found the alternative to be as effective as hospital treatment at slightly less than half the cost. (See *Result Seven* above, pages 263–266.)

In 1996, I joined my last professional organization, returning to California as the clinical director of San Diego County's public mental health system, which I was charged to reinvent. Within a short two years, I realized that it did not really want reform, in spite of what I had been told when recruited. Meaningful change cannot occur without commitment from the social and political leadership and support, expressed, among other things, in the form of resources. Neither was forthcoming in a county governed by five conservative Republicans.

In addition, I landed in the system just as the privatization bug bit the San Diego County Board of Supervisors, which promptly mandated countywide managed care. A year and a half after my arrival, I submitted a plan that would have decentralized and improved San Diego's mental health care system. But it also would have required hiring about two dozen new staff members, a move that the supervisors opposed.

A year later, I resigned to form, with my wife Judy, Soteria Associates, a consulting company that offers analysis and help to individuals, families, programs, and mental health systems. Our website is www.moshersoteria.com.

When my routine bill came from the American Psychiatric Association in late 1998, I decided it was time to act on my three decades of doubts about the cozy relationship between the professional organization and big pharmaceutical companies. When your paycheck comes from an establishment source, it is impolitic not to be a member of that powerful organization. Deinstitutionalized, I was free to quit.

I resigned in December 1998, with no attempt to be diplomatic. I firmly believe that the big drug companies virtually own psychiatry at this point in time.

Among other points, I wrote that the American Psychiatric Association "could not continue without pharmaceutical companies' generous financial support of its meetings, symposia, workshops, journal advertising, . . . unrestricted educational grants," and research.

Drug companies also affect psychiatric training, I continued. One of the most important parts of residents' curriculum is "the art and quasi-science of dealing drugs, that is, of writing prescriptions." As a whole, psychiatry no longer seeks to understand whole persons in their social contexts.

Instead, we are here "to realign our patients' neurotransmitters."

To make matters worse, I went on, the American Psychiatric Association has joined in an unholy alliance with the National Alliance for the Mentally Ill, a powerful group founded and controlled by the parents of "schizophrenics." The two organizations have similar public belief systems about the nature of madness.

While professing itself to be "the champion of its patients," the American Psychiatric Association is supporting nonclients, the parents of disturbed and disturbing children, to control—"via legally enforced dependency—their mad/bad offspring."

Embrace of "biologically based brain diseases," I pointed out, is convenient for families and practitioners alike. It offers no-fault insurance against personal responsibility by positing our helpless trap in a swirl of brain pathology for which no one, except DNA, is responsible.

I want no part of a psychiatry of oppression and social control. Psychiatry, as practiced today in this country, is mostly a hoax, I said.

The establishment, of course, disagrees. When *Psychology Today* solicited and published a piece summarizing my position in 1999, it was careful to encircle my contribution with four disclaimers from biopsychiatric spokesmen.[24] For a fuller account of the controversy, see *Psychology Today,* *32*(5), pp.40–44, or www.moshersoteria.com.

Deliverance recounts perspectives not only from me and Voyce, the only Soterians who lasted, stayed concerned, and invested energy in making the project's findings widely available but also of many of the residents and staff who lived and worked there. With the help of Washington, D.C., writer and editor Deborah C. Fort, we have come together, finally, to close the circle.

My own scars have healed. Here, finally is the bittersweet story— its warnings and its wisdom—of the time, space, and place that was Soteria. This mishandled, kidnapped child, with all its imperfections and strengths now speaks, and Soteria and Emanon are now themselves parents to a number of American and European children, grandchildren, and adoptees (see pages 2–3).

May the effort of the hundreds who participated in this extraordinary social experiment lead to more descendants, wherever dedicated people ease others' psychological distress by *being with* them in a safe place.

---

[24] They are Frederick K. Goodwin, MD, professor of psychiatry at the George Washington University Medical Center and former director of the National Institute of Mental Health; James Thompson, MD, deputy medical director of the Office of Education at the American Psychiatric Association; Steven E. Hyman, MD, director of the National Institute of Mental Health; and William Emmet, chief operating officer of the National Alliance for the Mentally Ill.

In short, Goodwin argues for medication, ideally combined with psychological treatment, asserting that today's antipsychotic drugs are so effective that some countries don't allow placebo groups in clinical trials for people with "illnesses" like schizophrenia and bipolar disorder. Thompson says that his organization controls the influence of the drug companies at its meetings and advocates psychotherapeutic as well as pharmaceutical interventions. Hyman believes that improved medicines are "safe and effective." Emmet says that, while individuals *should* have control over their own treatment, some with "brain disorders" are unable to act in their own best interest.

I dispute all their allegations.

For a fuller account of the controversy, see *Psychology Today,* *32* (5) pp. 40–44, or www.moshersoteria.com.

Voyce Hendrix, LCSW

One factor that helped me to survive at Soteria was my belief
that reality is liquid and essentially has no form. It can only
be caught in a photograph; after that instant, it is gone.
Once the photograph is developed, it can be infinitely
explored, but what is discovered will not have any necessary
implication about what will happen 10 minutes later.

UNLIKE PREPARATION FOR many careers, my life experience
was more important in my decision to go to work at Soteria and
remain there for its entire 12-year life than my formal education. It is
with this fact in mind that I approach this autobiography.

Moving

My African-American parents, born in the American South just after
the turn of the last century, migrated separately to California as young
adults in the 1920s. My mother, who had a high school education,
had taught grammar school in Arkansas, but my father had only
completed the third grade in Alabama before he had to quit
school and work to help the family survive. He left home at the
age of 16. My mother's marriage to my father at about age 30 was
her second; my four siblings and I would grow up, on occasion, with
six half sisters and brothers.

I was born in Delano, California, in 1938 and lived there until I was seven. My father and mother worked as farm laborers during my preschool and elementary school years.

Although we were poor until I was 14, we were able to live off my parents' income, mainly from farm labor. I did a variety of farm work from the time I turned 9 until I was 14, when I began to assist my father in his labor camp. The workers I met, and the way we interacted with them, turned out to be central to the way I played my role at Soteria.

My years at Delano were fairly stable. My four brothers, my parents, and I lived in one house, and we were an established part of the community. My father worked as a farmhand for several local growers of cotton and grapes; when my siblings and I were little, my mother was mainly a homemaker. Later, she joined my father in the fields.

My brothers and I grew up and went to school in a way traditional for the middle 1940s. All this changed when a freeway went through our neighborhood. The state condemned our house, paid our landlord, and took the property through the right of eminent domain. We moved North to Stockton to live with my father's parents, who had moved West from Alabama in the 1920s.

Although this arrangement was brief (we lived there for three summer months until it was just about time for school to start), it looms large among my childhood memories. There, for example, I learned to swim. There, for the first time, I got to know my cousins, aunts, and uncles on my father's side of the family. We became close to a number of members of his family.

I can recall hearing stories about how my uncle, who was light-skinned and could pass for white, was sent to Stockton to buy land. At that time, blacks were often discriminated against when they tried to buy property. He succeeded, however, in buying some fairly undesirable land which later—long after we had resold it, unfortunately—became prime development property.

I grew up, tall and thin, the second child among my parents' five children. My brother, OB, was four years older than I; Edmond and Charles were, respectively, two and four years younger. My sister,

Connie, was not born until we left Stockton. Edmond, intelligent and spoiled, got most of the family's attention.

The Value of Education

Not until we moved to Riverdale and I went to high school did I begin to feel more the older brother, a role reinforced by OB's graduating and going to college. All my brothers went to college—unusual, period, for members of any family whose parents' education stopped with high school, but particularly so for African Americans growing up in a highly segregated society. While our parents were proud of our efforts, they couldn't help us financially, and we all paid our own way. My "little sister," now 57, has recently completed her GED and is also contemplating higher education. OB's departure had a major impact on Edmond, who began to look up to me. His admiration in turn affected me. Finally, I was the dominant sibling.

My years from age eight until my teens were unsettled. We moved a great deal, and I went to three grammar schools, where my relationships with schoolmates were necessarily short-lived. These changes contributed to my later shyness. We stayed in the various living quarters provided by the labor camps—usually small cabins, one-to-three-room houses, never more than a few rooms and a kitchen. Only in Delano and Stockton did we have an indoor toilet. From 8 to 16, I used outhouses.

When I was 13, my father and mother separated temporarily, probably for financial reasons, and she moved with us children to a little town about 16 miles west of Delano called Allensworth. I always suspected that my father left home to get my mother to apply for welfare. She never did, and he was able to come home two years later. For the first and last time, however, we received public support in the form of donated food.

Allensworth is the only town I've ever seen housing only African Americans. Founded after the Civil War by Colonel Allensworth, a black Union officer who brought a group of freed slaves to the site after the Civil War, Allensworth is now a national monument. Its population was under 500 people when we lived there from 1950 through 1954.

My oldest sister from my mother's first marriage arranged for us to move into a four-room house near hers. Her husband's father, the mayor of Allensworth, owned both the gas station and the local store, which offered the only gas or groceries within a 10-mile radius. Farm work was the only employment available for my family though, and we couldn't make ends meet on what we brought in.

Oxymoronic as it may sound, the years from 10 to 14 were the best and the worst times of my childhood. We had close, consistent friends. We felt part of the community. By most standards, we were poor, but we were not much poorer than our neighbors.

My first teacher in Allensworth's one-room (occasionally partitioned-off) schoolhouse where 30 pupils attended was a burned-out veteran who was clearly divorcing herself from the community and preparing for retirement. Her replacement, a young, enthusiastic woman named Mrs. Allen, profoundly and essentially raised my self-esteem with her gentle, thoughtful encouragement.

I still can remember Mrs. Allen's observations as if they occurred yesterday. Small events have stuck in my mind that you would expect to disappear minutes after they had happened: At the end of a warm spring afternoon, as I was leaving school late, Mrs. Allen paused at the front gate to say how much she had appreciated my work that day. Her statement made me feel good about myself, and I ran happily the half-mile to the reservoir to join my friends, who were already swimming. Without looking around, I knew she was standing at the front gate watching my sprint. Knowing she cared enough to pay attention to me made me feel as if I could run forever. When she saw me the next morning, she greeted me, "You are a *good* runner."

I knew that I was *not* a good runner, but her undeserved praise made me feel special. No other teacher had that kind of impact. But just one year of her influence made a big difference. I have frequently wondered what my academic life would be like if Mrs. Allen had been my teacher from kindergarten on rather than just in sixth grade.

Under her influence, math became my favorite subject, and she made going to school seem meaningful.

One year at Delano High School dampened and nearly extinguished the flame she had lit, however. We were bussed about 16 miles to a school of over 1,500 students. I was lost.

Meanwhile, my father had set up a business in labor contracting. When I was about 15, we moved to Riverdale, a small town near Fresno, which could not have been less like Allensworth. Riverdale's minority population was only about 10 percent (and only about 3 percent black). Its entire high school enrollment of 300, while 10 times that of Allensworth Grammar School, was much easier for me to deal with than Delano High's crowds.

Settling Down

This turned out to be a permanent move. My father and we kids built the house in which we lived, and my parents stayed in Riverdale until they died. We also built a gas station and a small store, both of which I helped my father and uncle run.

I attended Riverdale Joint Union High School, where I played an active if nonacademic role. Maybe Mrs. Allen wasn't just being polite about my running ability. I was the first person in the history of Riverdale High to go to the state track meet. At that time, it was unusual for an African American to participate in an event such as pole vaulting, and I believe that I was the first nonwhite to win that event in California history. During my high school years, I was vice president of the student body, chairman of the band, president of the YMCA, and captain of three major sports teams—track, football, and basketball. I spent almost every evening involved in some school activity. In spite of all this joining, however, I was profoundly shy. I masked my lack of social skills and potential loneliness through commitment to athletics and school activities.

My academic work seemed necessary only to make me eligible for extracurricular activities—at least, that was what I thought at the time.

As I matured, I recognized that I was not alone in that misconception: The coach and other teachers and advisors encouraged my decision to see academic achievement as an irrelevant sidelight in high school. They routinely counseled me not to take difficult classes. They told me not to run for president of the student body (it would require too much work), but to go instead for the largely honorary vice presidential post.

My college career comprised three distinct periods: First, I functioned as an athlete, using my music major to maintain grade levels sufficient for participation in track. I was seen as a potential Olympic contender in pole-vaulting, and, at Fresno Junior College, I set the national junior college record for the pole vault in 1959. Although my athletic record attracted the notice of Fresno State College's coach Cornelius ("Dutch") Wammerdam, the first man to pole-vault 15 feet and then the holder of both the world and the Olympic records for that event, my athletic career ended abruptly when I was drafted into the Army in October 1961.

More Learning

This interruption turned into the catalyst that redefined my life. Because of the Berlin crisis, I was refused a college deferment. But the GI Bill, which financed my education after I was discharged, led to opportunities about which I would probably never have known without the doors it opened. Between 1966 and 1980, I was a desultory part-time student, using college courses to further whatever my current interest, eventually backing in 1980 into a bachelor's degree in American studies from San Jose State College.

My final college work, however, was as directive and serious as my first two forays were not. After Soteria closed, thanks to good advice from friends, I studied for a degree in social work at the University of Wisconsin at Madison. During this—by far the best—academic experience of my life, I took classes full-time without having to work simultaneously.

When I returned to civilian life after the Army, I saw myself as a musician, which I might actually have become if I had completed my bachelor's in music. As the super-star pop musician of tomorrow, however, I spent months on the road. I also lived six months in Los Angeles, hanging around and performing with friends playing the nightclub scene. Our band, the Blue Jays, backed up a good number of rhythm and blues singers. Some had singles on the top 10 chart, but they usually were one-shot successes who then sank back into obscurity.

After about a year and a half as a would-be rock star and another, working as a lineman for Pacific Gas and Electric, I realized that neither job met my needs. A lineman's job was dangerous. A musical career was unstable: While the income was adequate, not knowing where I might be living and working from week to week proved intolerable.

So I took my first job in a helping profession. I suppose I could lay the reason for this choice on my first wife, whom I had just begun dating and who had just gotten a job at the state hospital in Porterville, California. One night, coming off a particularly horrible two-week road trip through Arizona, West Texas, and New Mexico and ending in Barstow, California, near the Mohave Desert, I decided to end my musical career. I joined my wife-to-be at Porterville State Hospital as a psychiatric technician for $327 a month (about a third of my previous salary).

Helping and Accepting

I didn't intend to stay very long at the hospital, but it became quickly clear that I had an affinity for the work. I spent the next two years being trained half days about issues related to mental health. The first year, we spent the other half day with patients then called "mentally retarded" (now "developmentally disabled"). The second year, I worked half days with people described as "mentally ill" at Agnews State Hospital in San Jose.

My most vivid memories of training were of the incongruities between what we were taught about how to treat patients and the reality of the wards. According to our trainers, the patients were the most important people in the hospital, but on the ward, these VIPs were commonly beaten up. We also received warnings not to touch the patients to avoid getting their diseases, when it was clear to me that gentle physical contact was often just what the patients needed.

At Agnews State Hospital, where I worked for a couple of years, I slowly realized that many of the patients were similar to the people with whom I worked and lived as a teenager in my father's labor camp.

My father's camp had been located in an old grammar school that he converted into a large kitchen, dining room, and sleeping quarters. Unlike the migrant farm workers of today, who—though they have many problems as, largely, illegal immigrants of Hispanic origin—at least tend to center their efforts around their families, the farm workers of the 1950s were loners. When they were not picking crops, they inhabited large city slums and skid rows and lived much as do America's homeless now.

The farm laborers of yesterday were "winos" and "bums," faceless individuals outside of "normal" society. At the height of the cotton-picking season, the camp employed 300 to 400 of them. On reflection, I would guess that 30 to 50 percent of them were pathological to some level, having a range of disabilities from mild personality disorders to schizophrenia. It would probably be safe to say that 90 percent depended on alcohol, drugs, or both.

When I was not in school, I spent most of my time with this group of people. Although I recall that many of them spoke to someone I could not see or hear, I did not find it odd. I remember one man called "Kid Wilson" (a typical name) talking about the cricket in his ear. While I was never sure if he was really hearing a cricket, I never questioned that he heard something. Most of the laborers worked hard while they were in the camp; when the work season ended, they went back to their other worlds.

The camp experience prepared me for Soteria, though, of course, I didn't realize its helpfulness until much later. Another useful experience was living in a family of 11 children. You had to cooperate, and you had to help, if day-to-day life was to function at all. (In some ways, however, I feel as if I grew up with only three brothers and one sister because the five children born to my mother and her first husband had all moved out of the house by the time I was old enough to remember much of anything.) Although my mother and father were positive influences, they offered little control as we experienced our environment. Our response to this freedom was to become extra responsible.

In similar ways, my freedom from the mystifying capability of the medical model allowed me to have normal interactions with individuals whose approach to reality was unusual. Another useful difference that became important at Soteria was the expectation (*not* shared by mental institutions) that, with available housing and employment opportunities—albeit seasonal—one should do work and be paid. We never tried to change behavior that did not pose a problem for others either in the labor camp or at Soteria.

There was nothing wrong with hearing voices or having strange thoughts.

Education Continues

My wide-ranging education echoed my life. For example, my tastes and interest in music included both the work of Lightning Hopkins and Béla Bartók. Among my close friends were a country-and-western drummer from Bakersfield and a psychiatrist from Washington, D.C. When I was working as a musician, I played, on the one hand, authentic Portuguese music with a band whose members (with the exception of me) were all Portuguese. On the other hand, I worked frequently with the drummer in his chosen musical mode. I can spend hours working on my car or digging in the yard, but I can also lose myself for other hours in a book on chaos theory or super conductivity.

I find it easy to be comfortable with other people's lifestyles, and I feel comfortable in mine. I do not try to live a theoretical existential existence; my lifestyle grows out of my everyday experiences.

In the last 15 years, I have read a book a week either concerning science or social policy. In order to maintain an active political presence in the community, I have also funneled news items relevant to community mental health to the producers of WORT 89.9 FM, Madison's listener-sponsored community radio station.

My decision to work at Soteria had little to do with theory. I became aware that what I was doing at Agnews State Hospital did not seem to be helping patients get better. Anytime I suggested that there might be a better approach, I was made to feel like a traitor. It seemed to me that the only creative activity at the hospital was going on "Ward 11" (the study in which Loren was involved). I was told, however, that I was too important a resource for the hospital to be freed to work on that project, and my frustration was such that I decided to go back to school full-time and get out of the field altogether.

Before I left, however, Stanley Mayerson (the psychologist on Ward 11, see page 106) convinced me that I should talk to Alma and Loren about their experiment. The Soteria experience had a profound impact on my life not only professionally but also personally. One result, for example, was my divorce.

My first wife was actively pursuing her career as a nurse, a course that ultimately made our values differ dramatically. We had little in common, although we *seemed* to be in related fields, and we separated. The effect of the separation pushed me deep into the Soteria community. This period in my life now seems part of a natural and healthy growth process, one that I had to go through. As I was living it, however, it was filled with a great deal of both pain and happiness. Nonetheless, I am a better person because of the experience.

Weathering the Crises

Much of this book describes the tumultuous 12 years of my (and others') day-to-day lives at Soteria (and, to a lesser extent, at Emanon). The hardest times at Soteria were the last two years, during which I had to help close both houses. Shutting down Emanon was more difficult in some ways than closing Soteria because I had not forged significant connections with most of the residents. But I had close relationships with several staff members and the few residents remaining when I had to announce Emanon's closing. That Emanon's house director left just before I gave notice of termination put me in the unhappy position of giving bad news to a group of newly acquired friends. I tried to cushion the blow by spending about two months' time with that community after the house director quit and taking care of sad but necessary tasks.

When you are involved with a group of people in crisis times, you can make rapid and significant bonds with them. At Emanon, only five or six months after I had had to step in as house director, I had to give everyone layoff notices. I felt deeply sorrowful then, but, because I was able to help some of the staff members find jobs and other kinds of assistance, the process was not all negative. It left me with some long-term friends.

Closing Soteria was quite different. I did not even have enough time to grieve before I had to begin closure. To save money, I laid myself off as house director and cut my salary. This cost-saving measure temporarily avoided terminating regular staff, but it meant that I had to not only to serve as unpaid house director but also to cover some shifts. I often worked an 80-hour week, leaving little time for administration.

I also had to raise funds. Were it not for David L. Rosenhan, a member of Soteria's board of directors at the time who not only gave me a crash course in fund-raising but also provided the support that allowed me to deal with necessary day-to-day activities, I could not have survived the crisis myself or helped anyone else to do so. (See also page 122.)

Until the end, we never felt as if we were closing Soteria, because we were making the connections that we thought would produce local funding. For example, we had secured a promise of state money funded through the county for facilities like Soteria.

Then, suddenly, our landlord sold the house. At that point, reluctantly, taking this blow as a sign that it was time to close, we decided not to try to secure another site.

After closing Soteria and writing my part of the final report, not yet ready to make any major commitments even to relationships, I took some stopgap, odds-and-ends jobs. For 18 months, I worked in a private hospital. With a psychiatrist friend of mine, I helped a variety of people in the community cope with their life challenges. We also worked with a few families. This was not a stable time professionally, but it provided some powerful experiences. One family with whom we worked influenced me deeply, and—as is consistent with the Soteria experience—this family became an important part of my life.

Moving On but Remembering

I began to put my life back into focus when I accepted Larry Telles's invitation to join the annual gathering on the central coast of California at Esalen, an institute popular in the 1960s for sensitivity training and other activities. Each year, Larry brought together individuals that he thought could contribute some insight into ways of helping sufferers from mental illness.

As a result of that experience, I met many kind and wise people, including Mary Ann Test, who encouraged me to go back to school in social work at the University of Wisconsin at Madison. With the possible exception of Mrs. Allen's work with me in the sixth grade, this turned out to be my best educational experience. Not only did I get an outstanding academic education, but also I came to spend time with individuals who profoundly impressed me. To name but a few among many: Mona Wasaw, Jean Redpath, Debbie Alness, Steve Safian, and Pat Rukowski. These generous people made what could have been a lonely, difficult time into a wonderful, enlightening experience.

After graduating and moving back to California, I faced the traumatic process of becoming licensed as a clinical social worker. Fortunately, I married Stephanie Guth, also a newly graduated social worker, a wonderful woman with a wonderful family. Stephanie and I helped each other along the grueling path to our licenses. I knew that if we could survive that experience we could survive anything, and I was right. After we both earned our LCSWs, we practiced in the San Francisco Bay area before moving back to the heartland. There, in Wisconsin, our five-year-old twin daughters, Chloe and Simone, can see their loving grandparents Mary Jean and Donald Guth as well as having access to Madison's superior public education. Stephanie and I continue to be practicing social workers.

I worked for a while for the County of Santa Clara (the same area where Soteria existed) and frequently passed by the house that I knew as Soteria. While the experience there is bittersweet because the need it filled is now unmet, before it closed, Soteria turned my life—and a number of other lives—down meaningful paths. There is a simple reason why I stayed to the end. Soteria was never a job for me; it was my lifestyle. At times, it was difficult, but most of the time, it was rewarding.

I had never before had as my job description the charge to "create an environment that fosters psychological health." I have been (and, I expect will again be) asked to "build a case-management program" or to "administer a transitional residential program."

I probably never will have an assignment like that at Soteria. I am honored, however, to have had the chance to accept it once.

We did what we wanted to do and helped others deal with their problems so they could do what they wanted. We established a community that provided a safe environment where its often fragile members could live and flourish.

Soteria's center was *being with*—and thus helping—its wide community.

References

Barnes, M., & Berke, J. H. (1971/1994). *Two accounts of a journey through madness.* London: Free Association Books.

Basaglia, F. (1987). *Psychiatry inside out: Selected writings of Franco Basaglia* (N. Scheper-Hughes & A. M. Lovell, Eds., A. M. Lovell & T. Shtob, Trans.). New York: Columbia University Press.

Bateson, G., Jackson, D. D., Haley, J., & Weakland, J. H. (1956). Toward a theory of schizophrenia. *Behavioral Science, 1,* 251–264.

Beers, W. C. (1939). *A mind that found itself.* New York: Doubleday.

Bockoven, J. S. (1963). *Moral treatment in American psychiatry.* New York: Springer.

Bola, J. R., & Mosher, L. R. (2002). Predicting drug-free treatment response in acute psychosis from the Soteria project. *Schizophrenia Bulletin, 28*(4), 559–575.

Bola, J. R., & Mosher, L. R. (2003). Two-year outcomes from the Soteria project. *Journal of Nervous and Mental Diseases, 191*(4), 219–229.

Boss, M. (1963). *Psychoanalysis and daseinsanalysis.* New York: Basic Books.

Braden-Johnson, A. (1990). *Out of Bedlam: The truth about deinstitutionalization.* New York: Basic Books

Breggin, P. R. (1990). *Toxic psychiatry: Why therapy, empathy, and love must replace the drugs, electroshock, and biochemical theories of the "new psychiatry."* New York: St. Martin's.

Breggin, P. R., & Cohen, D. (2000). *Your drug may be your problem: How and why to stop taking psychiatric medication.* New York: Perseus.

Brown, G. W., & Birley, J. L. T. (1968). Crisis and life changes and the onset of schizophrenia. *Journal of Health and Social Behavior, 9,* 203–214.

Ciompi, L. (1997). The Soteria concept: Theoretical bases and practices: 13-year experiences with a milieu-therapeutic approach to acute schizophrenia. *Psychiatria et Neurologia Japanica, 9,* 634–650.

Cooper, D. G. (1967). *Psychiatry and antipsychiatry.* London: Tavistock Publications.

Crane, G. E. (1973). Clinical psychopharmacology in its 20th year. *Science, 181,* 124–128.

Deutsch, A. (1948). *Shame of the states.* Newt York: Arno.

Erikson, E. (1959). Identity and the hope cycle [Special issue]. *Psychological Issues, 1.*

Fairbairn, W. R. D. (1952/1994). *Psychoanalytic studies of the personality.* London: Routledge.

Fenton, W. S., Hoch, J. S., Herrell, J. M., Mosher, L. R., & Dixon, L. (2002). Cost and cost effectiveness of hospital versus crisis residential care for patients with serious mental illness. *Archives of General Psychiatry, 59*(3), 357–364.

Fenton W. S., Mosher, L. R., Herrell, J. M., & Blyler, C. R. (1998). A randomized trial of general hospital versus residential alternative care for patients with severe and persistent mental illness: Effectiveness and cost. *American Journal of Psychiatry, 155*(4), 516–522.

Fisher, S., & Cleveland, S. E. (1958). *Body image and personality.* Princeton: Van Nostrand.

Frank, J. (1972). *Persuasion and healing.* Baltimore: Johns Hopkins Press.

Freeman, T., Cameron, J. L., & McGhie, A. (1958). *Chronic schizophrenia.* New York: International Universities Press.

Fromm-Reichmann, F. (1948). Notes on the development of treatment of schizophrenia by psychoanalytic psychotherapy. *Psychiatry, 11,* 263–273.

Goffmann, E. (1961). *Asylums: Essays on the social situation of mental patients and other inmates.* New York: Doubleday.

Gould, S. J. (1981). *The mismeasure of man.* New York: W. W. Norton.

Guntrip, H. J. S. (1969). *Schizoid phenomena, object relations, and the self.* New York: International Universities Press.

Hirschfeld, R. M., Matthews, S. M., Mosher, L. R., & Menn, A. Z. (1977). Being with madness: Personality characteristics of three treatment staffs. *Hospital & Community Psychiatry, 28,* 267–273.

Jablensky, A. (1992). Schizophrenia: Manifestations, incidence, and course in different cultures: A World Health Organization ten-country study. *Psychological Medicine,* Suppl. 20, 1–95.

John Paul, II, Pope. (1995). *Crossing the threshold of hope* (V. Messoni, Ed., J. McPhee, & M. McPhee, Trans.). New York: A. A. Knopf.

Laing, R. D. (1960). *The divided self.* Chicago: Quadrangle Books.

Laing, R. D. (1967). *The politics of experience.* New York: Ballantine Books.

Leff, J. (1992). The international pilot study of schizophrenia: Five-year follow-up findings. *Psychological Medicine, 22,* 131–145.

Matthews, S. M., Roper, M. T., Mosher, L. R., & Menn, A. Z. (1979). A nonneuroleptic treatment for schizophrenia: Analysis of the two-year post-discharge risk of relapse. *Schizophrenia Bulletin, 5*(2), 322–333.

May, P. R. A. (1968). *Treatment of schizophrenia: A comparative study of five treatment methods.* New York: Science House.

May, R. (1958). *Existence: A new dimension in psychiatry and psychology.* New York: Basic Books.

Menninger, K. A. (1959). *A psychiatrist's world: The selected papers of Karl Menninger.* (B. Hall, Ed.). New York: Viking.

Moos, R. H. (1974). *Evaluating treatment environments: A social ecological approach.* New York: John Wiley and Sons.

Millett, K. (1990). *The loony-bin trip.* New York: Simon and Schuster.

Mosher, L. R. (1989). Community residential treatment/alternatives to hospitalization. In A. S. Bellack (Ed.), *A clinical guide for the treatment of schizophrenia* (pp. 135–161). New York: Plenum.

Mosher, L. R. (1991). Soteria: A therapeutic community for psychotic persons. *International Journal of Therapeutic Communities, 12,* 53–67.

Mosher, L. R. (1995). The Soteria project: First generation American alternatives to psychiatric hospitalization. In R. Warner (Ed.), *Alternatives to hospitalization for acute psychiatric care* (pp.111–125). Washington, DC: American Psychiatric Press.

Mosher, L. R. & Bola, J. R. (2004). Soteria-California and its American successors: Therapeutic ingredients. *Ethical Human Psychiatry and Psychology, 6*(1), 147–163.

Mosher, L. R., & Burti, L. (1989). *Community mental health: Principles and practice.* New York: W. W. Norton.

Mosher, L. R., & Burti, L. (1994). *Community mental health: A practical guide.* New York: W. W. Norton.

Mosher, L. R., & Goveia, L. (1971). *Community alternatives for treatment of schizophrenia* (Grant proposal, MH 19171–01). Washington, DC: National Institute of Mental Health.

Mosher, L. R., & Menn, A. Z. (1977). Soteria House: One-year outcome data. *Psvchopharmacologv Bulletin, 13*(2), 46–48.

Mosher, L. R., & Menn, A. Z. (1978a). Community residential treatment for schizophrenia: Two-year follow-up data. *Hospital & Community Psychiatry, 29,* 715–723.

Mosher, L. R., & Menn, A. Z. (1978b). The surrogate "family:" An alternative to hospitalization. In J. C. Shershow (Ed.), *Schizophrenia: Science and practice* (pp. 223–229). Cambridge, MA: Harvard University Press.

Mosher, L. R., & Menn, A. Z. (1979). Soteria: An alternative to hospitalization for schizophrenia. *New Directions for Mental Health Services, 1,* 73–83.

Mosher, L. R., Reifman, A., and Menn, A. Z. (1973). Characteristics of nonprofessionals serving as primary therapists for acute schizophrenics. *Hospital & Community Psychiatry, 24*(6), 391–396.

Mosher, L. R., & Vallone, R. (1992, March 14). *Soteria project: Final progress report.* (Final National Institute of Mental Health Report: Grant Nos. R12MH 20123 and R12MH 25570). Washington, DC.

Mosher, L. R., Vallone, R., & Menn, A. Z. (1995). The treatment of acute psychosis without neurolyptics: Six-week psychopathology outcome: Data from the Soteria project. *International Journal of Social Psychiatry.*

Mosher, L. R., Vallone, R., Menn, A. Z., Hendrix, V., & Fort, D. C. (1992). *Treatment at Soteria House: A manual for the practice of interpersonal phenomenology* (Final National Institute of Mental Health Report: Grant Nos. R12MH 20123 and R12MH 25570). Washington, DC.

National Institute of Mental Health Psychopharmacology Service Center Collaborative Study Group. (1964). Phenothiazine treatment in acute schizophrenia. *Archives of General Psychiatry, 10,* 512–517.

Perry, J. W. (1953). *The self in the psychotic process.* University of California Press.

Perry, J. W. (1962). Reconstitutive process in the psychopathology of the self. *Annals of the New York Academy of Sciences 96,* 853–876.

Rappaport, M., Hopkins, H. K., Hall, K., Belleza, T., & Silverman, J. (1978). Are there schizophrenics for whom drugs may be unnecessary or contraindicated? *International Pharmacopsychiatry, 13,* 100–111.

Rosenhan, D. L. (1973). On being sane in insane places. *Science, 179,* 250.

Safire, W. (1994, 13 November). On language: The word from the Pope. *The New York Times Magazine,* pp. 26, 28.

Schilder, P. (1950). *The image and appearance of the human body.* New York: International Universities Press.

Semrad, E. V. (1983). *Semrad: The heart of a therapist* S. Rako and H. Maze (Eds.). New York: J. Aronson.

Singer, M. T., & Wynne, L. C. (1965). Thought disorder and family relations of schizophrenics: III. Methodology using projective techniques, IV. Results and implications. *Archives of General Psychiatry, 12,* 187–212.

Strauss, J. S., Kokes, R. F., Klorman, R., & Sacksteder, J. L. (1977). Premorbid adjustment in schizophrenia: Concepts, measures, and implications, part I: The concept of premorbid adjustment. *Schizophrenia Bulletin, 3*(2), 182–186.

Straw, R. B. (1982). Meta-analysis of deinstitutionalization. Unpublished doctoral dissertation. Northwestern University, Evanston, IL.

Stroul B. A. (1987). *Crisis residential services in a community support system* (Report to the National Institute of Mental Health Community Support Program). Rockville, MD.

Sullivan, H. S. (1962). *Schizophrenia as a human process*. New York: Norton.

Szasz, T. S. (1961). *The myth of mental illness: Foundations of a theory of personal conduct*. New York: Harper and Row, Hoeber Medical Division.

Torrey, E. F. (1988). *Surviving schizophrenia: A family manual* (2nd ed.). New York: Harper and Row.

Wendt, R. J., Mosher, L. R., Matthews, S. M., & Menn, A. Z. (1983). A comparison of two treatment environments for schizophrenia. In J. G. Gunderson, O. A. Will, & L. R. Mosher (Eds.), *The principles and practices of milieu therapy* (pp. 17–33). New York: Jason Aronson.

Whitaker, R. (2002). *Mad in America: Bad science, bad medicine, and the enduring mistreatment of the mentally ill*. Cambridge, MA: Perseus.

Wilson, H. S. (1974). *Infracontrolling: The social order of freedom in an antipsychiatric community*. Unpublished doctoral dissertation. University of California, Berkeley.

Wilson, H. S. (1982). *Deinstitutionalized residential care for the mentally disordered: The Soteria House approach*. New York: Harcourt Brace Jovanovich (Grune and Stratton).

Wilson, H. S. (1983). Usual hospital treatment in the United States' community mental health system: A dispatching process. *International Journal of Nursing Studies, 20*(2), 75–82.

Winerip, M. (1994). *Nine Highland Road*. New York: Pantheon.

World Health Organization [WHO]. (1979). *Schizophrenia: An international follow-up study*. Chichester: John Wiley.

Wynne, L. C., & Singer, M. T. (1963). Thought disorder and family relations of schizophrenics: I. A research strategy, II. A classification of forms of thinking. *Archives of General Psychiatry, 9*, 191–206.

Appendices

Soteria in the Literature—
A Chronological Survey

1. Mosher, L. R. (1972). Research design to evaluate psychosocial treatments of schizophrenia. In D. Rubenstein & Y. O. Alanen (Eds.), *Psychotherapy of schizophrenia,* (pp. 251–260). Amsterdam: Excerpta Medica Foundation. (Reprinted in *Hospital & Community Psychiatry, 23,* 229–234)
2. Mosher, L. R., Reifman, A., & Menn, A. Z. (1973). Characteristics of nonprofessionals serving as primary therapists of acute schizophrenics. *Hospital & Community Psychiatry. 24*(6), 391–396. [Reprinted in English and Italian editions of P. Watzlawick & J. H. Weakland, Eds., (1977), *The interactional view: Studies at the Mental Research Institute, Palo Alto 1965–1974* (pp. 143–153). New York: W. W. Norton.]
3. Mosher, L. R. (1974). Psychiatric heretics and the extra-medical treatment of schizophrenia. In R. Cancro, N. Fox, & L. E. Shapiro (Eds.), *Strategic intervention in schizophrenia: Current developments in treatment* (pp. 279–302). New York: Behavioral Publications,
4. Mosher, L. R., & Menn, A. Z. (1974). Soteria: An alternative to hospitalization for schizophrenia. In J. H. Masserman (Ed.), *Current psychiatric therapies, Vol. 14* (pp. 287–296). New York: Grune and Stratton.

5. Mosher, L. R., Menn, A. Z., & Matthews, S. M. (1975). Soteria: Evaluation of a home-based treatment for schizophrenia. *American Journal of Orthopsychiatry, 45*(3), 455–467.

6. Menn, A. Z. & Mosher, L. R. (1976). The Soteria project. An alternative to hospitalization for schizophrenics: Some clinical aspects. In J. Jorstad & E. Ugelstad (Eds.), *Schizophrenia, 75* (pp. 347–372). Oslo, Norway: Universitetsforlaget.

7. Mosher, L. R., & Menn, A. Z. (1976). Dinosaur or astronaut? One-year follow-up data from the Soteria project. In M. Greenblatt & R. D. Budson (Eds.), A Symposium: Follow-up of community care. *American Journal of Psychiatry, 133*(8), 919–920.

8. Wilson, H. S. (1976). Presencing: Social control of "schizophrenics" in an antipsychiatric community. In C. R. Kneisl & H. S. Wilson (Eds.), *Current perspectives in psychiatric nursing* (Vol. 1, pp.164–175). St. Louis, MO: C. V. Mosby.

9. Wilson, H. S. (1978).Conjoint becoming: Study of Soteria, II [Report of postdoctoral study]. In C. R. Kneisl & H. S. Skodol (Eds.), *Current perspectives in psychiatric nursing* (Vol. 2, pp 135–148). St. Louis, MO: C. V. Mosby.

10. Hirschfeld, R. M., Matthews, S. M., Mosher, L. R., & Menn, A. Z. (1977). Being with madness: Personality characteristics of three treatment staffs. *Hospital & Community Psychiatry. 28*, 267–273.

11. Mosher, L. R., & Menn, A. Z. (1977a). Lowered barriers in the community: The Soteria model. In L. I. Stein & M. A. Test (Eds.), *Alternatives to mental hospital treatment* (pp. 75–113). New York: Plenum Press.

12. Mosher, L. R., & Menn, A. Z. (1977b). Soteria house: One-year outcome data. *Psychopharmacology Bulletin, 13*(2) 46–48.

13. Mosher, L. R, & Menn, A. Z. (1978a). Community residential treatment for schizophrenia: Two-year follow-up data. *Hospital & Community Psychiatry, 29*, 715–723.

14. Mosher, L. R., & Menn, A. Z. (1978b). Enhancing psychosocial competence in schizophrenia: Preliminary results of the Soteria project. In W. E. Fann, I. C. Karacan, A. D. Pokorny & R. L. Williams (Eds.). *Phenomenology and treatment of schizophrenia* (pp. 371–386). New York: Spectrum.

15. Mosher, L. R., & Menn, A. Z. (1978c). The surrogate "family", An alternative to hospitalization. In J. C. Shershow (Ed.), *Schizophrenia: Science and practice* (pp. 223–239). Cambridge, MA: Harvard University Press.

16. Matthews, S. M., Roper, M. T., Mosher, L. R., & Menn, A. Z. (1979). A nonneuroleptic treatment for schizophrenia: Analysis of the two-year post-discharge risk of relapse. *Schizophrenia Bulletin, 5*(2), 322–333.

17. Mosher, L. R., & Menn, A. Z. (1979). Soteria: An alternative to hospitalization for schizophrenics. In H. R. Lamb (Ed.), *New directions for mental health services: Alternatives to acute hospitalization* (pp. 189–206). San Francisco: Jossey-Bass. [Translated and reprinted in 1982 in *Psychiatria/Informazione, 4*(3), 7–17.]

18. Wilson, H. S.(1982). *Deinstitutionalized residential care for the mentally disordered: The Soteria House approach.* New York: Grune and Stratton.

19. Wendt, R. J., Mosher, L. R, Matthews, S. M., & Menn, A. Z. (1983). A comparison of two treatment environments of schizophrenia. In J. G. Gunderson, O. A. Will, Jr., & L. R. Mosher (Eds.), *The principles and practices of milieu therapy* (pp. 17–33). New York: Jason Aronson.

20. Mosher, L. R., & Menn, A. Z. (1983). Scientific evidence and system change: The Soteria experience. In H. Stierlin, L. C. Wynne, & M. Wirsching (Eds.), *Psychosocial interventions in schizophrenia* (pp. 93–108). Heidelberg, Germany: Springer-Verlag.

21. Mosher, L. R. (1983). Alternatives to psychiatric hospitalization: Why has research failed to be translated into practice? *New England Journal of Medicine, 309*(25), 1479–1480.

22. Wilson, H. S. (1983). Usual hospital treatment in the U.S.A's community mental health system. *International Journal of Nursing Studies, 20*(2), 75–82.

23. Mosher, L. R & Menn, A. Z. (1984). Soteria: An alternative to hospitalization for schizophrenia. In J. H. Masserman (Ed.), *Current psychiatric therapies* (Vol 21, pp. 189–206). New York: Grune and Stratton.

24. Mosher, L. R. & Menn, A. Z. (1984). Un'altemativa al 'ospedalizzazione nella schizofrenia: L'esperienza Soteria. In C. Faccinani, R. Fiorio, G. Mignolli, E. M. Tansella (Eds.), *Le psicosi schizofreniche: Dalla ricerca alla pratica clinica* (pp.143–164). Bologna, Italy: Patron.

25. Wilson, H. S. (1986). Presencing: Social control of schizophrenics in an anti-psychiatric community: An illustration of grounded theory. In P. L. Munhall & C. J. Oiler (Eds.), *Nursing research: A qualitative perspective.* (pp.131–144). Norwalk, CT: Appleton-Century-Croft.

26. Mosher, L. R, Kresky-Wolff, M., Matthews, S. M., & Menn, A. Z. (1986). Milieu therapy in the 80s: A comparison of two alternatives to hospitalization. *Bulletin of the Menninger Clinic, 50*, 257–268.

27. Wilson, H. S. (1986). Deinstitutionalized residential care in the U.S. community health system. In C. Chennitz & J. Swanson, (Eds.), Qualitative research (pp. 181–190). Menlo Park, CA: Addison-Wesley.

28. Mosher, L. R. (1989). Community residential treatment/ alternatives to hospitalization. In A. S. Bellack (Ed.), *A clinical guide for the treatment of schizophrenia* (pp. 135–161). New York: Plenum.

29. Mosher, L. R., Vallone, R.,. & Menn, A. Z. (1989). The Soteria project: New outcome data. In A. Migone, G. Martini & V.Volterra (Eds.), *Il progetto Soteria: Nuovi risultati emersi* (pp. 313–330) [translation of New trends in schizophrenia]. Caserta, Italy: Edito dalla Fondazione.

30. Wilson, H. S. (1990, January). Replicating a low EE environment: The Soteria approach ten years later. *Florida Nursing Review, 13,* 1–8.

31. Mosher, L. R. (1991). Soteria: A therapeutic community for psychotic persons. *International Journal of Therapeutic Communities, 12,* 53–67

32. Mosher, L. R., & Burti, L. (1994). Alternatives to hospitalization. In L. R. Mosher & L. Burti (Eds.), *Community mental health: A practical guide* (pp. 119–142). New York: W. W. Norton. [Translated into Italian, German, Japanese, Swedish, and Danish]

33. Mosher, L. R., Vallone, R., Menn, A. Z., Hendrix, V., & Fort, D. C. (1992). *Treatment at Soteria House: A manual for the practice of interpersonal phenomenology* (Final National Institute of Mental Health Report: Grant Nos. R12MH 20123 and R12MH 25570). Washington, DC. (Translated and published in German as Psychosoziale Arbeitshilfen, 7: Dabeisein: *Das Manual zur praxis in der Soteria.* Bonn, Germany: Psychiatrie Verlag.)

34. Mosher, L. R. (1995). The Soteria project: The first generation American residential alternatives to psychiatric hospitalization. In R. Warner (Ed.), *Alternatives to hospitalization for acute psychiatric care* (pp. 111–125). Washington, DC: American Psychiatric Publishing.

35. Mosher, L. R, Vallone, Robert, & Menn, A. Z. (1995). The treatment of acute psychosis without neuroleptics: Six-week psychopathology outcome data from the Soteria project. *International Journal of Social Psychiatry, 41*(3), 157–173.

36. Mosher, L. R. (1996). The Soteria Project: Therapeutic communities for psychotic persons. In P. R. Breggin & M. Stern (Eds.), *The psychotic patient* (Vol. 9, No.3/4, pp. 43–58) [Also published as *Psychosocial approaches to deeply disturbed persons*]. Binghampton, NY: Haworth.

37. Ciompi, L. (1997). The Soteria concept: Theoretical bases and practices: 13-year experiences with a milieu-therapeutic approach to acute schizophrenia. *Psychiatria et Neurologia Japanica, 9*, 634–650.

38. Mosher, L. R. (1999). Soteria and other alternatives to acute psychiatric hospitalization: A personal and professional review. *Journal of Nervous and Mental Disease, 187*, 142–149. (Reprinted in *Changes 17*[1], 35–48, 1999)

39. Mosher, L. R., & Bola, J. R. (1999). Das Soteria Project: Einschtäzung des Affects un Interventions formen. In W. Machleidt, H. Halternet, & P. Gaslipp (Eds.), *Schizophrenia—Eine affective Erkrankung?* (pp. 243–257). Stuttgart, Germany: Schattauer.

40. Mosher, L. R., & Bola, J. R. (2000). The Soteria project: Twenty-five years of swimming upriver. *Complexity and Change, 9*(1) 68–74.

41. Mosher, L. R. (2001).Die Anwendung von therapeutischen Prinzipien der Soteria in der gemeindepsychiatrischen Versorgung [Application of Soteria principles to community psychiatric care]. In M. Wollschlager (Ed.), *Socialpsychiatrie: Entwicklungen-Kontroversen-Perspektiven* (pp. 497–503). Tubingen: Verlag.

42. Mosher, L. R. (2001a). Soteria-California and its successors: Therapeutic ingredients. In L. Ciompi, H. Hoffmann, & M. Broccard (Eds.), *Wie wirkt Soteria?—Ein atypische Psychosenbehandlung kritisch durchleuchtet* [Why does Soteria work?—An unusual schizophrenia therapy under examination] (pp. 13–43). New York and Bonn, Germany: Huber.

43. Mosher, L. R. (2001b). Treating madness without hospitals: Soteria and its successors. In K. J. Schneider, J. F. T. Bugental, & M. Broccard (Eds.), The handbook of humanistic psychology (pp. 389–401). Thousand Oaks, CA: Sage.

44. Bola, J. R., & Mosher, L. R. (2002a). Clashing ideologies or scientific discourse? [response to Carpenter and Buchanan]. *Schizophrenia Bulletin 28*(4), 583–588.

45. Bola, J. R., & Mosher, L. R. (2002b). Predicting drug-free treatment response in acute psychosis from the Soteria project. *Schizophrenia Bulletin, 28*(4), 559–575.

46. Fenton, W. S., Hoch, J. S., Herrell, J. M., Mosher, L. R., & Dixon, L. (2002). Cost and cost effectiveness of hospital versus crisis residential care for patients with serious mental illness. *Archives of General Psychiatry, 59*(3) 357–364.

47. Bola, J. R., & Mosher, L. R. (2003). Two-year outcomes from the Soteria project. *Journal of Nervous and Mental Diseases, 191*(4), 219–229.

48. Bola, J. R., Mosher, L. R., & Cohen, D. (2004). Treatment of newly diagnosed psychosis without anti-psychotic drugs: The Soteria project. In S. Kirk (Ed.), *Mental disorders in the social environment: Critical perspectives.* New York: Columbia University Press.

49. Mosher, L. R. (2004). Non-hospital, non-drug interventions with first episode psychosis. In J. Read, L. R. Mosher, & R. Bentall (Eds.), *Models of madness: Psychological, social, and biological approaches to "schizophrenia."* London: Brunner-Routledge.

50. Mosher, L. R. & Bola, J. R. (2004). Soteria-California and its American successors: Therapeutic ingredients. *Ethical Human Psychiatry and Psychology, 6*(1), 147–163.

After studying at Stanford University, **Loren R. Mosher** received his MD from Harvard Medical School in 1961. His psychiatric training took place at Harvard and at the National Institute of Mental Health's Intramural Program in Bethesda, MD. After working with Anna Freud, John Bowlby, R. D. Laing, and others in London, Dr. Mosher served as Chief of the Center for the Studies of Schizophrenia at the NIMH from 1968 to 1980 during which time he designed and implemented the Soteria Project. He also established and was first editor-in-chief of the *Schizophrenia Bulletin.* In 1980, he studied Italy's radical new mental health law. From 1981 to 1988, he was professor of psychiatry at the Uniformed University of the Health Sciences (Maryland). From 1988 to 1998 he was medical director of two county-wide public mental health systems in Maryland and California. His last posts were as clinical professor of psychiatry at the University of California at San Diego and director of Soteria Associates in San Diego. *Soteria* was complete and at the publisher when Dr. Mosher died in 2004.

After earning his undergraduate degree in American Studies with a minor in sociology from California State University—Fresno, **Voyce Hendrix, LCSW,** took an MS in social work at the University of Wisconsin—Madison. Before completing his formal studies, he worked in the field of mental heath in state institutions, private hospitals, and community-support programs. Hendrix took part in research examining alternatives to treatment in psychiatric hospitals in the community (Soteria) and at the Mental Research Institute in Palo Alto. This research was funded by the National Institute of Mental Health. Hendrix also worked as a licenced psychiatric technician and served as an administrator. He is now a licenced clinical social worker practicing in Wisconsin. His 40-year career has offered him comprehensive experience with a wide spectrum of services and models for helping those who suffer and experience alternative states of reality and has taught him that there are no simple answers for disturbed and disturbing persons in pain.

Washington, D.C.-area freelance writer and editor **Deborah C. Fort** earned her PhD in comparative literature from the University of Maryland in 1974. After a decade of teaching English and writing at the college level, she turned full-time to writing and editing, specializing in science, education, and women's issues. Of the numerous books on which she has worked, she is proudest of her service as association editor on *Gifted Young in Science: Potential* Through *Performance* (National Science Teachers Association, 1989) and *A Hand Up: Women Mentoring Women in Science* (Association for Women in Science, 1993, 1995). Among other projects, she is currently working on a study of the influence of Paul F. Brandwein on science education in America

Printed in the United States
110743LV00002B/216/A

9 781413 465235